BEARS

From gentle pandas to fearless polar bears

BEARS

From gentle pandas to fearless polar bears

i|m|p

inspiring & informing you

This edition published by International Masters Publishers, Inc.
225 Park Avenue South
New York NY 10003
U.S.A.

ISBN 9781930560055
Library of Congress: 2008921071

Written by Christina Curwen
Kim Bryan pp.8–23, 170–9
Ben Hoare pp.104–115
Rob Huston pp.56–67

Produced, edited, and designed by
Writeline and Dot 2 Dot Design Ltd

Project manager: Belinda Wilkinson
Editor: Patricia Burgess
Picture researchers: Amanda Montoura, Griselda Barrett
Designers: Kristine Hatch, Melissa Roskell
Production controller: Nicky Bowman

Printed and bound in China
Color separations by Fresh Media Group

For more IMP publications, please visit our website at:

www.imponline.com

IMP product code US P C302 17006

IUCN and SSC

The intitials IUCN stand for International Union for the Conservation of Nature and Natural Resources, usually called the World Conservation Union. Within the IUCN is the Species Survival Commission (SSC), a global network of volunteer experts working to conserve the world's existing levels of biodiversity. This continually assesses the degree of risk for different species, and those most in danger of global extinction are highlighted in the IUCN Red List of Threatened Species. The current assessment for each species featured in this book is included on the final page of its section.

Contents

Introduction

Ever since cave people first stumbled upon a huge and hairy bear curled up asleep in its winter den, with cuddly cubs clutched close in a furry embrace, bears have inspired mixed feelings. At different times and in different cultures bears have been both revered and feared, petted and persecuted, celebrated and exterminated. Today, with several species seriously threatened, the rarest but best-known bear, the giant panda, has become a worldwide icon of precious wildlife.

With just eight living species, the modern bear family, or Ursidae, might seem surprisingly small, but each species varies markedly in size, habitat, and diet, from the dog-like, jet-black, tropical sun bear to the mighty ice-white polar bear, the world's largest land carnivore. Despite diverse size and color, every member of the clan looks unmistakably "bearish," with a broad "teddy" head, long, dog-like muzzle, and round, furry ears. Apart from the sleek sun bear, most ursids are shaggy-haired and hulking, their bulky, barrel-shaped bodies equipped with massive shoulders, muscular limbs, spreading paws, and slashing, non-retractile claws. Most bearish of all—unlike many other carnivores—every ursid can stand upright, with its feet planted flat on the ground. Other more predatory carnivores, such as cats, race about on their toes. Built for strength rather than speed, but far from slow, bears are bright, supremely adaptable all-rounders. With their short, sturdy limbs and dextrous paws, ursids can scale glaciers, unscrew honey jars, uproot bulbs, snorkel under water, catch leaping fish, and pack a powerful punch.

The first bears

The bear story began over 65 million years ago, soon after the dinosaurs died out, when a new tribe of fox-like hunters (miacids) flourished in the treetops. Evolving piercing canines and cutting carnassial teeth, the miacids became successful flesh-eaters, and in time spawned a dog-like (caniform) line of hunters, from which sprang the first "dawn" bear, *Ursavus elemensi*, about 30 million years ago. Little bigger than a terrier, but more bear-like, with flatter teeth for crushing plants, the dawn bear in turn gave rise, around 13 million years ago, to the larger *Protursus*, from which in time evolved the modern bear family.

Wide rangers

Today bears live on every continent except Africa, Antarctica, and Australia, but are most widespread in the northern hemisphere. Only two species, the sun and spectacled bears, live south of the equator. Ursids have adapted to diverse habitats, from subzero polar pack ice to searing Indian scrublands and steamy tropical rainforests. Between extremes, the panda wanders the bamboo forests of China, while the world's brown and black bears roam the temperate tundra, woods, or swamps of the northern rim.

A taste for diversity

Despite their carnivorous ancestry, most bears are "dining room opportunists," shifting seasonally between plants and flesh, from spring sedge to summer salmon. Four species, though, have quite particular tastes. The polar bear, the only true meat-eater, dines mainly on seal; at the other extreme, the panda chews bamboo all day. Two other specialists—the sun bear and the sloth bear—feast almost entirely on insects outside the fruiting cycle.

With a taste for fat-rich fish, an Alaskan brown bear races after spawning salmon.

Bears make model moms. Giant pandas are no exception, nursing and nurturing their vulnerable cubs with utmost devotion.

Sleepyheads

Shuffling along at a leisurely pace, bears can seem sleepy and slothful, but with good reason. Giant, shaggy-haired bodies easily overheat. To stay cool, bears rarely run, and often rest in shady daybeds. Even shaggy coats, though, cannot protect from seasonal snow and food scarcity. To escape the worst weather, most northern bears den for the winter, living off fatty reserves in a sleep-like state. By binging in the fall, they shore up fat, doubling their spring-time weight. Unlike small mammals, though, bears do not hibernate fully. To do so, they would need to drop their metabolic rate too low for gestation and birth, which are crucially timed to occur in the safety of the den. Birth in a snug, secluded den is vital for the survival of the unusually tiny cubs—born 10–20 percent smaller than dogs or cats. To ensure a midwinter birth, the embryos, which are usually fertilized in the summer, float free until the fall, when they implant on the uterine wall and develop. Once born, the helpless cubs suckle avidly on bodybuilding milk, piling on vital fat before venturing out in the spring. Even in deep sleep, without food or water, mothers nourish their needy cubs—an extraordinary feat.

Mental mapping

To survive seasonal variation, many bears have developed super memories and navigation skills, enabling them to return to the same ripe berry patch time and again. Even "nuisance" bears, shifted up to 168 miles (270 km) away, can find their way home. Experts believe that bears navigate by some mental compass, possibly linked to the earth's magnetic fields.

Bear appeal

Perhaps no other wild animal has inspired a cuddly toy as popular as the teddy bear. Modeled on cute bear cubs, it is a far cry from the ursid giants that roam the tundra, forests, and ice floes of the world, but hints at the enduring appeal of bears. For primal hunting cultures, bear fat, flesh, and fur provided vital energy and warmth. Peeking from behind the bushes, early tribespeople marveled at the bear's dextrous paws, its ambling, upright gait, almost "human" footprint, and motherly devotion. Stripped of its shaggy fur, the bear's slim body seemed even more human, especially in the northern hemisphere, where apes—our closest relatives—remained unknown until modern times. For primal peoples, who imagined all life pervaded by one sacred force, the kindred bear spirit, "brother bear," commanded, at the very least, family respect, and often much more: In the north, especially, many tribes credited bears with supernatural powers. It is little wonder, as the great brown and black bears disappear each winter, surviving in a death-like sleep, only to emerge "miraculously" in the spring. Often revered as a mighty spiritual force, sometimes as Lord of the Animals, with power to control the supply of game, the bear was richly honored and celebrated. Over time, as bears and people competed for resources, the great bear fell from grace—no longer venerated, but baited and persecuted. Only recently have bears recovered something of their original charisma, inspiring wonder once again.

The future of bears

Sharing similar diets and habitats, bears and people have jostled for position and power for over 20,000 years. Right across their range—in Europe, Asia, and the Americas—bears have lost vital ground to human homesteads. Even in the Arctic, far from civilization, the polar bear's survival is threatened by industrial pollution and global warming. Despite such overwhelming forces, breakthroughs in conservation abound. Even in deprived regions, such as Peru, Cambodia, and India, innovative refuges have sprung up against the odds. Elsewhere, in model American bear zones, many bears now lead natural, secluded lives, while people watch from afar. The future lies in extending sanctuaries, such as the Great Bear Rainforest in British Columbia, where people can gaze in wonder while bears wander on their way.

Strolling across the drifting ice floes, an intrepid polar bear leads her cubs to the edge of the pack ice, where she will lie in wait for blubber-rich seal.

Giant Panda

CLASS: Mammalia   **ORDER:** Carnivora   **FAMILY:** Ursidae   **GENUS & SPECIES:** *Ailuropoda melanoleuca*

Cuddly and charismatic, the giant panda is arguably one of the planet's best-loved animals—adored by adults and children alike for its winsome features, toy-like appearance, and peaceful reputation. So universally recognized is this distinctive-looking black and white bear that it today appears as the logo for the World Wide Fund for Nature (WWF), and its image is used to represent a symbol of peace. Ironically, however, it is humans who now threaten its survival—its natural, bamboo-rich habitats ever encroached on by the expanding population of China. Today, though considered a national treasure by the Chinese, its existence is precarious to say the least; with only about 1600 giant pandas left in the wild, and a reluctance to breed in captivity, they remain one of the world's most endangered animals.

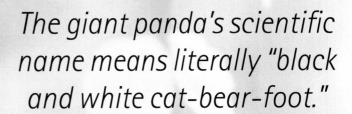

The giant panda's scientific name means literally "black and white cat-bear-foot."

Key Features

- Lives mainly on the ground, but can climb trees if necessary.

- Does not hibernate in winter, as it must eat almost continuously in order to maintain enough energy to survive.

- Can grasp objects in much the same way as humans, thanks to the development of a "false thumb."

- Unlike all other bears, it cannot walk on its hind legs.

In Focus

Looking much like other bears in general shape, the giant panda's black and white markings make it instantly recognizable. This coloration is believed to help the bears stand out against their surroundings, thus enabling these solitary animals to avoid contact with each other. The wide "teddy bear" head and clown-like eyepatches give them a friendly appearance, but the broad, muscular chest and immensely strong teeth indicate that they are not to be toyed with.

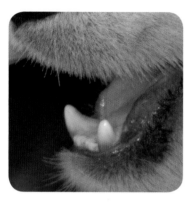

Crushing teeth

Giant pandas usually have 40 teeth—two fewer than other bears. They have lost one of the lower molars (cheek teeth) seen in other bears, and instead have large, broad, flat-topped molar teeth used for crushing fibrous bamboo. While it very rarely eats meat, the giant panda has large carnivorous canines, ideal for seizing prey.

Flexible forepaws

These are modified for grasping. An enlarged bone in the wrist—the radial sesamoid—acts as a thumb, while a degree of flexibility in the pads on the first two digits allows these to function as "fingers." The whole paw therefore operates much like a human hand.

Pigeon-toed paws

The giant panda walks on four legs, never upright, with the heel of the hindlimb touching the ground. Pandas walk awkwardly, with their paws turned inward, only running if disturbed or frightened.

Panda pupils

Unlike other bears, the pupil of the giant panda's eye is slit-like rather than round, which allows better control of how much light enters the eye. However, compared with its acute senses of smell and hearing, the giant panda's sight is relatively poor.

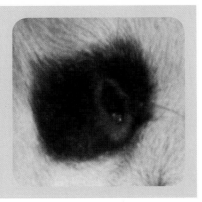

Waterproof fur

The giant panda's fur is coarse and dense. At its longest, it grows to 4 in (10 cm) on the belly, and at its shortest to 1.5–2 in (3–5 cm) on the rump. The density is for warmth, while an oily coating on each hair keeps it waterproof—adaptations to living in a cool, moist habitat. With its coat also resistant to compression, a panda can sleep even on snow.

Tuft-like tail

The short furry tail, no more than 4–6 in (10–5 cm) long, is usually held close to the body. It protects a naked area that contains scent glands. With the tail raised, the panda rubs its slightly acetic scent secretions against trees and rocks.

Vital Statistics

Weight: Male 165–352 lb (75–160 kg); female 155–220 lb (70–100 kg)

Length: 4–5 ft (1.2–1.5 m)

Height: 2.4–2.8 ft (70–80 cm) at the shoulder

Color: White back, belly, and head; black arms, legs, ears, and eyes

Sexual maturity: 5.5–6.5 years

Gestation period: 97–163 days, depending on period of delayed implantation of the fertilized egg

Number of young: 1–3 cubs, but usually only a single cub is raised

Birth interval: 2 years

Typical diet: Predominantly bamboo, but will sometimes consume other plants, birds' eggs, insect larvae, and small rodents

Lifespan: About 20 years in the wild; up to 34 years in captivity

Did you know?

● A baby panda is one of the smallest of mammals at birth relative to its adult size, weighing only 3.2–4.6 oz (90–130 g).

● About 99 percent of a panda's diet is bamboo, and it consumes up to 40 lb (18 kg) of it each day.

● Rather than simply roaring or growling, pandas make 11 different vocalizations.

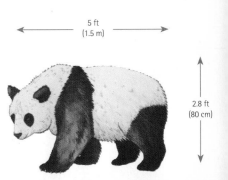

5 ft (1.5 m)

2.8 ft (80 cm)

Habitat

Today, giant pandas are found in just a few remote highland areas on the eastern edge of the Tibetan plateau. In the past, when the bamboo flowered and died, they could migrate to another area, but now that their remaining habitat is much reduced and fragmented, they are unable to do this, and risk starvation.

Distribution

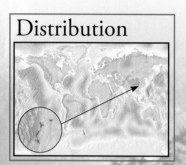

Qinling Mountains

Situated in Shaanxi Province, this is the most northerly of the giant panda's habitats. About 200–300 pandas live on the southern slopes of the mountains, but only in the 970 square miles (2425 square km) where suitable bamboo species grow. Pandas in this area sometimes show different coloration, being brown and white rather than black and white.

China

Pacific Ocean

Min Mountains

At 1320 square miles (3300 square km), this is the world's largest area of panda habitat, and is home to about 585 individuals. Straddling the provinces of southern Gansu and northern Sichuan, it contains most of China's 50 panda reserves.

Indian Ocean

Wolong

Nestled in the Qionglai Mountains, Wolong covers about 800 square miles (2000 square km) and is the largest of China's giant panda reserves. Thanks to the abundance of palatable bamboo species, it supports about 150 giant pandas.

During Pleistocene times (1.8 million to 10,000 years ago) pandas were much more widespread, with fossils having been found at localities of 1650 ft (500 m) and above in eastern China as far north as Beijing, and in northern Burma and Vietnam. Today, because of climate change, habitat destruction, and hunting, pandas are restricted to small blocks of land, which leaves them vulnerable to extinction from disease, inbreeding, and starvation if there is no bamboo to eat.

In southwestern China there are just a few mountain ranges in which the giant panda survives. The towering peaks, often shrouded in mist and cloud, are separated by steep-sided valleys covered with a mix of broadleafed and coniferous forest. The understory is made up of forbs (nongrass species of plants) and different species of bamboo that grow in dense, tall stands. Pandas are solitary and each one occupies a small territory of 1.6–2.6 square miles (4–6.5 square km). During the year they range from altitudes of 11,220 ft (3400 m) in summer down to 3960 ft (1200 m) in winter. None now ventures below this level because the forest and its bamboo have been largely replaced by cultivated crops.

Risk of isolation

Since pandas live only in mountainous areas, they can easily become isolated if the valleys in between those mountains are settled and become barriers to movement. Most people tend to live in valleys where the climate is milder, and then cultivate or graze livestock on the surrounding mountain slopes. In this part of China people can cultivate areas high on the hillsides because even at 1650 ft (500 m) the climate is mild enough to grow wheat, rice, and other vegetables. As a result, little of the natural vegetation is left, and the giant panda can be restricted to a narrow belt of forest, sometimes little more than 0.75 miles

(1.2 km) wide. If a panda has to move from its territory for whatever reason, it invariably has to cross a valley where there is no food and, despite being legally protected, is still at risk of injury or death from dogs and/or humans.

Giant pandas roll bamboo leaves into bite-sized wads before chewing them thoroughly.

Dependence on bamboo

Bamboo is an essential part of the giant panda's habitat. So close is the association of the two that, without palatable bamboo species, there are no pandas. Bamboo has an unusual life cycle. Most of the time it reproduces vegetatively (asexually) by sending out more shoots, but periodically it flowers, produces seeds, and then dies. To ensure the flowers are cross-fertilized and remain vigorous, all bamboo of a particular species flowers at the same time. This results in a large die-off of bamboo, which, coupled with the fact that the seeds may take up to three years to produce new shoots, considerably reduces the stock of food available. In the past, giant pandas would simply move on to another area, but now that their habitat is so fragmented and small, they cannot easily do this. Sadly, about 40 years ago, when the umbrella bamboo flowered over large areas of the Min Mountains and subsequently died off, at least 138 pandas died as a result, so specialized is their diet.

Classification

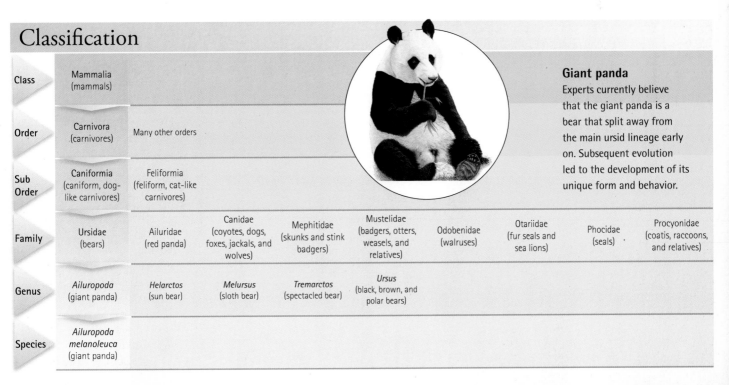

Giant panda
Experts currently believe that the giant panda is a bear that split away from the main ursid lineage early on. Subsequent evolution led to the development of its unique form and behavior.

Class	Mammalia (mammals)									
Order	Carnivora (carnivores)	Many other orders								
Sub Order	Caniformia (caniform, dog-like carnivores)	Feliformia (feliform, cat-like carnivores)								
Family	Ursidae (bears)	Ailuridae (red panda)	Canidae (coyotes, dogs, foxes, jackals, and wolves)	Mephitidae (skunks and stink badgers)	Mustelidae (badgers, otters, weasels, and relatives)	Odobenidae (walruses)	Otariidae (fur seals and sea lions)	Phocidae (seals)	Procyonidae (coatis, raccoons, and relatives)
Genus	Ailuropoda (giant panda)	Helarctos (sun bear)	Melursus (sloth bear)	Tremarctos (spectacled bear)	Ursus (black, brown, and polar bears)				
Species	Ailuropoda melanoleuca (giant panda)								

Adaptation and Behavior

Giant pandas are solitary animals, despite living in territories that overlap with one another. Males often range through the territories of neighboring females and sub-adults, but they rarely make contact except during the breeding season. Females spend most of their time in a core area of their territory, and will not tolerate the presence of other pandas within it. Communication is mainly by scent marking, though pandas are capable of making 11 different vocalizations. Males move silently along the boundaries of their range, marking trails either by clawing trees, spraying them with urine, or rubbing on secretions from the glands under their tail. They sleep in hollow trees, rock crevices, or caves; some may even climb into the fork of a tree, but most live mainly on the ground. With no permanent dens to return to, and with generally abundant bamboo to eat, they seldom travel more than about 650 yards (600 m) in a day.

Protection against the elements
Although temperatures in southwest China are not extreme, the giant panda has a sedentary lifestyle, so it needs a thick coat to minimize the amount of body heat lost to its surroundings. Its coat also needs to be capable of repelling moisture, as the relative humidity of its forest habitat is high—on average about 80 percent.

Daily life
The giant panda has several adaptations for eating bamboo, including forepaws that are capable of clutching stems. However, the scanty amount of nourishment it obtains from this diet means that it is unable to lay down vast fat reserves and sleep out the winter like some other bears. Instead, pandas spend around half the day eating bamboo to meet their basic needs, the peak activity times being early morning and late afternoon. In between they pass an hour or two grooming and scent-marking, but the remainder of the day is spent resting to conserve the little energy they have created.

Hunting and Feeding

Around 99 percent of the giant panda's diet comprises bamboo shoots and roots, but it will also eat other food, including meat and eggs, when available. This would suggest that the panda's diet is restricted to bamboo only because there is little else to choose from, particularly during the winter.

Thirst quenching
Most gullies in the panda's mountainous habitat contain water, which is fortunate, as it needs to drink every day through much of the year. Only spring bamboo shoots contain enough water to balance the amount lost in the panda's urine and feces.

In keeping with most members of the bear family, the giant panda is omnivorous, eating opportunistically when suitable food comes its way. After bamboo, the remaining 1 percent of its diet consists of flowers, vines, mushrooms, grass, fish, small rodents, occasionally wild parsnips, and even carrion. Like the American black bear, it has been observed to scratch bark from certain conifers to eat the nutritious layer underneath.

Carnivorous heritage
Bone fragments and the hair of musk deer, tufted deer, and golden monkeys have been found in the droppings of a few individuals, and certainly the powerful cheek teeth would

Types of food
Different parts of the bamboo plant are eaten at different times. Stems and new shoots are preferred between March and June, when the leaves are avoided. Leaves and stems become more important during the winter. Any insects resting on the bamboo are also eaten.

Ants on bamboo stem

Arrow bamboo

serve equally well for crushing bones as bamboo stems. In practice, though, meat is rarely eaten because the giant panda lacks both the speed and stamina to catch anything.

Eating bamboo

A giant panda usually eats while in a sitting or half-lying position, leaving its forepaws free to clasp bamboo stems. It spends about 10–14 hours a day feeding, consuming about 15 percent of its body weight. Food passes through the gut in 8–11 hours, and only a fifth is actually digested. Because of this, panda feces are often greenish in color, and different parts of the bamboo, such as the leaves, are still clearly recognizable—only the stems disappear completely.

Digestion

Plants are made of cells, the contents of which are enclosed in indigestible cellulose. The giant panda has none of the special adaptations seen in grazing animals, such as stomach bacteria that convert cellulose into digestible cellulase, and long intestines to allow for slower absorption of nutrients. However, some of the panda's cheek teeth are broader and flatter than those of true carnivores—such as the polar bear—and these, assisted by the powerful jaw muscles, are used to crush the bamboo before swallowing it. In addition, the esophagus has tough, longitudinal folds that protect it from the sharp, fibrous bamboo stalks. The short intestine gives little time for the uptake of nutrients: Most occurs in the colon, which has a larger surface area than in other bears.

Sitting comfortably

Pandas adopt a sitting or semi-reclining position while feeding in order to leave their forepaws free to hold and manipulate bamboo stems. Adopting these relaxed positions also saves energy.

Bamboo leaves

Bamboo shoots

Dragon spruce

Life Cycle

Giant pandas live for about 20 years, but mature slowly, not breeding until they are five or six years old. Females rear a cub every two years, and if they give birth to twins, they usually elect to raise just one. Helpless at birth, the cubs are weaned at 8–9 months, and are independent of their mother at 18 months, by which time she may be pregnant again.

Producing young

Mating
Males may accompany a female for a short period prior to mating. In captivity, females may encourage the male to mount her by backing into him as shown here.

Newborn
Females carry newborn cubs either in their mouth, as shown here, or cradled in a forepaw. The helpless cub relies on its mother for warmth, food, and protection.

Growing up
Born pink, giant pandas develop their adult coloring over a period of about three weeks. During these early days they spend most of their time sleeping and feeding.

The mating season of the giant panda lasts from March to May, and is the only time when pandas are sociable or vocal. The female is sexually receptive for about three weeks, during which time her behavior changes dramatically. She stops eating, makes bleating and chirping noises, and increases the frequency of her scent-marking.

Males attracted to the female compete for mating rights. The union is brief, lasting only a couple of minutes, but may be repeated many times over 1–3 days. Gestation time varies considerably from 97 to 163 days, depending on how long the fertilized egg floats in the uterus of the female before implanting and developing. This floating time can be anything up to 100 days. The reason

Twins
It is very rare for a female panda to rear twins to adulthood; a single cub is much more common. Here a mother plays with her cubs. Only when accompanied by young does a giant panda socialize with others of its kind.

for this delay is to ensure that cubs are always born sometime during August and September, when bamboo leaves are at their most nutritious.

Birthing
Females give birth in a den that is about 3 ft (1 m) in diameter, and high enough for them to sit upright to hold and suckle their cub. Offspring are born naked, blind, and helpless. About the size of a rat, the cub does not develop black markings until it is about a

week old; at three weeks it has the same markings as an adult. Often two cubs are born, but lactation is expensive in terms of energy, so if both survive the first few weeks of life, one of the cubs is usually abandoned. In the wild, females may leave their offspring for periods to feed, but in captivity a cub is often held continuously by the mother for the first few weeks of life: With dextrous forepaws, she holds the cub close to her chest for warmth and to suckle. The den is abandoned when the cub is one or two months old. Although its eyes are now open, it is still helpless, so the mother carries it around in her mouth, allowing it to suckle 3–4 times a day.

Cub life

At three months the cub can walk in a coordinated manner and suckles only 2–3 times a day. It is more playful, starts to climb, and is generally much more adventurous. At six months it has most of its milk teeth and starts to eat bamboo. Cubs are completely dependent on their mother until they are fully weaned at 8–9 months. In captivity, cubs that are kept together will play with each other, much as other young animals do, but as they get older, they revert to a more solitary existence.

A taste for bamboo

Juveniles start to eat bamboo at about six months of age, by which time they have milk teeth to chew with. While there are 1000 species of bamboo, pandas eat only 42 of them. The young bears learn all about the palatable types as they accompany their mother on foraging trips.

Growing up

At about 18 months old, young pandas are independent. Some will set up territories that overlap with those of their mother, but others, often female, will travel further afield. Like adult giant pandas, they spend most of their time eating. Where food is abundant, they need not move far to find it. Interacting with other pandas uses energy and reduces feeding time, so is avoided. Scent-marking of territory reinforces this message to other pandas.

Adult life

In adulthood the sedentary lifestyle of the giant panda is balanced between the limited amount of energy it obtains from its food and what it expends on its basic needs. These bears spend the majority of their time alone, eating for most of the day, with rest periods in between. They may sleep at any time of the day or night, usually for periods of 2–4 hours. In captivity, these two activities tend to be reversed, with pandas sleeping most of the time, and feeding only for a short while. Little time is wasted on defending a territory or producing offspring.

Young climbers

Like other bear cubs, young pandas learn to climb trees. Adult pandas, though, do this only rarely, probably because it requires so much energy. They tend to climb if harassed, or occasionally to sun themselves.

Legend and History

Although the giant panda is considered a symbol of peace in China—possibly as it rarely attacks or eats other animals—its remote habitat and scarcity mean that it was not well known until relatively recently. This perhaps explains why it features in fewer recorded myths and legends than one might expect, and was apparently never used in oriental medicine.

The peaceful image of the giant panda possibly arises also from the ancient belief that it fed on copper and iron—metals often associated with peacetime. When pandas occasionally wandered into villages, they were seen licking copper and iron cooking pots. Since in times of war, metal pots were turned into weapons, people believed that the panda went hungry in wartime, but prospered in peacetime.

Decorative skins

Writings from 3000 years ago mention a mysterious white creature, variously said to be a fox, tiger, or leopard. Of course, it might have been a panda, but the first confirmed account relating to the animal dates from around AD 621 during the T'ang Dynasty. Later, in 685, the Japanese recorded a gift from the Chinese, probably Empress Wu Tse-Tien, of two white bears and a number of skins. From that time on the panda is noted more often, perhaps because traders passed through its habitats along the Silk Route towards Beijing. Generally, though, the giant panda roused little interest, although its skins were valued as decorative and luxurious possessions.

M am. David

Great naturalist

Best remembered for discovering a species of deer and the giant panda, Père David (above) made many other discoveries during his years in China, including 58 species of bird, 100 types of insect, and many different plants.

Sensational achievement

Ruth Harkness (left) fulfilled her late husband's ambition by capturing a live panda cub and taking it to the U.S.A. Su-Lin, as the cub was called, not only survived the arduous journey, but was also probably the first "wild" animal to be seen at close quarters, unconfined by a cage, in 1936.

Diplomatic relations

In the 19th century, as Western powers pressed China into allowing more foreigners into the country, various exploratory expeditions were mounted. These revealed a wealth of plants and animals new to science. Père David, a French Lazarist missionary who lived in China between 1862 and 1874, first managed to secure the skins of a baby and adult giant panda, which he sent to Paris. His description of the animal was, at his request, published in 1869, prior to the specimens arriving at their destination. In subsequent anatomical studies the panda was referred to by various names, such as the clawed bear or bamboo bear. It was not until 1901 that the name "great panda" was suggested by E. Ray Lankester, the then director of the Natural History Museum in London, to distinguish it from the red panda, with which it was then classified. "Great" soon succumbed to "giant," and the panda now had a common name that was known to most English-speaking peoples.

Live capture

Over the next 30–40 years the elusive panda was sought by many game hunters, including the sons of U.S. president Theodore Roosevelt. A number of skins and skeletons made their way to Western museums, but fortunately the challenge then shifted, with hunters instead vying to bring a live giant panda to the West. An expedition led by William Harkness came to nothing when he died in Shanghai in February 1936 before ever reaching his destination. His wife, however, took up the challenge, and by November of that year, despite numerous hardships, she had obtained a baby panda weighing less than 3 lb (1.3 kg). Called Su-Lin, the baby panda aroused great interest among the Chinese, but that was nothing compared to its reception at San Francisco dock on December 18th, 1936, and in Chicago two days later, where the young panda caused a sensation. Su-Lin's appeal was such that the hunting of pandas rapidly fell out of favour. She was eventually housed in Brookfield Zoo in Chicago, where she died about a year later.

Strategic value

With the popularity of the giant panda assured, the Chinese government quickly saw its value as a potential diplomatic tool. Two pandas were presented as gifts to the Bronx Zoo in 1941 to thank the Americans for their help during World War II. Over 30 years later, in 1972, more pandas were donated—this time by Chairman Mao Zedong. He first presented a pair to President Richard Nixon, and then made gifts to Tokyo, Paris, London, and Mexico City. China then went through a period of loaning out pandas in return for money, but in 2007 this practice was stopped, and today they are lent only for breeding and research purposes rather than for political gain.

Why is the panda black and white?

According to Chinese legend, the giant panda was not always black and white, but was once pure white all over. The story goes that, while mourning the death of a little girl who gave her life defending a panda against a leopard, the black dye of the panda's mourning armbands began to run as tears rolled down its face and body. When the panda rubbed its eyes, it smudged the dye in black circles around them, and as it covered its ears to block out the sound of wailing and crying, these were left blackened as well. The panda has been colored black and white ever since.

Panda politics

Diplomatic gifts

The first documented record of the giant panda is probably attributable to the only woman ever to have ruled China—Empress Wu Tse-Tien (left). Known as the "white bear," its skin was valued both for its rarity and as a luxury item, being comfortable to sit or lie on. It is therefore not surprising that giant panda pelts, or even the animals themselves, would be considered suitable gifts for visiting dignitaries, or as diplomatic tools—in this case to facilitate a trade agreement between China and Japan.

Outstanding attraction

So few pandas exist outside China that they are a huge attraction in zoos that are lucky enough to have them among their collections. Here Queen Sophia of Spain visits a panda in Madrid Zoo.

Threats and Conservation

As human populations expand further into the panda's natural habitat, the challenge to survive becomes ever greater. All is not doom and gloom, though, as research has shown that where conservation measures have been put in place, giant pandas are flourishing, if not increasing in number.

Loss of habitat

Logging is a major threat to what remains of the panda's habitat, and in 1998 the Chinese government banned commercial logging within its reserves. Agriculture and grazing are also regulated, but in practice these laws are difficult to enforce.

The only real threat to panda survival is from humans, as adult pandas have no predators. The population of China is increasing, and large areas of the panda's habitat have been cleared and turned over to agriculture. In fact, the period 1974–89 saw half the forest areas of Sichuan province lost to farming. This has forced pandas to retreat to higher altitudes within their range, often isolating them in pockets of mountainous forest.

In addition to the loss of their habitat, this isolation has made giant pandas more vulnerable to the cyclic flowering of bamboo, as it means that they are unable to move into new areas, and might simply die of starvation. Those pandas that do wander into settled areas are disoriented and risk injury or death.

Poaching

Despite pandas being a protected species, the value of a pelt is so high relative to what a local person can earn that poaching has become a significant problem. However, tourism is providing another source of revenue, and some of that money is going towards conservation work. Sadly, even that can have negative effects because it has been discovered that animals can develop abnormal behaviors when observed for long periods, or not given sufficient rest or time to feed undisturbed.

Ongoing problems

Although the giant panda is now bred successfully in captivity, and numbers in the wild are relatively stable, small populations are always at risk from inbreeding and subsequent loss of genetic variation, which render them vulnerable to birth defects and disease. The smallest viable population size is thought to be about 50 individuals, and there are already populations of pandas in isolated areas that number less than this.

Even if the panda does survive, its habitat may not. Pandas need bamboo, but they also need large trees, such as fir and hemlock, to use as scent posts and birthing dens. Once removed, these trees take many years to regenerate, and often they do not succeed because other species, such as birch, compete more successfully for the space.

It remains to be seen whether or not this slow-maturing, highly specialized bear and its shrinking habitat will survive in the modern world.

Hope for the future

Today there are only about 1600 giant pandas left in the wild, and they are highly endangered. Various measures are in place to ensure their survival, but it is unlikely that numbers will increase significantly in the wild as there are few places left where they can live. The Chinese government has, with the help and advice of WWF, created more than 50 reserves, which means that over 45 percent of remaining panda habitat is protected. Creating "corridors" between islands of forest may also help to maintain genetic diversity by allowing some movement.

Research stations, such as that at Wolong, allow scientists to study giant pandas in great detail. They research both wild and captive populations, and have successfully reared many of the second cubs that females have abandoned. Outside China there are very few giant pandas, and even fewer pairs that have bred successfully. However, as our knowledge of these animals increased, so too did the number of births—aided by artificial insemination. Zoos also cooperated in lending pandas to one another, even though they were the main attraction of their collections. Zoos in Mexico, Spain, and the U.S.A. have bred successfully from their giant pandas on more than one occasion.

Distant friends

These captive sub-adult pandas are drinking together, but there is little interaction between them. Solitary creatures by nature, they might have played together as cubs, but as they mature, they go their separate ways, even if kept in the same enclosure.

Human help

As our knowledge of the giant panda increases, so too does the survival of cubs bred in captivity.

How can we help?

● Make donations to organizations such as WWF, which are providing funds for wild panda conservation. It costs around $600,000 a year to protect one panda in its native habitat.

● "Adopt" a panda at a zoo that requires funding for its artificial insemination programs.

● Support reforestation projects that create "corridors" between isolated patches of panda habitat.

current status: **Critically endangered**

Species Survival Commission

IUCN
The World Conservation Union

Sun Bear

CLASS: Mammalia   **ORDER:** Carnivora   **FAMILY:** Ursidae   **GENUS & SPECIES:** *Helarctos malayanus*

As it scampers through the tropical rainforest, the little Malayan sun bear, the world's smallest bear, is dwarfed by some of the planet's tallest trees. Quite undeterred, the intrepid and surprisingly nimble bear blithely scales the heights of tropical giants without a backward glance. Perched high in leafy boughs, it whiles away the time, feasting on fruit and grubs, snoozing and musing, sunning, humming, and sucking its paws. Seldom seen in the wild, rarely studied, and little understood, the sun bear remains one of the world's most elusive and endangered creatures.

Defying gravity, sun bears sink sickle-shaped claws into giant rainforest trees and shin up trunks in seconds.

Key Features

- No larger than a dog, sometimes called the "dog bear," it has a sharp bark and a sharper bite.

- The only bear to live in the tropical rainforest.

- The sun-like crest on its chest inspired its common name.

- Nicknamed "honey bear" for its sweet tooth.

In Focus

By bear standards, the sun bear is surprisingly small—ten times smaller than the polar bear, and not much larger than a black bear cub. Yet it has a compact and powerful body, with muscular forelegs, ideal for climbing. The sun-like crest on its chest probably helps exaggerate its size and startle its foes.

Beady eyes

Although the sun bear's eyes are small, beady, and shortsighted, it can probably distinguish the bright colors of tropical fruit, and spot distant movement even in the dark. It compensates for any myopia by having an acute sense of smell, catching the whiff of food over 3 miles (5 km) away.

Sickle-like foreclaws

The large forepaws and long, curved claws are well suited to scaling giant hardwood trees. On the jungle floor, the sun bear uses its 4 in (10 cm) claws to rake through rotten wood and termite mounds.

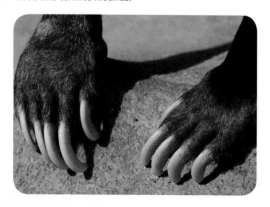

Close-cropped fur

The sun bear's sleek, short-haired coat easily sheds forest mud and rainwater. Swiveling around in its loose and baggy skin, it can bite any predator intrepid enough to attack.

Extra long tongue

The superlong tongue, which can grow up to 10 in (25 cm) long, is ideal for sucking up every last drop of honey from bees' nests, and scooping out grubs from deep termite mounds.

Streamlined ears

Set low on its head, the bear's small, round ears allow it to slip through the jungle's dense understory without getting tangled in leaves and branches.

Powerful teeth

Its four unusually large canine teeth help the bear to smash open logs and termite mounds in search of insects; as sharp as tigers' teeth, they can inflict slashing cuts on predators. The broad, flat molars are ideal for grinding up fruits and plants.

Gripping pads

The bear's furless footpads give it a firm grip on tree branches, while its pigeon-toed feet and bow legs hug the wide trunks of tropical trees.

Vital Statistics

Weight: Male 60–145 lb (27–65 kg); female 60 1b (27 kg)

Length: 4–5 ft (1.2–1.5 m)

Height: 2.3 ft (70 cm) at the shoulder

Color: Glossy black with a golden, orange, or creamy crescent or doughnut-shaped mark on the chest

Sexual maturity: 3–4 years

Gestation period: 3–8 months, including delayed implantation

Number of young: 1–3, most often 2

Birth interval: Unknown

Typical diet: Sweet fruits, especially figs; beetles, termites, ants and their grubs; bees, their honey, and larvae; small rodents, snails, lizards, and birds

Lifespan: 33 years in captivity; unknown in the wild

Did you know?

● Although the world's smallest bear, *Helarctos malayanus* is the largest carnivore on the island of Borneo.

● Sun bears build tree nests up to 130 ft (40 m) above the ground.

● Over 24 hours a sun bear can cover up to 3.5 miles (5.5 km) in search of food.

← 5 ft (1.5 m) →

2.3 ft (70 cm)

Habitat

The sun bear thrives best in the steamy, mist-shrouded rainforests of tropical Southeast Asia. Straddling both sides of the equator, its range stretches from Burma and Bangladesh across to Laos, Cambodia, Vietnam, and Thailand, peninsular Malaysia, and the islands of Sumatra and Borneo.

Distribution

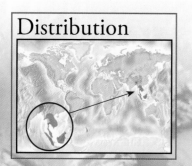

Laos montane forest
Laos, with its remote, rugged terrain and unbroken block of forest, might be one of the sun bear's last strongholds. When montane trees shed their leaves in the dry season, light floods the jungle floor, nourishing a green understory teeming with edible bugs and grubs.

China

Thailand

Laos

Vietnam

Pacific Ocean

Sumatra

Borneo

Indian Ocean

Sumatran swamps
Peat swamp forests along coastal lowlands provide an alternative home for sun bears. Swamps, however, are even more endangered than terrestrial rainforests, as they provide ideal waterways for transporting logs, and good soil for growing rice.

Tropical rainforest, Borneo
Lush lowland rainforest, the sun bear's prime habitat, provides ample shelter and water, and a staple supply of insects outside of the fruiting cycles. Dominated by tall, broadleafed trees with wide, sheltering canopies, tropical rainforest is the oldest and richest habitat on earth.

As it darts through the forest's dark understory, the sun bear is sheltered from the sweltering sun by some of the world's oldest giant hardwoods, such as the mengaris, which towers 130 ft (40 m) high. Down on the forest floor a mass of greenery teems with diverse life, nourished by more than 100 in (254 cm) of rainfall each year. With little seasonal variation in temperature, the forest remains warm—at least 80°F (27°C)—and wet throughout the year. In some parts of its range, such as Thailand and Vietnam, the sun bear lives in higher montane rainforests, which have a cooler dry season.

Tree dwellers
Being natural and nimble climbers, sun bears spend much of their time hanging out in the treetops, foraging for fruit and bugs, napping, and lapping up fresh rainwater dripping from evergreen leaves. Soon after they can walk, cubs learn to clamber up giant trees, clinging on with sharp, curved claws.

A place to crash
Like their northern cousins, sun bears create a variety of safe, secluded shelters or "daybeds", where they can crash out, chill out, and dry out. Some are built high in leafy boughs. Such tree or stick nests, made from a mass of bent and broken branches, provide soft and stable shelters. Ideal trees for stick nests seem to be large Shorea, such as the honey bee tree, with its strong, shady boughs. Sun bears seem to build tree nests more often in disturbed habitats—whether recently logged, close to human settlements, or where tigers and leopards prowl, as on Sumatra and the Asian mainland. In less disturbed habitats the sun bear seems happy to make its bed on the ground, often in the hollow trunk of a huge tree. The forest's mighty hardwood trees, such as Philippine mahogany and Borneo ironwood, with trunks up to 3 ft (90 cm) wide, offer ideal bedding sites for both day and night rest. Fallen tree logs seem particularly comfortable, providing roomy cavities carpeted with soft, dry layers of woody debris. Tucked away in the forest undergrowth, such daybeds sometimes double up as birthing dens. The sun bear also makes its bed in dirt dugouts between exposed tree roots.

> *Despite its name, the sun bear spends little time in the sun, preferring the shade of trees.*

Rainforest neighbors
In parts of its range the sun bear coexists with its Asian cousins, the Asiatic black bear in Southeast Asia and the sloth bear in northeast India, but the overlap seems too borderline to cause conflict. The sun bear's main enemies are hungry tigers or leopards, although reticulated pythons in Borneo have been known to swallow weakened individuals whole. Sun bears also share their tree home with other fruit-eaters. In fig trees, they regularly pick ripe fruit alongside binturongs (bearcats), helmeted hornbills, and other colorful birds of the forest.

Classification

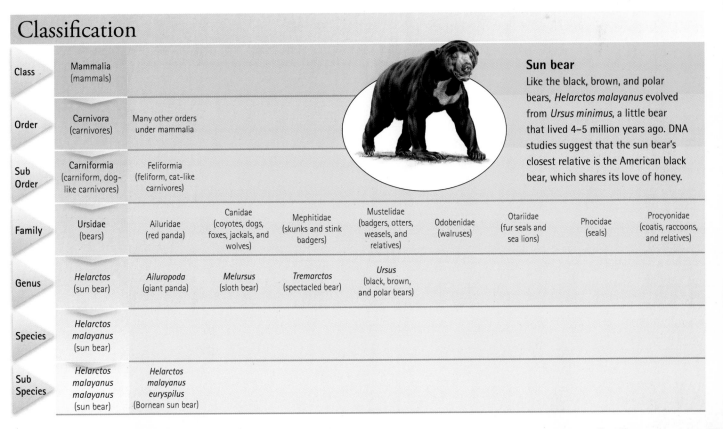

Sun bear
Like the black, brown, and polar bears, *Helarctos malayanus* evolved from *Ursus minimus*, a little bear that lived 4–5 million years ago. DNA studies suggest that the sun bear's closest relative is the American black bear, which shares its love of honey.

Class	Mammalia (mammals)									
Order	Carnivora (carnivores)	Many other orders under mammalia								
Sub Order	Carniformia (carniform, dog-like carnivores)	Feliformia (feliform, cat-like carnivores)								
Family	Ursidae (bears)	Ailuridae (red panda)	Canidae (coyotes, dogs, foxes, jackals, and wolves)	Mephitidae (skunks and stink badgers)	Mustelidae (badgers, otters, weasels, and relatives)	Odobenidae (walruses)	Otariidae (fur seals and sea lions)	Phocidae (seals)	Procyonidae (coatis, raccoons, and relatives)	
Genus	*Helarctos* (sun bear)	*Ailuropoda* (giant panda)	*Melursus* (sloth bear)	*Tremarctos* (spectacled bear)	*Ursus* (black, brown, and polar bears)					
Species	*Helarctos malayanus* (sun bear)									
Sub Species	*Helarctos malayanus malayanus* (sun bear)	*Helarctos malayanus euryspilus* (Bornean sun bear)								

Adaptation and Behavior

A native of the rainforest, *malayanus* is supremely adapted to the warm, steamy atmosphere and dense undergrowth of its tropical home. Dark fur provides the perfect camouflage for a retiring animal that likes to melt into the shadow of the forest. Dark colors also absorb heat, which helps at night when temperatures drop to 55°F (13°C). Despite its name, the sun bear spends little time in direct sunlight, preferring the soft, cool shade of logs and trees. Its unusually short hair—just 5 in (13 cm) long—easily sheds splattered mud and moisture, and protects against insect bites and scratches from branches.

Life in the treetops

Sun bears climb trees to forage, build nests, and escape predators, swarming insects, and monsoon rains. Lithe and natural climbers, they grip giant trunks between their short bow legs and pigeon-toed paws, clinging on with powerful forearms and hook-like claws. Wherever sun bears climb, they leave their "signature"—an imprint of teeth and claw marks—on the bark. Although usually active from dawn to dusk, *malayanus* becomes more nocturnal when disturbed by human presence.

Biting backs

When attacked or threatened, the sun bear flashes its sharp canines, barks loudly, and rises on its hindlegs, flaunting its startling yellow chest crest. Twisting and turning easily in its loose skin, it can inflict sharp bites on any predator, even tigers. Small, but ferocious once aroused, it is regarded locally as one of the most dangerous animals in the jungle.

Hunting and Feeding

With its nose close to the ground, the sun bear scurries across the forest floor, sniffing and grubbing around in the verdant undergrowth. Although essentially a fruit-eater, the bear subsists on insects, snails, lizards, small rodents, and even carrion when fruit is scarce.

Coconut craze
Ripping through the outer shell with rake-like claws, five-year-old Kong feasts on a coconut, his favorite fruit. Despite his blindness, Kong has no problem manipulating the fruit with deft paws, and sucking out its sweet flesh.

Dwelling in the luxuriant rainforest, where hundreds of sweet, nutritious fruits grow, sun bears are spoilt for choice, but limited to the fruiting cycles between May and July. For most of the year the bears survive on forest insects, particularly termites, beetles and their young, occasionally wasps and bees, cockroaches, and the odd scorpion. As insects provide a fairly staple food supply, sun bears wander less than their northern cousins, although they can roam quite widely during the relatively brief fruiting cycles.

Feast or famine
Periodically, the lush fruit trees in tropical rainforests flower en masse, then produce little or no seed for a season or more, when sun bears and other fruit-eaters can starve. Fortunately, even after a barren spell, *malayanus* can subsist on insects, which remain fairly constant.

Types of food

During the fruiting season, sun bears feast on a wide variety of sweet tropical fruits, such as peach palm, figs, and palm hearts. For the rest of the year they forage for beetles, termites, ants, and bees, but will also tackle larger prey, such as tortoises, pheasants, and fish.

Guavas

Bees' nests

During the short-lived fruiting season, sun bears easily compete with other fruit-eaters, reaching the top boughs in seconds. Any branches beyond easy reach are yanked over until the fruit can be nipped off. After smashing shells and skins with its claws and jaws, the bear scoops out the delicious pulp with its extra long tongue. Figs, an all-time favorite, are guzzled up whole.

Hard graft

Unlike fruit, which provides high energy with minimal effort, insects demand maximum effort with little reward. To get the most out of a termite nest, the bear first laps up the high-fat nymphs (young), eggs, and alates (reproductive members), leaving the less nutritious soldiers and workers to the end. To break into hard termite mounds, the sun bear smashes the crust into chunks, then licks up the swarming insects. Bees' nests, hidden high in treetops, are no safer. After ripping open a nest with its claws, *malayanus* sucks out honey and larvae, howling with pain from angry bee stings. Although its fondness for the sweet liquid inspired its nickname, "honey bear," it is probably keener on the bees' more nutritious larvae.

A fast worker

As fallen fruit and dead animals rot quickly in the warm, moist jungle, the sun bear has evolved a rapid "skimming" technique. Setting out at dawn, it scurries across the forest floor, nose to the ground, sniffing out and gobbling up any fallen fruit, snails, eggs, lizards, termites, and rodents.

When living close to farms, sun bears raid crop fields for papayas, bananas, oil palm, and coconut hearts, the last being a special favorite. As eating the coconut buds destroys the tree, sun bears are often killed as pests.

Forest feast
To reach insects nesting within hollow trees, the sun bear gnaws through hard wood with its razor-sharp canines. Once it has broken through, it probes inside with its superlong tongue, scooping up the hapless bugs.

Palm fruits

Termites

Watermelon

Life Cycle

With tropical warmth all year round, the Malayan sun bear can breed at any time of year, but usually mates during the fruiting season, when energy-high sugar is abundant. In Burma, unusually, breeding is seasonal, tied to the hottest weather, while in captivity, breeding peaks in the spring and fall.

Mating and birth

Forest courtship
Couples mate repeatedly during the breeding season. As females do not ovulate spontaneously, frequent mating is needed to stimulate ovulation.

First steps
Leaving his den for the first time, four-month-old Duma yelps for his mother, while struggling over a branch twice his size. In the dense forest, vocal sounds keep mother and cub in touch.

Courtship is triggered by the onset of estrus at the start of the breeding season, when females grow lethargic and lose their appetite. Marking their scent along major bear trails, they attract the interest of roving males, who grow increasingly restive. Calling loudly from the trees, courting males track and visit prospective mates for a couple of weeks. Courtship is relatively brief by bear standards, lasting from two to seven days. It is quite a noisy and boisterous affair, with much clucking, barking, sparring, chasing, hugging, head bobbing, and kissing. When the female finally reaches peak receptivity, the male initiates copulation. If the female fails to conceive during the spring estrus, she

Watch and learn
Watching intently, a bright young cub exactly mirrors his mother's posture and gesture. By copying her every move, he will learn the vital lessons of jungle survival.

might mate later in the year. As with other bears, the egg's implantation on the uterine wall seems delayed until the female has feasted and stored enough fat to nurse her cubs after birth. Gestation varies between three and eight months.

Forest birth
Although little is known about birth in the wild, the local Indonesians report that sun bears give birth in secluded forest arbors, or within the trunk of a

First-year cubs scamper up trees soon after they leave the den. After hectic antics in the treetops, they often fall asleep, coiled snugly around a tree branch, paws all a-dangle.

hollow tree or log. Giant hardwoods with capacious cavities, sometimes 3 ft (90 cm) wide, provide ample and comfortable shelters, carpeted with soft, dry matting. Tucked away in the dark forest undergrowth, such log and tree-trunk dens afford safe refuge for growing cubs. Dirt dens are also sometimes dug out beneath the massive roots of tropical trees.

Generally, twins are born, sometimes triplets. Like all bear cubs, the newborns are deaf, blind, and helpless. Minute and mouse-like, they weigh no more than 7–10 oz (225–325 g). At birth their skin is nearly transparent and hairless. For the first two weeks, the little bears cannot walk, but after feeding on their mother's creamy milk, they gain strength and develop rapidly. Although their eyes open after 25 days, the cubs remain virtually blind for up to 50 days.

During the first two months, the mother constantly licks her cubs, stimulating urination and defecation. To achieve the same result in captivity, orphaned cubs need to be sponged several times a day, or they will die.

Once on their feet, the playful cubs bounce and bob along behind their mother. Watching her every move, they learn fast how to forage and survive in the forest. Within three months they are running and romping through the undergrowth.

Although quite as devoted as grizzly moms, mother sun bears do not always defend their cubs quite so ferociously. If threatened, they might attack, but have also been known to take fright and drop their cubs rather than fight. Occasionally, fathers stay to help raise their young—sun bears, unlike their larger relatives, are thought by some to be monogamous. Although generally weaned sometime after the third month,

cubs stay with their mother until fully grown, at about two or two and a half years old. Some months after weaning, usually in the seventh month, the little bears shed their milk canines, but do not grow a full set of adult teeth until around 18 months.

Much like children who suck their thumbs, sun bears often suck their paws and hum, possibly contentedly, but more probably as a sign of uncertainty or boredom. Parent sun bears communicate with hoarse grunts, a bit like male orangutans.

Going it alone

When leaving their mother's protection, littermates often set off together and share the task of foraging. Juveniles reach sexual maturity at three years old, but might not mate until four or five, depending on how well nourished they are.

Although captive sun bears can live up to 25 years, their wild cousins probably die younger, from disease or starvation, or by falling prey to tigers, poachers, and farmers.

Best tree
A wistful-looking yearling hugs a tree as though it is his only friend. It is easy to see why young sun bears are kept as pets throughout their range.

Legend and History

Less awesome and compelling than either grizzlies or polar bears, the little Malayan "man-bear" (*beruang orang*) nonetheless won a place in the hearts and folktales of the local people. Smiling at *beruang's* treetop antics, the Malayans call him *basindo nan tenggil*—"he who sits high"—and sit high he does, sometimes 130 ft (40 m) up a tree.

The original tribes who shared the rainforest with the sun bear imagined all life as essentially sacred and inextricably linked by one all-pervasive life force, soul, or spirit. For the Kelabit of Borneo, the wild life force (*lalud*) pervaded the dense primary forests, where fearless heroes hunted, bringing back not just vital meat and hide, but the life-giving *lalud* force itself.

In common with the first peoples of America and Europe, rainforest tribes evolved elaborate rites and taboos to summon, placate, and honor the powerful spirits of the forest. When, for example, the Dusuns and Dayak of Borneo cut down trees to make way for rice paddies, they traditionally left one tree standing in the center of the ricefield, as a refuge for the forest spirits.

Claw power

After harvesting the bear's meat and hide, the rainforest peoples fashioned its claws into dagger sheaths, earrings, and ceremonial necklaces. More than simply decorative, bear claws were badges of valor—talismans charged with the bear's legendary courage.

Hunting valor

Armed with a spearpoint dagger and deadly *sumpit* (blowpipe), a Penan Daya hunts in the dense Bornean rainforest. The Dayak and Kelabits harvested sun bears for fat and fur. Killing a bear was a rite of passage and feat of valor.

In the beginning

In Malayan legends the bear plays its inimitable part in creating the world at the dawn of time. The Kintak Bong tell how the earth was fashioned by the dung beetle, who unearthed some powdery clay from beneath the ground. The powder rose and rose, billowing up to the sky, until the bear reared up on its hindlegs, and crashed down, stamping the earth into shape with its paws. The tale reflects the harmony between great and small, and the extraordinary potential in the most ordinary events.

The tiger and the bear

Closer in spirit to *Aesop's Fables*, early Malayan folktales describe the bear's legendary sweet tooth, strength, courage, and rivalry with tigers. One story tells how the bear lost its tail.

Why the bear has no tail

"A thin water buffalo grazing quietly along the river was startled by a tiger sniffing at her hoofs. 'A feast for sore eyes!' he purred. The buffalo's fur stood on end, but she thought on her hoofs and replied enticingly: 'But I shall be so much fatter after a week's grazing.' The tiger reasoned that he could only be hungrier in a week's time. 'I'll be back,' he growled over his shoulder.

"A week later, the buffalo moped along the riverbank, not knowing where to turn, when a crippled monkey called from the trees, 'Why so low?' After the buffalo sighed out her story, the monkey shrugged his tail and huffed, 'Give me a ride, and I'll show you the way to go!' Soft rustling warned them of the tiger's presence. Immediately, the monkey popped a fleshy brinjal fruit in his mouth. Munching noisily, he murmured, 'Mmm… tigers' heads are so tasty.' The tiger stared, took fright, and bolted. Running through the forest, he bumped into a bear with his nose in a bees' nest—bears don't see very well. The tiger told his story and asked the bear to take a look. The bear replied politely that it was not his affair, but he'd come along if it would help. As both were growing anxious about the strange turn of events, they tied their tails together to prevent either running away.

"As soon as they found the buffalo, her monkey friend noisily munched his 'tiger's head.' Bear and tiger stared, took fright, and bolted, pulling their tails apart. When they stopped running, the bear looked behind, but couldn't find his tail. The tiger swirled his around, boasting, 'Your loss is my gain.' To this day, the bear has a stump for a tail."

The mythic bear comes off with a short tail but good nature, while the tiger is cast as a selfish schemer.

What a pet!

Although a familiar character in old Malayan folktales, the sun bear was unheard of in the West until the 19th century, when Sir Thomas Stamford Raffles, an English civil servant with a passion for natural history, "discovered" the sun bear and named him *Ursus malayanus* Raffles in 1821. A gifted linguist, Raffles rose through the ranks of the East India Office, serving as governor of Bencoolen (Sumatra) from 1818, and founding Hong Kong in 1819. While in Bencoolen, Raffles reared a sun bear cub that apparently joined the family for dinner, feasting on mangoes and drinking champagne. Similarly, many people of Bencoolen, as well as the neighboring Malayans and Thais, kept sun bears as pets. The tradition of raising sun bears continues today, encouraged by Buddhist ideals of harmlessness and "right effort," epitomized by monks who fearlessly tend the wildest animals. As playful as puppies, "dog bears" clearly make delightful pets, but can grow too big and bad-tempered to keep, when they might be donated to zoos and sanctuaries, or returned to the wild, or sometimes, sadly, sold to the bear parts market.

Pet sun bears

Governor's pet
Sir Thomas Stamford Raffles, governor of Bencoolen (Sumatra) "discovered" not only the Malayan sun bear, but also the long-lost Borobudor Temple of Indonesia. A Renaissance man, with a passion for culture and nature, he filled his menagerie with exotic creatures, including a pet sun bear that joined the family for dinner.

In the right spirit
Epitomizing Buddhist harmlessness, monks at the Thai "Tiger Temple" fearlessly tend the wildest animals, not only stray dogs and sun bears, but tigers and lions. Throughout Thailand, people look after pet sun bears, inspired by Buddhist ideals of kindness and "right effort."

A walk in the park
Not much larger than a Labrador, young sun bears, or "dog bears" as they are sometimes called, make energetic and engaging pets. Some pet bears in Thailand enjoy all the home comforts—cool baths, warm blankets, peeled fruit, and walks in the park.

Threats and Conservation

Sun bears once roamed far and wide through the tropical rainforests of Southeast Asia. Now they cling on, in isolated patches, to a fraction of their former homestead, their shrinking habitat systematically plundered and fragmented by relentless logging and burgeoning human settlement.

The two biggest threats faced by sun bears are erosion of their habitat and poaching. The bears' natural home has been reduced and fragmented by human settlements and massive logging programs. Every year more rainforest is cut down to build houses and make way for roads, farms, and plantations, slashing through wildlife habitat. As villages and plantations overrun the sun bear's home, clashes become inevitable, especially when the bears raid precious crop fields. Particularly bitter conflict arises over the lucrative coconut palm heart, which sweet-toothed *malayanus* loves to gorge on. Unfortunately, devouring the palm buds destroys the entire harvest, provoking farmers to shoot the animal as a pest.

Bear trade

Although poaching is illegal in Southeast Asia, sun bears are still hunted for the thriving trade in bear parts, particularly paws and gallbladders. Paws, a delicacy served up in paw soup, are much prized in Asia. Gallbladders are used in traditional Chinese medicine to treat wide-ranging ailments, from baldness to rheumatism. The trade in gallbladders is highly lucrative, dried gall selling for 18 times the price of gold. Bear cubs are particularly at risk, being poached mainly for bile farms, where their bile is "milked," but also for the bear market, where they are sold as pets. When they grow up, some are returned to the wild, where they often fall victim to poachers or angry farmers.

Short shrift

Ripping through Malaysian rainforest to clear a logging path, a bulldozer wipes out in weeks what took thousands of years to grow—one of the world's most ancient, rich, and biologically diverse rainforests.

Stuff of nightmares

Trapped in coffin-like "crush-cages," bears are milked for their bile from a steel tube inserted in their gallbladder. Stressed, sick, and in constant pain, they are literally tortured to death. Although bear bile, a traditional Chinese cure-all, does contain a healing chemical, artificial substitutes now exist.

Safe reserves?

The sun bear's future depends on the survival of enough secluded forest habitat to support healthy populations. Even where trees have been logged, sun bears might survive, provided the forest is left to revive rather than being overrun by new settlements or plantations. To safeguard the sun bear's habitat, national parks and forest reserves have been set aside, and hunting made illegal in Malaysia. Unfortunately, in Borneo and much of Southeast Asia conservation law is not strictly applied. Without legal enforcement, reserves merely serve as a magnet, drawing poachers after easy pickings.

Future sun bears

To boost the falling numbers of wild sun bears, several U.S. zoos tried captive breeding during the 1990s, but with limited success. Fearing that the captive population in North America might die out, Woodland Park Zoo in Seattle called in panda experts from San Diego Zoo to try artificial insemination. In June 2004 Suntil, a bear from Borneo, became the world's first sun bear to undergo artificial insemination. Although she failed to conceive, the experiment broke new ground, providing valuable data for future trials.

Sanctuary for the sun bear

To combat the trade in bear parts, a variety of reserves and refuges have sprung up in Cambodia, Thailand, and Vietnam, where bears, rescued from the wildlife market or bile farm, are rehabilitated, housed, and fed. At Phnom Tamao Wildlife Rescue Center in Cambodia, over 30 sun bears are kept in safe, clean enclosures funded and staffed by Free the Bears.

To publicize the cruelty of bile farms and change traditional attitudes, Pro Fauna Indonesia, supported by the World Society for the Protection of Animals (WSPA), have successfully staged exhibitions in crowded malls in Java. The star attraction is a mechanical bear developed in London—shown caged, with a steel tube stuck in its gallbladder, the arresting model graphically illustrates the horrors of bile milking for traditional Chinese medicine.

Upstaged by the superstars, sun bears have often been overlooked by conservationists. But research is now underway in Sumatra and Borneo to help protect the sun bear from continued poaching and further loss of habitat. Unless rapid headway is made, however, the rare sun bear could disappear before it can be saved. In the words of bear biologist Christopher Servheen, the situation is "ominous."

Saving the sun bear
On his way to a better life, a puzzled sun bear wriggles in protest as he is lifted to freedom by animal activists during an operation to rescue wild animals caged in a small hotel zoo in Sulawesi, Indonesia. After a spell in quarantine, the animals recuperate at rescue centers.

In safe hands
A tiny cub confiscated from illegal traders is hand-reared at the Phnom Tamao Wildlife Rescue Center in Cambodia. Rescued cubs often arrive dehydrated, disoriented, and starving.

How can we help?

● Help Free the Bears Fund to save sun bears from torture and poaching; contact www.freethebears.org.au.

● Sponsor a sun bear at Cambodian Wildlife Rescue, which provides refuge for victims of the illegal wildlife trade: www.cambodianwildliferescue.org.

● Support the Wildlife Friends of Thailand rescue center at www.wfft.org.

current status: **Vulnerable**

SSC
Species Survival Commission

IUCN
The World Conservation Union

Sloth Bear

CLASS: Mammalia   **ORDER:** Carnivora   **FAMILY:** Ursidae   **GENUS & SPECIES:** *Melursus ursinus*

Busily scratching and snuffling for ants and termites, the sloth bear seems far from slow or slothful. It sets a steady pace, sniffing intently as it rustles through dry brush and thicket in India's baking forests and scrublands. But, as the most unlikely looking bear—with long disheveled hair and mobile, trunk-like snout—it was originally mistaken for a sloth. The first reports to reach Europe in the 18th century described a curious creature with scythe-like claws and unkempt hair that hung upside down from jungle boughs for hours on end, and cried like a child. Believed to be a giant sloth, it was dubbed *Bradypus ursinus* (bear sloth), until a lively specimen reached Paris, and scientists realized that the bear-like sloth was instead a sloth-like bear.

> *"It is accepted local wisdom that a sloth bear possesses ten men's strength and twelve men's cunning."*
>
> Brian Payton, *In Bear Country* (2006)

Key Features

- The only bear endemic to the Indian subcontinent.

- Specially adapted to feeding on insects, particularly ants and termites.

- The only bear to carry its young around for up to nine months.

- Unusually vocal, its sounds can be heard up to 330 ft (100 m) away.

In Focus

Although relatively small by bear standards, the sloth bear has a compact and muscular build. Its powerful forelegs help it to scale smooth trees with ease, while its short, sturdy hindlegs provide stable support from behind. The bear's long, rumpled coat and shaggy mane, along with the blaze of white on its chest, probably help exaggerate its size and startle its enemies.

Poor sight
By all accounts, the sloth bear is nearsighted. Its lack of distance vision means that it can easily be surprised, especially at night when deeply engrossed in noisy feeding.

The "lip bear"
Once known as the "lip bear" (*Ursus labiatus*), the sloth bear has long, mobile lips, which are ideal for picking berries or scooping up scurrying bugs. The long, flat tongue can lick up grubs deep inside insect nests.

Sucking tube
The sloth bear's teeth and palate are specially adapted for feasting on ants and termites. It has a gap in its front teeth, where two upper incisors are missing, while the bony upper palate is hollowed out, creating a vacuum-like nozzle for sucking termites out of their mounds.

Mobile muzzle

Unusually long and flexible, the trunk-like snout can be twisted and pressed into tight holes to feed on insect nests. A flap at the tip of the nostrils allows the nose to be closed at will, preventing dust and debris entering as the bear feeds. Short hair on the muzzle might help shed the stinging secretions of angry insects disturbed in their nests.

Vital Statistics

Weight: Male 175–320 lb (80–145 kg); female 120–210 lb (55–95 kg)

Length: Male 4.6–6.2 ft (1.4–1.9 m)

Height: 2–3 ft (60–90 cm) at the shoulder

Color: Black, with a creamy "U," "V," or moon-shaped crescent across the chest, and pale gray hair around the muzzle

Sexual maturity: 5–6 years

Gestation period: 4–7 months, including delayed implantation

Number of young: 1–2, rarely 3

Birth interval: 3 years

Typical diet: Insects, especially termites, ants, and bees; fruits, some flowers, and honey

Lifespan: Averages 20 in the wild; 30–35 in captivity

Long-haired coat

At first sight the bear's shaggy fur might seem rather hot for an Indian summer, but the flowing hair probably acts like loose clothing, allowing air to circulate, while the lack of any under-pelt prevents overheating. The long hair also probably protects against insect bites.

Did you know?

● Sloth bear hair can grow up to 1 ft (30 cm) long.

● A sloth bear can jump down from a height of 10 ft (3 m).

● The oldest captive sloth bear lived to 40 years.

● *Melursus ursinus* can scale tree trunks as smooth and straight as poles.

● When angry or frightened, sloth bears can break into a gallop and outstrip a running person.

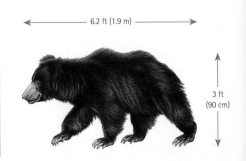

6.2 ft (1.9 m)

3 ft (90 cm)

Digging claws

The bear's strong, sickle-shaped foreclaws, up to 3 in (8 cm) long, enable it to rip into caked termite mounds, or sun-baked soil and rotten logs sheltering ants. The bow legs and bare soles give it a firm grip when climbing rocks and trees.

Habitat

Whether digging for underground streams, sheltering from drenching downpours, or chilling out in cool rock caves, the sloth bear shows canny good sense in its choice and use of resources. With typical bear flexibility, it dwells in diverse habitats, ranging from moist forest to dry savanna, from grassy floodplain to rocky outcrop.

Distribution

Terai grasslands, Nepal
On the fertile *terai* (damp) grasslands and moist riverside forests among the foothills of the Himalayas, sloth bears thrive in the highest densities, possibly as high as 0.4 per square mile (2.6 square km). Unfortunately, the populations on the *terai* floodplains and nearby Shivalik Hills are probably now isolated from the rest of India's sloth bears.

Nepal

Bhutan

India

Sri Lanka

Dry forest, central India
Populated with tall, broadleafed trees, such as teak, Indian laurel, and palash, India's dry deciduous forests provide prime habitat for local wildlife, including tigers, leopards, and sloth bears. In Panna, in central India, rocky outcrops of caves and boulders offer ideal shelter from both rain and heat.

Dry zone, Sri Lanka
The subspecies *Melursus ursinus inornatus* survives in a small population of around 300 in the dry evergreen forests of the island's northern and eastern lowlands, mostly below 1000 ft (300 m). In ideal bear habitat, densities reach 0.6 per square mile (2.6 square km).

Indian Ocean

Commonly known as the Indian sloth bear, *Melursus ursinus* is endemic to the Indian subcontinent, where it probably evolved. Its full range encompasses India, Nepal, Bhutan, possibly Bangladesh, and Sri Lanka, where a local subspecies dwells (*Melursus ursinus inornatus*). The majority of India's bears—up to 13,000—live in lowland deciduous forests, both dry and moist, although well over half seem to prefer the dry variety. A handful—up to 600—thrive on the *terai* (damp) grasslands and moist riverside forests among the foothills of the Himalayas in northern India, southern Nepal, and Bhutan. The sloth bear's strongholds in India today lie in the dry deciduous forests of the Central Highlands and the moist deciduous forests of the Western Ghats.

Chilling out

Although the sloth bear does not den up for winter sleep like its northern cousins, it does need to shelter from extreme heat in the dry season (from March to June), and from drenching downpours in the rainy season (from June to October). The average annual temperature in much of its range remains bearably hot at around 77–80°F (25–27°C), but can soar to 122°F (50°C) in the dry season, and then drop in the winter (from November to February) to 48°F (9°C), or even as low as 32°F (0°C) on the northern *terai* grasslands. For refuge from glaring sun and searing heat, the sloth bear shelters in dense thickets, tree cavities, and natural caves in rocky outcrops. Inside shady stone caves, daytime temperatures can drop 15°C (60°F) lower than outside, offering cool respite from sizzling heat. The rocky dens make ideal daybeds, where the bears can spend much of the day resting and sleeping between bouts of

nighttime foraging. Some small hillocks in India are laced with a network of caverns, where several bears—both males and females with cubs—seem content to rest in nearby caves.

Other ways to keep cool in the dry season include lying belly down on earth or stone, with mouths agape and legs spread wide. As the bear's stomach and underlegs are sparsely covered, they can "dump heat" by lying face down.

As many as 10 sloth bears can rest close together on one small hillock.

Watering well

To keep hydrated, sloth bears drink daily during the dry season. If fresh springs have dried up, the bears might travel far in search of underground streams, which they can detect up to 6.5 ft (2 m) down. The wells they dig provide water for smaller mammals, insects, and birds during the peak of the dry season.

Drying out

During the rainy season, rock caves provide ideal shelter, but the bears also create ground nests in dense lantana thickets. In Nepal the *terai* plains often flood from June to October, when many bears take refuge in upland sal forests. When the rains subside and the ground dries out in November, the bears return to the floodplains to forage for termites.

Classification

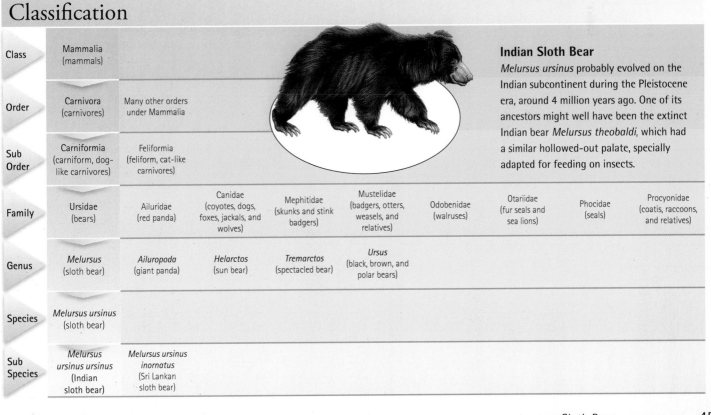

Indian Sloth Bear
Melursus ursinus probably evolved on the Indian subcontinent during the Pleistocene era, around 4 million years ago. One of its ancestors might well have been the extinct Indian bear *Melursus theobaldi*, which had a similar hollowed-out palate, specially adapted for feeding on insects.

Class	Mammalia (mammals)								
Order	Carnivora (carnivores)	Many other orders under Mammalia							
Sub Order	Carniformia (carniform, dog-like carnivores)	Feliformia (feliform, cat-like carnivores)							
Family	Ursidae (bears)	Ailuridae (red panda)	Canidae (coyotes, dogs, foxes, jackals, and wolves)	Mephitidae (skunks and stink badgers)	Mustelidae (badgers, otters, weasels, and relatives)	Odobenidae (walruses)	Otariidae (fur seals and sea lions)	Phocidae (seals)	Procyonidae (coatis, raccoons, and relatives)
Genus	Melursus (sloth bear)	Ailuropoda (giant panda)	Helarctos (sun bear)	Tremarctos (spectacled bear)	Ursus (black, brown, and polar bears)				
Species	Melursus ursinus (sloth bear)								
Sub Species	Melursus ursinus ursinus (Indian sloth bear)	Melursus ursinus inornatus (Sri Lankan sloth bear)							

Adaptation and Behavior

The dramatic extremes of India, alternating between searing drought and drenching rain, helped shape the sloth bear's body and behavior. Its long, flowing hair keeps insects at bay, while the lack of underfur and low metabolic rate prevent overheating when temperatures soar to 122°F (50°C). Sparse hair on the soles, belly, and underlegs also helps release heat when the bear splays out on its belly or presses its feet flat on the ground. To avoid intense heat, most adult sloth bears are active at night and during twilight hours, although mothers and juveniles tend to forage by day, possibly to avoid nocturnal predators and hostile male bears.

Defensive reflexes

Defensive, rather than aggressive, the sloth bear reacts violently if surprised at close quarters. Its legendary fierceness might be a natural defense against powerful predators, such as tigers and leopards. Inevitably, when local people wander through the forests gathering firewood, fruits, and flowers, they run the risk of ferocious bear attacks. If disturbed unexpectedly, the bear usually reacts with a threatening upright display and bluff charge. Most attacks in central India occur during the rainy season at dawn or dusk, usually when bears are foraging. Sloth bears commonly attack by running on all four legs and knocking the intruder down. Another tactic is to rear upright and maul, slashing the victim's upper body, face, and eyes. Afterwards the bear often flees the area.

Making connections

True to bear custom, sloth bears claw and rub trees on prime bear trails, particularly during the breeding season, possibly advertising status and readiness to mate. Although mostly solitary, sloth bears seem relatively tolerant of their fellows, sometimes sharing breeding rights, and overlapping home ranges. Equally, they seem more overtly communicative than other bears, using facial expressions, along with a fulsome range of roars, howls, huffs, puffs, rattles, and gurgles.

Hunting and Feeding

Through much of the year sloth bears sniff out ants, termites, and bees, eagerly lapping up whole colonies, including fat-rich nymphs, larvae, and pupae, along with any sweet honey. During the fruiting seasons they switch to a sugar-rich diet of fleshy, fragrant fruits, such as Indian jujube berries and mangoes.

Fruit feast
Balancing skillfully on sturdy hindlegs, a sloth bear nips off ripe berries with its long lips. Although it might pick figs and small berries in the treetops, the sloth bear usually prefers to shake plump fruits to the ground, where it can feast at leisure.

Sloth bears enjoy a mixed diet of insects and fruits, along with some flowers and honey. While insects provide a fairly staple diet through the year, most fleshy flowers and fruits are short-lived treats. Only the fig species, an all-time favorite, grows throughout the year. Unlike its relatives, the sloth bear eats little carrion, relying almost entirely on insects for the protein in its diet.

The ratio of insects to fruits varies by season and region. In Nepal's Chitwan valley, along the riverside forests and *terai* grasslands, where termites abound, insects make up the bulk of the bears' diet. By contrast, in Panna, in central India, fruit comprises over half the annual diet, with termites and ants making up the rest, along with some seasonal flowers. During the fruiting season in Panna, fruit consumption

Types of food

For the essential protein in its diet, the sloth bear relies on insects, especially termites and ants, including fat-rich grubs. Although less plentiful in the dry season, insects remain fairly constant all year round. Most fruit, by contrast, is only briefly available when in season.

Black ants

Indian jujube berries

peaks at 70 percent, while insect meals drop to a mere 16 percent. When insects become more abundant (during the rains), they provide over half the diet, with figs or late fruits comprising more than a third, supplemented with some flowers and honey.

Expert insect hunter

Rather than compete for meat with prize hunters, such as the tiger and leopard, the sloth bear evolved special lips, snout, and claws for feasting on ants and termites. With few competitors, apart from pangolins, the sloth bear just has to sniff out and expose insect nests hidden under boughs, rocks, logs, and mounds. To get at termites, it rips into rock-hard mounds with its sickle-like claws. When the caked crust breaks, the bear inserts its mobile snout, blowing away dust and dirt. Pressing elastic lips to the nest, it breathes in, sucking up the luckless termites and their nymphs (young). The rhythmic puffing and sucking can be heard up to 330 ft (100 m) away. Some ants nest underground, but the sloth bear can smell them up to 3 ft (1 m) below, and dig 5 ft (1.5 m) down to reach large colonies. Like its tropical relative, the Malayan sun bear, the sloth bear loves honeycombs. It scales high trees, rips open hanging nests with its claws, and sucks out the larvae and honey, while swatting angry bees with its paws. To descend, the bear slides backward, clinging on to creepers.

Passion for fruits and flowers

As the trees start to blossom, sloth bears make a beeline for the fragrant mohwa tree, which flourishes in India from late March into early May. Its pearly, lychee-like flowers float to the ground like drifts of snow. As the locals also prize the aromatic blossom for making wine, clashes are inevitable. Sri Lankan sloth bears

show a similar passion for palu fruit, its sweet scent drawing them from their shady hideouts. In both Sri Lanka and India an exotic variety of sugar-rich fruits grows at different times of the year, but the sloth bear always seems to know what ripens where, reaching the plump fruit just as it falls. If spoilt for choice, it will pick the most nutritious. Apart from fig, its favorites include East Indian ebony, Indian jujube, jamun, bel, guava, and mango.

Fatal opportunism

Like all bears, the sloth bear will make a play for any "fast food" found in crop fields. It is especially fond of sugar cane and maize, peanuts, and millet. Inevitably, its raids cause conflict with local farmers.

Digging for ants

After sniffing out underground ant and termite nests, the sloth bear bores deep into the sun-baked soil with long, hooked claws. Once the nest is exposed, the bear blows dirt away, then sucks up the insects through its tube-like mouth. Foraging is easiest during the monsoon and post-monsoon seasons, when the soil is soft, and breeding colonies with fatty larvae or nymphs are most plentiful.

Rock bee nest

Mohwa flowers

Termites

Life Cycle

As the first flowers blossom in March or April, the mating season gathers momentum. Males broadcast their intentions loud and clear by barking or whining, and clawing and rubbing trees with scent—probably to attract mates, while warding off rivals. In India the mating season runs until June or July, while in Sri Lanka sloth bears breed at any time of year.

Cub life

Cub naps
Tiny twins nap peacefully after suckling. Splayed out, belly down, they might be trying out the art of "heat dumping" by laying bare bellies on cool ground.

Free riding
Slung over their mother's back like a pair of furry saddlebags, cubs get a free ride for the first 6–9 months of life. With eyes fixed on mom's every move, the twins learn quickly.

Rival males gather around a breeding female and, rather than fighting off competitors, wait their turn in pecking order. Some jostling for power erupts in flamboyant threat displays and loud roars. Courtship among sloth bears is, by all accounts, a boisterous affair, with much hugging, barking, clucking, and mock fighting. Mating itself lasts just a few days, with frequent copulation to stimulate ovulation. As with other bears, the egg floats free for a spell of arrested growth until it implants on the uterine wall and develops.

Cave birth
With warm tropical temperatures and a fairly stable food supply, sloth bears do not need to hibernate, but expectant

Rocky homestead
A mother and cub rest on rocky outcrops beside their shady cave den (top right). Most sloth bears sleep in the heat of the day, but mothers and cubs often forage by day, to avoid nocturnal predators.

mothers prepare secluded birthing dens in the post-monsoon season. Many females seem to favor natural caves in rocky hillocks. Elsewhere, dirt dens are dug out of the ground beneath boulders or brush piles. Mothers shelter in dens for 6–10 weeks, living mainly off fat reserves and metabolized body water, and making just a few forays outside for food.

Sometime in the cool winter, one or two cubs are born in the cosy warmth of the den. Tiny, blind, hairless, and helpless, the newborns are kept warm on their

First steps
Intrigued by the teeming life outside his den, a three-month-old cub peers intently, sniffing everything. When his mother sets off on her feeding forays far from the den, he will ride on her back, clinging on to the long clutch of hair between her shoulders.

mother's body until they grow fluffy coats of fur. Nourished on her rich milk, they develop rapidly, and open their eyes within three weeks. Growing faster than their northern relatives, the cubs are strong enough to venture out after six or eight weeks.

Mobile nest
Unlike other cubs who rarely hitch a lift on their mother's back, young sloth bears free-ride from the day they leave the den for up to nine months. After scrambling up their mother's legs, the new cubs grab on to a thick clutch of maternal hair. Usually one cub settles on the rump, the other on the shoulders. If the twins accidentally clamber up the wrong end, a wild scramble for position ensues until both feel secure again. If either slips offcenter, the mother will shake, shuffle, or nudge them back into place. Carrying cubs protects them from predators lurking in the tall

grass and patchy shrub underbrush. It is also energy-efficient, as a mother is much less impeded with lightweights on her back than she would be with frolicking cubs lagging behind. For the first month, mothers forage close to the den, fearing to venture far afield until the cubs have grown stronger. Although well guarded by her vigilance, many still fall victim to leopards, tigers, wild dogs, and jackals.

Family dynamics
Quite unlike grizzly and polar bear fathers, male sloth bears seem gentle with their offspring, although they have little to do with their upbringing. Most cubs stay with their mother until their second or third year. Some even remain after she mates again, traveling in family groups with younger siblings. When the cubs do leave home, they often pair up for a year or two to share the burden of foraging and warding off predators. Sub-adults, especially males, disperse widely in search of their own stamping ground. In common with other bear young, the "teenage" years are tough, with probably a high rate of mortality.

Making contact
Sloth bears are unusually vocal, with a repertoire of up to nine call sounds. Roaring signifies aggressive intent; howling, screaming, and squealing express anger or fear during stressful situations; huffing acts as a warning, while chuffing signals distress in non-aggressive circumstances. Cubs also yelp when upset. Adults sometimes sound a rarely heard, long-distance call, possibly to make contact. Mothers grunt and whicker, probably in alarm, or to round up cubs. The loud huffing and puffing made when feeding might serve to ward off rivals.

En garde!
Littermates bark and snarl in boisterous sparring matches, testing their boundaries and toning muscles. Mock fighting can be noisy, with much toothy threat display, but hair never stands on end, as in real fights, and blood is rarely drawn.

Legend and History

In the Indian epic *Ramayana* the hero Rama wrestles with the forces of darkness to restore light and beauty to his realm. In the mythic struggle the bear king Jambavan lends his weight to the cause, leading his legions of warrior bears to fight alongside the allied forces of gods and monkeys. Legend has it that Jambavan still watches over his bears on the hills of India.

When Prince Rama's radiant wife Sita is abducted by the scheming demon Ravana, and spirited away to the island of Lanka, the monkey god Hanuman and the bear king Jambavan come to her rescue with legions of loyal monkeys and brave bears, who fight on the side of Rama and right. At a crucial stage in the struggle, the monkeys falter on the beach before the churning sea that separates India from Lanka. Doubting their ability to leap across the dark waters, but mostly fearing Ravana on the other side, the monkeys loiter on shore, chattering the time away. With ageless wisdom, Jambavan inspires the monkeys to cast aside fear, draw forth their innate powers, and leap boldly across the ocean to reach Lanka and Sita on the other side. The monkeys follow Jambavan's advice and soar safely across. After an epic struggle with hordes of demons, the allied forces of gods, monkeys, and bears overcome Ravana, and restore Sita to Rama.

The Seven Sages in the night sky

As ancient and wise as Jambavan, the Seven Rishis (Sages), sometimes called the Seven Bears, sparkle in the night sky as they turn on their heavenly course in the Great Bear constellation. The Hindus believe that the Great Bear keeps the universe whirling and the seasons changing, causing fruits to ripen and leaves to fall in a divinely ordered cycle of renewal. Turning the

Force of bears

Brave bears and loyal monkeys fight shoulder to shoulder with Rama in the epic battle to overthrow the dark demon Ravana. (*Ramayana*, 17th century)

wheel of birth and death, the Great Bear safeguards childbirth and smooths the passage of souls incarnating on earth. Mirroring the whorl of the Great Bear in the sky, the Hindus paint red spirals on the houses of expectant mothers. The red spirals are depicted turning to the right, encouraging the unborn to turn the right way round before entering the birth channel.

Forest guardian

In local legends the bear plays less exalted but no less helpful roles, sometimes consoling weeping women, sometimes guiding children through the forest, bearing them on its back, much as a mother sloth bear carries her cubs:
"A twin boy and girl who lived with their parents in the forest were gathering firewood when night drifted in like a dark cloud. Before they knew it, they could no longer see their feet, and started wandering in circles. The evil spirits of the forest, seeing the twins stumbling in the gloom, gathered in a swarming shadow around them. Feeling their hair stand on end, the twins took fright and bolted. As they crashed through the rustling undergrowth, they tripped over a dozy bear hidden

under a brush pile. He mumbled grumpily, 'Watch your step!' But when the twins sobbed out their sorrows, the bear took pity. Whisking the children up in his paws, he perched them on his hairy back and bounded through the brush until he came to a tree so high that its top boughs melted into the night sky. Reaching up with his hook-like claws, the bear scampered up the trunk until he touched the treetops swaying beneath the stars. After making a leafy nest, he laid the children to rest and slid backward down the trunk, peeling bark off as he went. The stripped trunk shone as white as the moon. The bear ran his paw over the smooth tree oozing with sticky sap, and nodded approvingly. Then he melted into the forest. When the evil spirits gathered in a pulsing shadow at the base of the tree, they shrieked, as the toxic sap stung, and they could find no foothold on the smooth, shining trunk. The fretful spirits lingered darkly all night until day broke, scattering the shadows away. The twins slid down the tree and ran all the way home."

Of bears, ants, and men

Like their cousins in the Americas and Eurasia, some Indian elders still remember tales of a time when bears, like monkeys, talked and lived like people, turning into men and back into bears again. Some legends tell of Indian beauties who, like their northern relatives, fell for handsome bears, and produced strong, hairy sons. Even today, some tribes fear that sloth bears might lure women from their families.

Other legends, more in the spirit of *Aesop's Fables*, tell how the bear gained its white collar, and why it spends so much time huffing and puffing over anthills: "In the time before time, when Earth was a beautiful virgin, the gods held a council to find her the best of all husbands. At first they thought of Cloud, who was quite a catch, but then realized that if Cloud and Earth married, the two would chase each other around the pole like two parts of a grindstone, crushing the world to bits. The gods threw their hands in the air in despair, and lightly brushed a rain spirit floating in the sky. Catching the spirit, they rolled it like tobacco until it turned into a strong, hairy bear. The bear married Earth, whose breasts, as everyone knows, are anthills."

Tigers beware!

Sloth bear courage is legendary—rather than flee tigers and leopards, sloth bears stand and fight. Equipped with deadly defense reflexes, they lash out at any surprise intruder, including local people. Despite, or perhaps because of, the sloth bear's reputation for savage maulings, many local Indians revere its superhuman strength, virility, and vitality. Like the American Andeans, they regard the bear spirit as guardian of the forest, nurturing the trees and rains. Belief in the life-renewing power of the sloth bear endures today in folk customs and cures. Sick children are placed on "dancing" bears; bear fat is smeared on bald scalps to regenerate hair growth, while baculum (penis bone) is used as an aphrodisiac, and claws and teeth are worn as amulets. Despite the risk of attack, many local people respect the bears and their right to remain, guarding their ancient home.

Sloth bear epics

The Seven Sages
For the Hindus, the seven bright stars in the heavens, known as the Seven Sages, or Seven Bears, keep the universe whirling on course.

Rajput courage
In the days of the martial Rajputs, princelings displayed their warrior prowess (much like American braves and Nordic *berserkers*) by over-coming fiercesome bears single-handedly with nothing more than a bow and arrow. (Indian miniature, Mughal school, 17th century)

Baloo the sloth bear
Perhaps inspired by local legends, Rudyard Kipling, author of *The Jungle Book* (1894), cast Baloo the bear as a wise guide, teaching the man cub Mowgli the ways of the jungle. The original illustrations show Baloo as a shaggy sloth bear.

Threats and Conservation

The greatest threat faced by the sloth bear is diminishing habitat. Once widespread across the Indian subcontinent, it now clings to a reduced and fragmented range—a fraction of its former homestead—competing with expanding human populations for space, shelter, and vital resources.

Originally sloth bears roamed throughout the lowland forests of the Indian subcontinent. During the 19th century, trophy hunting slashed bear populations, while in the 20th century burgeoning settlements diminished bear habitat. Many forests were plundered for prized hardwoods, such as ebony and teak, as well as for vital subsistence fuel, fodder, and fruit. Other forests were cleared for plantations, farms, villages, and roads. By the 1950s, the sloth bear had almost become a rarity, until the Wildlife Protection Act in India (1972) forbade hunting and bear trade. Even so, the Indian population has declined by 30–49 percent over the past 30 years, while in Bangladesh sloth bears have possibly disappeared.

Poaching is the second gravest threat to sloth bears, which are captured for the black market in bear parts, or for illegal street shows of "dancing" bears. Gallbladders and dried gall, much prized in traditional Chinese medicine, are exported to Asia. On a far lesser scale, bear parts, such as fat, claws, and penis bone, are traded locally for folk cures. Although poaching and trading are illegal, enforcement remains patchy.

Illegally captive cub
The nomadic Kalandars of India eke out a living by training sloth bear cubs to "dance." For the families, living with the bears is a way of life and livelihood, but the capture, mutilation, and forced "dancing" of little bears is cruel and illegal.

Expanding sanctuaries
One solution would be to expand wildlife sanctuaries. Many sloth bears already live within the safety of India's 174 reserves, but as many—at least half—live in the wild, where they are vulnerable to poaching and conflict with local people. In Sri Lanka, too, more than half the bear's range remains unprotected. As sloth bears tend to react violently to intrusion, maulings can be frequent. In central India, for instance, bear attacks can occur twice a month, usually when people graze their livestock, or gather mohwa flowers, fruits, fodder, and fuelwood. Until lost habitat is restored, conflicts are unlikely to decrease, or bear numbers to increase.

Restoring habitat
The Daroji Bear Sanctuary in Hampi, Karnataka, is a shining example of restored habitat. Brainchild of the nature photographer M.Y. Ghorpade, the sanctuary covers about 20 square miles (55 square km) in the Billikallu forest reserve. Despite a shortage of resources, the heavily quarried site was rejuvenated with fruit trees. Now a haven for many bears, it offers hope for future sanctuaries.

Disturbed and degraded habitat
Behind a lopped tree a sloth bear feeds furtively on a termite nest. Innately shy and secretive, sloth bears are easily disturbed by trespassers. As forests are plundered for resources, the bears shrink into ever smaller and poorer ranges.

Release for the sloth bear

In a tradition dating back four centuries, the wandering Kalandars (street performers) captured, trained, and exhibited "dancing" sloth bears in traveling shows. Although the custom was outlawed in 1992, it still continues in some parts of India, where more than 1000 dancing bears entertain locals and tourists. Traditionally, the Kalandars abducted cubs from their dens, removed their claws and canines, then inserted a red-hot poker in the snout to create a hole through which a rope or ring could be threaded. By pulling the rope or ring upward, the cub could be trained to stand upright and sway its paws as though in dance. As many Kalandars depend for their livelihood on dancing bears, wildlife activists have persuaded them to develop alternative lifestyles. In 2005 the World Society for the Protection of Animals (WSPA), working in partnership with the Wildlife Trust of India (WTI), initiated the Integrated Sloth Bear Conservation and Welfare

project. Designed to be far-sighted and holistic, the program aims to tackle several interrelated issues, including the rescue and rehabilitation of dancing bears, alternative support and training for the Kalandars, prevention of poaching, and widespread education to raise public awareness.

Free to play

Finally freed from its lifelong chains, an old dancing bear relaxes at Agra Bear Rescue Facility. Run by India's Wildlife SOS, the center is funded internationally by Free the Bears, One Voice of France, and Animal Rescue.

How can we help?

- Refuse to watch dancing bears when traveling in India.

- Lobby central governments to protect sloth bears and enforce laws against poaching.

- Find out what the WSPA and WTI are doing locally and nationally to rescue dancing bears (www.indianbears.com).

- Adopt a sloth bear and support bear sanctuaries (www.wildlifetrustofindia.org).

- Support conservation of sloth bears in the wild: http://nationalzoo.si.edu.

current status: **Vulnerable**

Species Survival Commission

IUCN
The World Conservation Union

In the field

Sloth bear biologist Yoganand Kandasamy and an assistant radio-collar an Indian sloth bear to study its ecology, behaviour, and diet, and to assess current threats. As suitable habitat rapidly diminishes, the race is on to find out exactly how sloth bears tick, and to plan practical conservation.

Spectacled Bear

CLASS: Mammalia   **ORDER:** Carnivora   **FAMILY:** Ursidae   **GENUS & SPECIES:** *Tremarctos ornatus*

The spectacled bear, also known as the Andean bear, is the only type to be found in South America, and is one of only two species of bear to live either side of the equator. Easily recognizable from the facial markings that inspired its name, this bear is intensely shy, preferring the high-altitude seclusion of the Andean cloud forest, far from humans. Thanks to its reclusive nature, little is known about it, but with its numbers rapidly dwindling as a result of human encroachment on its habitat, the race is on to discover more about this vulnerable bear before it disappears from even its last refuges.

"Ukuku," an Andean name for the spectacled bear, mimics the gentle trilling sound made by this shy species.

Key Features

- Usually a timid vegetarian, but occasionally takes the opportunity to attack livestock.

- Never hibernates, since its food is available all year round.

- Unlike other bears, it has 13, rather than 14, pairs of ribs.

- Has longer front legs than rear legs, making it an excellent climber.

In Focus

Smaller than the grizzly or polar bear, yet much larger than the Malayan sun bear, the spectacled bear has slightly shaggy fur, usually black, but sometimes brown or with a reddish tinge. The pale markings around its eyes—its most distinctive feature—may sometimes extend over the snout and on to the chest, giving the impression that it is wearing a bib.

Shortsighted

Although its eyesight is said to be poor, some experts think that the spectacled bear communicates visually, leaving scratch marks on tree bark around rich feeding sites. The scratches might act as visual landmarks to help the bear locate the food source again in future.

Curved claws

The big, curved claws are specially adapted for climbing, but are also useful for tearing apart bromeliads (tropical plants with long, stiff leaves) and for digging into earth and rotting wood in search of worms and insects, such as bark beetle larvae.

Acute sense of smell

Smell dominates this bear's sensory world, and is vital for finding food and communicating with other bears over great distances. The ethmoid bone within the cavity of the nose has many complex projections covered in nasal membrane, which is the sensory surface for picking up smells.

Plant-grinding teeth

Like other bears, the spectacled bear has a full set of 42 teeth, but its cheek teeth (the premolars and molars) are wide, blunt, and massive—ideal for pulverizing fibrous vegetation. Despite being mainly a vegetarian, it has retained the long, sharp, canine teeth of its more carnivorous ancestors.

Furless footpads

Unlike some other bears, the soles of the feet are not furred, but there is a continuous band of fur between the toe-pads and the ball of the foot.

Vital Statistics

Weight: Male 220–330 lb (100–150 kg); female 136–176 lb (62–80 kg)

Length: 4.3–6.6 ft (1.3–2 m)

Height: 2.3–3 ft (70–90 cm) at the shoulder

Color: Black or sometimes brown or reddish, with white rings around the eyes

Sexual maturity: 4–7 years

Gestation period: 5–8 months, including delayed implantation

Number of young: 1–3, most often 2, occasionally 4

Birth interval: Unknown

Typical diet: Fruit, hearts of bromeliads and palms, bamboo shoots, corn, sugar cane, insects, carrion

Lifespan: 20–25 years in the wild; maximum 39 years in captivity

Did you know?

● Males can occasionally grow to a length of 7.9 ft (2.4 m) and a weight of 440 lb (196 kg).

● Its direct ancestor, the giant short-faced bear (now extinct), was the biggest carnivore in the Americas.

● Its trademark eye markings are unique in every individual, or may be absent altogether.

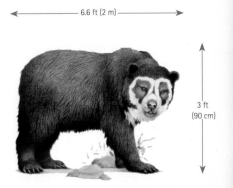

6.6 ft (2 m)

3 ft (90 cm)

Habitat

The few thousand surviving spectacled bears live mainly in isolated parts of the Andes Mountains. Typically of bears, they are adaptable and roam a variety of habitats, from desert to rainforest and high-altitude grassland. However, it is clear that they thrive best in the lush seclusion of the Andean cloud forest.

Distribution

Caribbean Sea

Colombia

Ecuador

Brazil

Pacific Ocean

Bolivia

Atlantic Ocean

Argentina

Colombian grasslands
Like spectacled bears elsewhere, those in Colombia prefer to live in the cloud forest, but often wander above the treeline on to the grassy slopes of the high Andes—the páramo—where fields of espeletia (yellow-flowered plants) grow.

Ecuador's mountain slopes
Enveloped by cloud forest, this is the place the spectacled bear really likes to call home. In general, these lush, misty forests reach up to 10,500 ft (3200 m), though here at the equator, they can be 1000 ft (300 m) higher.

Cloud forest interior
Bears in Bolivia live in mountain forest on the eastern flank of the Andes, beating paths through the dense undergrowth. The vegetation shrouds their movements from observers, but the bears might be glimpsed in places where large rivers part the canopy.

Before the 20th century, the spectacled bear ranged throughout the Andes—particularly the moist eastern slopes—from the cordilleras of Venezuela in the north, through the Andes of Colombia, Ecuador, Peru, and Bolivia, to northernmost Argentina in the south. Today, while small populations still survive in most of these countries, in Argentina they are probably now extinct, and the bear's absence from Chile can be explained by the extremely dry Atacama Desert, where there is insufficient food, water, or shelter.

Mountain dwellers

While in the past the spectacled bear probably thrived in a range of habitats, including lowland rainforest, it is now confined to inaccessible mountainous regions. Today it is rare to find bears below an altitude of 3200 ft (1000 m), though they may sometimes roam over forested habitats from about 1600 ft (500 m) above sea level to around 10,500 ft (3200 m), where the forest peters out to leave the high-altitude grassland known as páramo. They will climb higher too, wandering the páramo on foraging trips up to heights of 14,000 ft (4300 m).

Head in the clouds

The bears' preferred habitat is cloud forest—a particularly lush, high-altitude type of tropical rainforest that spends much of the year shrouded in fog. Cloud forest is a dense tangle of trees, ferns, palms, and climbers, where every branch drips with moisture, and some plant communities live rooted not to the ground but to the limbs of trees. These so-called epiphytic communities feature mosses, lichens, orchids and, most importantly for the bears, fleshy bromeliads, the hearts of which provide their staple food. While in cloud forest, the bears spend much of their day in the trees, hunting down not only bromeliads, but the fruits of the cloud forest trees. They climb as high as 33 ft (10 m) above the ground in pursuit of food.

Spectacled bears play a crucial role in the forest ecosystem, providing a seed-dispersal service for trees.

Solitary wanderers

Spectacled bears range widely across huge territories, wearing paths across the landscape along ridges and down ravines. Being mountain creatures, and good climbers, they can cope even on very steep slopes. Sometimes they roam out of the cloud forest into areas of dry forest and desert scrub, where they feed on the fruit of cactus and sapote. Such movements may follow the seasonal ripening of fruit in different areas, but scientists have only recently begun to track individual bears' movements and have much to learn. What we do know is that a spectacled bear's life is nearly always solitary. The males patrol huge ranges of up to 60 square miles (150 square km) and, as far as we know, hardly ever meet. The females have smaller ranges of around 13 square miles (34 square km), and allow their territories to over-lap, so they must encounter one another from time to time.

Classification

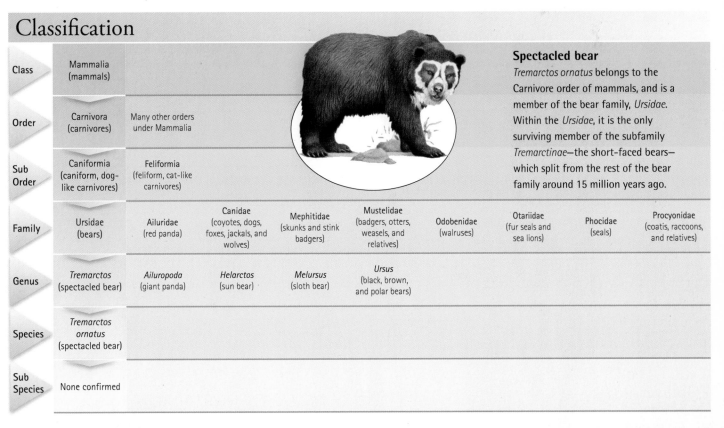

Spectacled bear
Tremarctos ornatus belongs to the Carnivore order of mammals, and is a member of the bear family, *Ursidae*. Within the *Ursidae*, it is the only surviving member of the subfamily *Tremarctinae*—the short-faced bears—which split from the rest of the bear family around 15 million years ago.

Class	Mammalia (mammals)								
Order	Carnivora (carnivores)	Many other orders under Mammalia							
Sub Order	Caniformia (caniform, dog-like carnivores)	Feliformia (feliform, cat-like carnivores)							
Family	Ursidae (bears)	Ailuridae (red panda)	Canidae (coyotes, dogs, foxes, jackals, and wolves)	Mephitidae (skunks and stink badgers)	Mustelidae (badgers, otters, weasels, and relatives)	Odobenidae (walruses)	Otariidae (fur seals and sea lions)	Phocidae (seals)	Procyonidae (coatis, raccoons, and relatives)
Genus	*Tremarctos* (spectacled bear)	*Ailuropoda* (giant panda)	*Helarctos* (sun bear)	*Melursus* (sloth bear)	*Ursus* (black, brown, and polar bears)				
Species	*Tremarctos ornatus* (spectacled bear)								
Sub Species	None confirmed								

Adaptation and Behavior

Spectacled bears are rarely seen in the wild. They are so elusive that most experts assumed until recently that they were nocturnal. In fact, the inaccessibility of the mountainous terrain and the impenetrability of the cloud forest vegetation were the main reasons that the bears remained hidden. Since scientists have tracked them with radio collars, we know that they are in fact more active during the day than the night. In cloud forest they have only short rests between bouts of climbing and foraging activity, though in dry forest and desert scrub in Peru they stop and find shade from the midday heat.

Resourceful nature

These bears live most of their life up in the trees. For such large animals they are extraordinarily agile, climbing from tree to tree without having to return to the ground. Many upper branches cannot support their weight, so the bears construct platforms, or "day nests," for stability while feeding. A bear begins by bending over several slender tree limbs to form a rough, disorganized latticework of branches, sometimes supported by the thick fork of a tree. On this the bear places a layer of smaller branches to form a mattress-like surface. If the animal has recently been resting in its day nest, a compacted oval depression can be seen—a useful sign for field scientists tracking the bear's activities. In areas where bear country and farming land overlap, bears have taken to using their tree nests as safe havens and vantage points from which to watch for farmers, before conducting raids on their sugar cane and cornfields.

Night nests

The bears do not sleep in the canopy—it is too dangerous, since high winds can pick up in the night. For sleeping at night, they make a similar mattress of small branches on the ground, dug into cliff faces, under boulders, or sheltered within the large buttress roots at the base of trees.

Hunting and Feeding

Bears are generally omnivores—that is, they feed on both plants and other animals—and spectacled bears are no exception. They are, however, one of the most vegetarian of omnivores. Plants make up the greater part of their diet, so hunting usually means tracking down the juiciest palm, bamboo, or bromeliad.

Well-wrapped food

The puya is a bromeliad of the high mountains, and grows itself a thick, fibrous coat to insulate it against the cold, the bright sunlight, and the drying wind. To reach the nutritious soft interior, a spectacled bear must rip the plant apart with its paws.

What spectacled bears eat often seems to depend on what they can find in the locality. For this reason some experts have described them as "dining room opportunists." However, scientists are beginning to discover, through tracking of individual animals, that far from passively eating what is around it, each bear roams great distances in search of the best food. The purpose of their journeys is probably to synchronize with the cycle of various ripening fruit. Other than the occasional meal of meat, fruit is the most nutritious part of the spectacled bear's diet. At fruiting time, bears may roam into desert scrub, where they have been observed climbing prickly cacti to reach the fruit at the top. The páramo is not bountiful in fruit, but on ground-hugging

Types of food

In season, spectacled bears eat fruit, nuts, and berries, but otherwise subsist on a diet of the fleshy, nutritious parts of plants such as bromeliads, bamboos, and palms, enlivened by the occasional insect, bird, or rodent.

Bromeliads

Espeletia

shrubs the bears might find the heather berries known as mortiño—relatives of blueberries and of the cowberries eaten by grizzlies on the Arctic tundra. Fruit in the forest is usually up in the canopy, and the bears are amazingly agile in climbing from tree to tree, following the ripening of figs, nuts, and berries. While waiting for fruit to ripen, a bear may stay in a single tree for 3–4 days (the entire ripening period).

Staple favorites

Outside the fruiting season, spectacled bears concentrate on their staple food of bromeliads. In cloud forest these fleshy plants live as epiphytes (plants that grow upon or are attached to other plants for physical support) on the upper branches of trees, so again the bears must climb to find their food, ripping the bromeliads apart to access the tender leaf bases, and eating them as humans would eat an artichoke. Palmitos—the fleshy hearts of palms—provide another valuable food source, but these trees are not strong enough to support the bears as they feed. A bear will therefore climb a neighboring tree and eat the palm from there if it can, or, in typically destructive fashion, it might break the palm apart, later eating the soft interior parts on the ground. Up on the páramo, the bear favors giant ground bromeliads known as puya, or achupaya, from which it has acquired the Spanish name *oso achupayero*, or "achupaya-eating bear." Back in the cloud forest, spectacled bears eat a great deal of bamboo (of a type known locally as suro), snapping the stems with their paws to reach the soft, growing shoots in a way remarkably reminiscent of the giant panda. The bears' exceptionally powerful jaws also enable them to access the hardest cloud forest foods, such as orchid bulbs, palm nuts, and the bark of trees, which are inedible to other forest animals.

Reluctant carnivores

Like other bears, spectacled bears love to eat honey when they can find it. However, their sweet tooth has led them to raid crops of sugar cane and sweetcorn in areas where farmers have settled in bear country. The bears also use their claws to dig for insects and worms, and take larger animals, such as rabbits, birds, rodents, and carrion, when they can. They do not hunt large, native mammals, but cattle are slow, docile, and defenseless, so some bears overcome their natural shyness and mostly vegetarian ways and learn to exploit the abundance of

Agile eaters

Here a succulent bromeliad forms part of a community of plants (epiphytes) living on the upper limb of a tree. The branch is sturdy enough for the bear to feed on in comfort, but in flimsier parts of the canopy spectacled bears construct stable platforms on which to enjoy a relaxing meal.

hoofed food where cattle farms expand on to bear-inhabited lands. Upsettingly, such bears have no way of efficiently killing cattle, so they jump on to a cow's shoulders and simply begin eating, later dragging the dead or traumatized cow off into the forest. These attacks are rare and are stopped either when the farmer shoots the bear illegally, or when a conservation agency moves the bear to an area uninhabited by people.

Heather berries

Insects

Grasses

Life Cycle

Despite being widely scattered, shy, and reclusive, spectacled bears somehow manage to track one another down to court, mate, and raise offspring. There are still many questions about exactly how they achieve this in the wild, but scientists hope that further research will reveal more about this fascinating bear.

While it remains something of a mystery exactly how male and female spectacled bears meet, researchers think that the bears communicate by leaving messages beside the paths they wear through the forest. It has been observed that they make frequent and prominent scratch marks in bark by the side of paths. These are clearer and more deliberate than the scratch marks made incidentally while climbing, and the bears seem to prefer cedar trees for these messages. They also rub their back against trees, leaving traces of fur and probably scent. While all of these signs may be territorial warnings to rival males, they may also act as a lonely hearts column for bears seeking mates.

Brief encounters

Couples are seen together any time between March and October, and remain together for one or two weeks, mating frequently. The female's ovary releases an egg only when stimulated by these repeated matings. Once the egg is fertilized, the female may take any length of time from

Another mountain to climb
From the age of three months, a spectacled bear cub can forage for food with its mother, but it may take the opportunity to ride on her back when it is tired or faced with danger.

Producing young

Den of secrecy
For the birth, the mother prepares a den in a secluded, sheltered place, such as under a rocky overhang or within the roots of a tree. Locals estimate that the heaviest females are more likely to have large litters of three or, exceptionally, four cubs.

Goggle eyes
A brood of two cubs is common in the wild. These individuals, which are a few weeks old, sport particularly clear examples of the delightful and distinctive goggle-like eye markings that give this species its name.

Playful littermates relax together on a rocky slope. They will probably remain with their mother until they are about a year old. It is a measure of how little these bears have been observed in the wild that it is not known when cubs become independent.

5–8 months to give birth. This large range can be explained by delayed implantation: Sometimes, as in other mammals, the fertilized egg implants in the wall of the uterus immediately and begins development; in other cases, it floats in the uterus until it is triggered to implant by some later hormonal change. Some experts think that delayed implantation is an adaptation to a climate subject to El Niño variations. In most years, cubs are born between November and February, meaning that when the rainy season arrives with its abundance of fruit several months later, the cubs are old enough to be weaned and can take advantage of the bounty of food. In an El Niño year, the seasons are disrupted. The first signs of the changed climate pattern, such as rains in the Peruvian desert, for instance, trigger a hormonal adjustment in the timing of the birth (according to this idea) to cope with the changed seasons.

Cub life

A spectacled bear mother normally gives birth to between one and three cubs, occasionally four. The size of the litter seems to correspond to the bear's environment: Larger litters are born when there is a great diversity and abundance of fruit in the area, and when fruiting is predictable. The cubs are blind at birth and weigh only 11–12 oz (310–335 g), but after six weeks they open their eyes, and in three months they can begin to accompany their mother on foraging trips, as they will do for another 6–8 months. Some field researchers have seen a mature male, presumably the father, accompanying a family group, but this is rare. No one knows when the cubs leave the family group, but since one wild mother was seen to stay with the

Vertical challenges
For this most arboreal of bears, tree climbing is one of the most important early skills to be learned. It is aided by the fact that its forelimbs are longer than its hindlimbs, which helps posture when climbing vertical tree trunks. Climbing ability is useful not only for reaching food—it is also escape behavior when danger threatens. A cub may have to survive some wobbly moments, but these animals are tough: Bears have been known to jump from the canopy without harm when alarmed.

same litter of cubs for a period of 13 months, it is thought to be between the ages of 12–14 months. Neither is it known when the wild cubs begin courting, but judging by those in captivity, it will not be until they are between four and seven years old, whether they are male or female.

Distinctive sounds

In captivity, the sounds that pass between mother and cubs have been recorded in detail. The mother makes two sounds: A growl, which carries a threat, and a trill, which sounds like "ucucu." Captive cubs respond to the trill only about half of the time, but in the wild the sound may be useful as a contact call when mother and cubs are out of sight of one another in dense forest. The cubs make at least five sounds: They trill when in contact with their mother, suggesting that trilling is a signal of contentment, like purring in cats; when suckling they whimper and yelp; and when anxious they may squeal or scream.

Legend and History

Under starlit skies the early Andeans sang tales of a time when "people were animals, but were also people," when the spectacled bear roamed through the clouds, talking with gods, nurturing the trees, and guarding the Andeans. Later, after the Spanish invasion in 1492, the mountain bear slipped from grace—no longer revered, but reviled as *El salvaje* (the savage).

From time older than memory, the spectacled bear was revered throughout the Andes, where it is immortalized in ancient rock carvings. Dwelling near the clouds, close to the heavens, it was regarded by many tribes as half-human, half-divine, with the power to travel between heaven and earth, just as it roamed from the dense jungle to the high plains.

For the Queruchas of Peru, the Andean bear, named Ukuku, clearly had the ear of the gods, and was blessed with quite unusual powers. Only Ukuku could save the *condenados* (cursed souls) that haunted the ice fields: A lethal lash from the bear's sacred paw broke the curse, and sent sinful souls straight to heaven. Something of Ukuku's original role emerges in the legend of *ukukus*—bear-children born of a human mother and bear father. Endowed with supernatural strength, *ukukus* alone were able to banish *condenados* from the ice fields. The mythic role of *ukukus* is still enacted in Peru today during the festival of

Machu Picchu, lost citadel of the Inca
Like the ancient Moche people before them, the Inca revered the Andean bear as a sacred being that bridged the gulf between heaven and earth, light and day, gods and mortal men.

Qoyllur Rit'l, when people clad as *ukukus* struggle up Mount Colquepunku, sacred home of the *apus* (mountain spirits). On the perilous glaciers, the *ukukus* defeat the doomed *condenados*. Before returning home, the victorious *ukukus* gather sacred ice, symbolizing the mountain's curative power and life-giving rain.

Manoba, the older brother
The U'wa tribe of Colombia looked up to the Andean bear, called Manoba, like a protective elder brother. Out of respect for Manoba, the U'wa never hunted brother bears. An U'wa legend tells how the god Sira first made bears at the dawn of time:

The first man that ever was

"At the beginning there was nothing. Only light, only Sira. There were no mountains, nor trees, nor fish. Sira made it all, mountains, trees, and fish. When Sira wanted to make U'wa, he made the bear. Then Sira looked at the bear. He did not like what he had made. Then he made the U'wa once again, just as we are now. The first people were the U'wa. U'wa do not kill the bear because the bear is the father of the U'wa, the Older Brother—the first man that ever was."

El salvaje

With the arrival of the Spanish conquistadors in 1492, the Andean bear gradually lost its spiritual status, being cast instead as *El salvaje* (the savage), a bully and abductor, embodying the macho qualities of conquerors. Throughout the Andes local legends still tell of bears stealing girls and boys, prompting anxious fathers to shoot any bear on sight. A famous case of legendary abduction involved Juan Oso (John Bear):

"Long ago, Juan Oso abducted a local woman, and made her his wife. Soon a child was born, called Juan Osito. Suspecting that his wife might run away, Juan hid his young family in a cave sealed with a giant boulder. All day long he gathered food and water for his family. As time passed, little Juan grew big, strong, and bright. One day he had an idea, and asked his father to bring the water in a grass basket. Keen to please his son, Juan filled the basket with water, but before he was halfway home, all the water had leaked out. Frustrated, Juan tried again and again, working faster and faster. While his father was distracted with his thankless task, little Juan pushed the boulder from the cave's entrance and escaped with his mother. When Juan Oso discovered how he had been tricked, he wept with sorrow and rage. In time he tracked down the runaways and attacked his wife. Rising to his mother's defence, little Juan slew his father."

Sequels to the folktale describe Juan Osito happily settled in his mother's home village, where his titanic strength and heroic deeds become legendary.

Latin lover

Along with his bluebeard image, the Andean bear enjoyed a reputation for superhuman virility, backed up by local observations of bears mating non-stop for up to two hours. Some truth might lie behind the fiction, as female ovulation is not spontaneous, but needs to be stimulated by sustained penetration, aided by the male's rigid penis bone (baculum). Inevitably, baculum is much prized as an aphrodisiac.

Folk healer

In light of the bear's legendary strength, his parts remain in constant demand. In Peruvian markets bear fat is still sold for a range of complaints, from pain to sexual impotency, while gallbladders are bought to prevent blindness and cataracts; ground bear bone is fed to children to build strength, while warm blood is drunk as a general tonic. In one way or another, brother Manoba still looks after the people of the Andes.

Andean bear myth

Sparkling Pleiades

In the southern hemisphere the Pleiades shine brightly in the June sky, coinciding with the festival of Qoyllur rit'l (Lord of Snow Star) when *ukukus* (bears) traditionally fetch life-giving ice from the mountain. The summer stars, called *collca* (storehouse), herald a time of order, light, and plenty after chaos, darkness, and sterility.

Festival of Qoyllur rit'l

During the festival of Qoyllur rit'l, a ritual procession of pilgrims and *ukukus* (bears) clamber up icy Mount Colquepunku, sacred home of the *apus* (mountain spirits). On steep glacial slopes, the *ukukus* symbolically defend the village by battling with the cursed souls that haunt the ice fields.

Paddington Bear

A stowaway from darkest Peru, the lovable teddy of the children's classic *A Bear Called Paddington* owes his name to the London station where he was found. Courteous and caring, with a curious taste for marmalade, Paddington reflects the cuddly cuteness of Andean bear cubs.

Threats and Conservation

One of the rarest species of bear in the world, only a few thousand spectacled bears now survive in remote and isolated pockets of the Andes Mountains. However, local conservation efforts are finding a variety of constructive solutions that might ensure the bear's survival.

The spectacled bear is what is known as a "keystone" species, which means that it plays a vital role in the functioning of the ecosystem. The bears are key dispersers of seed, especially of laurels, a role otherwise performed only by howler monkeys. Even more crucially, by foraging in the canopy and breaking so many branches in the process, spectacled bears effectively change the architecture of their forests, letting light through to the undergrowth and stimulating the sort of regrowth and regeneration on which many other forest plants and animals depend. No doubt for these reasons it has been found that, in Bolivia, for example, sites where the spectacled bear lives also support 63 percent of South America's other mammal species. The presence of bears can be used by conservationists as a measure of a healthy, pristine environment. Sadly, however, the areas in which the bear performs its role as a keystone species are becoming increasingly small and fragmented, its forest home being rapidly cleared for agriculture as farmers exhaust lower-level farmland and push ever further up into the mountains.

Isolation and poaching

Bears need a lot of room in which to live. Venezuelan experts estimate that bear-occupied land can support a density of only one bear for every 10 square miles (26 square km). Estimates of

Destructive practices

As farmers illegally set fire to the páramo to clear shrubs and improve pasture for their cattle, the bears' food, such as espeletia and mortiños, is destroyed in the process, and the bears are pushed into ever-smaller refuges.

the world population of the bears are now as low as 2000–3000, and this total is split into tiny, isolated populations that cannot interbreed. As a result, the bears' genetic diversity in Ecuador is now half that of the jaguar, and much lower than that of other bears worldwide. To make matters worse, where the bear encounters humans, it is usually persecuted. Some cultures value the hunting of a bear, although illegal, as a mark of manhood. Bears are also poached for their claws, skin, and fat, as well as their meat, for local use as food or medicine. The gall bladders may be exported to Asia for the traditional medicine trade, in which they can fetch around US$150 each—five times the average monthly wage in Ecuador. Spectacled bears are also trapped or shot because of conflict over land and food, since they raid crops and occasionally threaten livestock.

Menace from the skies

Once remote and undisturbed mountains, the Peruvian Andes are today a busy place. The tourist industry at Macchu Pichu now fuels a railway and even a helicopter service, which ecologists claim frightens the bears.

Protection

World numbers of spectacled bears are so low that captive breeding programs are underway locally and internationally to prevent extinction, and to replenish numbers in the wild. Since the mid-1990s, bears have been returned to the wild in Ecuador, Colombia, and Peru. Beyond release programs, a larger-scale and more permanent solution is protection of habitats and prevention of poaching. Some 56 new areas have been set aside in the last 30 years, but only eight of these are more than 750 square miles (1950 square km) in area—considered the minimum size necessary to maintain a viable population.

Working together

Conservation organizations have been at loggerheads with settler-farmers in the past, but local communities must be involved in any efforts to save the bear. In Ecuador the Andean Bear Conservation Project offers compensation to farmers for damage done by bears, which fosters community support and involvement. In Venezuela most people were unaware of the spectacled bear 20 years ago, but now it is a conservation icon. In Chaparri in Peru a successful project has involved the community in purchasing land to create a private nature reserve for the bears. With land ownership, the villagers gain more rights over their natural resources, such as water, and jobs in running the reserve as a tourist attraction. Here the spectacled bear has risen quickly from cattle-killing villain to proud mascot of conservation.

Flagship reserve
Incorporating 3.7 million acres (15,000 square km) of rainforest, mountain grassland, and, as here, cloud forest, Peru's Manu National Park is one of the world's largest protected areas of spectacled bear habitat.

Learning to be wild

In Peru, bears taken from the wild illegally may be confiscated. The lucky ones reach a conservation project, such as this one at Chaparri. Here they learn to forage again and are rehabilitated for release into the reserve.

How can we help?

- Support the LiBEARty appeal run by the World Society for the Protection of Animals (WSPA), which campaigns against the persecution of spectacled bears.

- "Adopt a Bear" in Peru and help fund its rehabilitation, and ultimately its release back into the wild, with the Wildlife Protection Foundation.

- Visit the Chaparri reserve in Chcilayo, Peru.

current status: **Critically endangered**

 SSC
Species Survival Commission

 IUCN
The World Conservation Union

American Black Bear

CLASS: Mammalia   **ORDER:** Carnivora   **FAMILY:** Ursidae   **GENUS & SPECIES:** *Ursus americanus*

Shy, secretive, and easily startled, the American black bear has always walked in the shadow of its grand cousin, the grizzly. While the grizzly lorded it over the open plains, the black bear shrank into the shadows of the forest. For the first peoples of the plains, the black bear was simply *kyaio* (bear), whereas the grizzly was *nitakyaio* (real bear). For the first white settlers, the "poor, timid, bashful" black bear was really nothing to write home about. Yet *Ursus americanus* is the oldest and only true native American bear. Older, more watchful, and perhaps wiser than the grizzly, the black bear adapted far better to people. The most tolerant and possibly the brightest of the world's bears, the "all-American black bear" is currently the healthiest and most widespread.

Black bears come in more than one color, ranging from raven through cinnamon, honey, and, very rarely, glacier blue-gray or even white.

Key Features

● Twice as numerous as all other bears combined, with a total population of around 800,000.

● *Ursus americanus* is the only bear exclusive and native to North America.

● Adaptable and tolerant, it can live on the edges of cities virtually unseen.

● Avoids conflict—even mothers with cubs choose flight over fight.

In Focus

Although similar to grizzlies, black bears are usually smaller and less bulky, with a straighter back—lacking the grizzly's shoulder hump—and a distinctively droopy backside. The black bear's much sleeker head, narrow muzzle, and straight Roman nose give it a more aquiline profile. Although named for its black coat, the color varies by season and region.

Color vision

Living in the forest, black bears do not need to see far, but can detect movement well over a mile (1.6 km) away. Their color vision is excellent. Studies suggest that they can perceive different colors in all lights, and can distinguish between different shades of the same color.

Keen nose

Using its keenest sense, a black bear in northern California once marched 3 miles (5 km) in a straight line, tracking the upwind scent of a dead deer. When sniffing the wind for scent, the black bear tilts its head at an angle and cocks its ears to listen.

Flexible lips

The bear's long, mobile tongue can scoop insects out of crevices and suck up sugary tree sap, while its flexible lips are ideal for picking berries from shrubs. When foraging, the bear extends its upper lip, using its incisors to nip off plant and grass stems.

"Teddy bear" ears

Large, round, and upright, black bear ears seem always cocked, as though listening attentively. In youth, the ears are large in relation to the face, giving cubs a "teddy bear" look. Black bears can hear the click of a camera 55 yards (50 m) away, but can seem deaf by streams, when rushing water drowns out the sound of footsteps.

Vital Statistics

Weight: Male 130–500 lb (60–225 kg); female 90–330 lb (40–150 kg)

Length: Male 4–6.2 ft (1.2–1.9 m)

Height: 2.3–3.3 ft (0.7–1 m) at the shoulder

Color: Black, brown, cinnamon, blond, or (rarely) blue-gray or white, with a paler muzzle and occasional white blaze across the chest

Sexual maturity: 4-6 years

Gestation period: 6.5–8.5 months, including delayed implantation

Number of young: 1–6, usually 2 or 3

Birth interval: 2 years

Typical diet: Mainly berries and nuts, shoots, buds, and catkins; also insects and small rodents, spawning salmon, and young elk, moose, or deer

Lifespan: Averages 25 years, but can live up to 35

Glossy coat

The thick, sleek fur easily sheds rain and snow, and provides natural camouflage in the forest shadows. Like its ursine cousins, *americanus* has a double-layered coat: An inner layer of soft, dense, wooly under-fur affords warmth and insulation, while an outer layer of long, coarse, overlapping guard hair keeps the underpelt clean and dry.

Did you know?

● Bears who eat lots of corn can weigh as much as 880 lb (400 kg).

● The oldest wild black bear lived to the age of 31, while the oldest captive bear survived to 44, the equivalent of 100 in human years.

● Black bears can consume as many as 20,000 calories a day in the fall—the equivalent of 42 hamburgers.

Climbing claws

Short and strong, with hook-like points, black bear claws are ideal for climbing. Like pickaxes, the tips sink into tree bark, giving the bear a firm grip. At not much longer than 1–1.5 in (2.5–3.5 cm), they are too short for digging, but ideal for ripping open rotten logs for grubs.

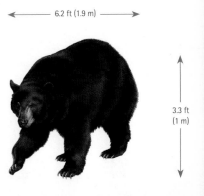

← 6.2 ft (1.9 m) →

3.3 ft (1 m)

Habitat

A creature of forest and thicket, the black bear roves through the diverse woodlands of Canada and North America, from sea level to over 6560 ft (2000 m). At home in both dry and moist forests, its range includes the mossy rainforests of coastal Alaska, the scrubby chaparral of Mexico, and the steamy swamps of the southeast.

Distribution

Maine's mixed forests
Historically a logging state, Maine offers prime black bear habitat, with vast stretches of conifer-deciduous second-growth woods. In eastern parts spruce forest is interspersed with blueberry barrens, making it particularly appealing to berry-loving black bears. Maine's growing population of *americanus* is the largest in America.

U.S.A.

North Atlantic Ocean

Pacific Ocean

Washington's primal forests
At any time of year, black bears delight in Washington's lush primeval rainforests of Sitka spruce, western hemlock, and western red cedar. Douglas fir in particular draws spring bears, who gorge on its sugar-rich sap. To minimize the harm done to the fir, Washington has traditionally managed the bear as a game species.

Yosemite, California
Yosemite's blend of valleys and verdant forests, interspersed with wildflower meadows and waterfalls, provides ideal habitat for black bears. In the 1980s it was renowned for its "mugging bears," who learned to waylay hikers, scaring them into dropping their lunch-filled backpacks.

Although driven from half their original range, black bears remain widespread throughout the forests of Canada (bar Prince Edward Island), northern Mexico, and 41 of the Lower States. They are most abundant in forests with plenty of shrubbery and understory, such as the vast coniferous woodlands rimming the Pacific northwest, and the mixed hardwood forests of the east. The best woods for black bears are small and interspersed with open marshes and meadows, where edible grasses and berries grow close at hand in the spring and summer. Ideally, the forest itself should not be too dark or dense, but filled with sun-dappled glades, where the bears can roam within easy reach of tree cover.

Fire, flood, and decay

Natural disasters, such as fire or flood, often leave ideal glades of burnt or sodden snags interspersed with living trees. The rotting trunks can become rich sources of nesting grubs. Experts even suggest that modern efficiency in putting out fires has deprived black bears of prime habitat. Arbors also open naturally in ancient forests, where giant trees have crashed to the ground. The black bear's liking for glades, however, means that it is fatally attracted to man-made clearings, where tantalizing scents tempt it to raid cropfields, leading to conflict with farmers.

Diverse daybeds and dens

For rest and refuge, the forest's cool, shady understory provides natural cover from rain, sunlight, and swarming mosquitoes, while tall trees offer retreat from the bear's main enemies—hunters, grizzlies, wolves, and, in southern swamps, alligators and snakes. Black bear dens and daybeds are as diverse as its woodland habitats. In the north, the bears often dig dens underground, well hidden beneath root masses, or a mound of snow, where they might sleep for more than seven months, or even eight in the coldest parts of Alaska. A typical dugout den has an entry tunnel 3–6 ft (1–2 m) long, leading to a cozy, oval sleeping chamber. It is usually lined with a soft bedding of

Bear dens covered in a blanket of snow are virtually invisible.

moss, grass, and leaves, sometimes 6–8 in (15–20 cm) deep. In the south bears often create "ground nests" from brush piles, or the branches of fallen treetops. In southern swamps black bears usually den up in trees, sometimes as high as 100 ft (30 m). Many daybeds are also made in the treetops, where they might double up as feeding platforms. Tree nests are often built in the crown of beech, black cherry, wild apple, and oak trees.

Grizzly-free tundra

Historically, black bears have steered clear of grizzly stamping ground on the open plains and mountain slopes. But on the remote, treeless tundra of northern Labrador, where no grizzlies roam, black bears have settled down and spread out, although to date they show a relatively low reproductive rate.

Classification

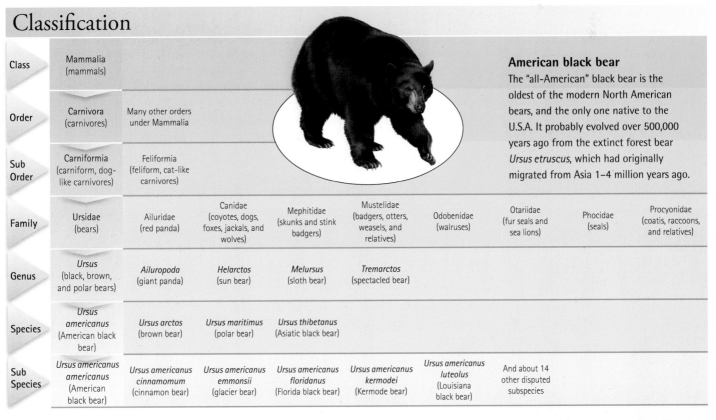

American black bear
The "all-American" black bear is the oldest of the modern North American bears, and the only one native to the U.S.A. It probably evolved over 500,000 years ago from the extinct forest bear *Ursus etruscus*, which had originally migrated from Asia 1–4 million years ago.

Class	Mammalia (mammals)								
Order	Carnivora (carnivores)	Many other orders under Mammalia							
Sub Order	Carniformia (carniform, dog-like carnivores)	Feliformia (feliform, cat-like carnivores)							
Family	Ursidae (bears)	Ailuridae (red panda)	Canidae (coyotes, dogs, foxes, jackals, and wolves)	Mephitidae (skunks and stink badgers)	Mustelidae (badgers, otters, weasels, and relatives)	Odobenidae (walruses)	Otariidae (fur seals and sea lions)	Phocidae (seals)	Procyonidae (coatis, raccoons, and relatives)
Genus	Ursus (black, brown, and polar bears)	Ailuropoda (giant panda)	Helarctos (sun bear)	Melursus (sloth bear)	Tremarctos (spectacled bear)				
Species	Ursus americanus (American black bear)	Ursus arctos (brown bear)	Ursus maritimus (polar bear)	Ursus thibetanus (Asiatic black bear)					
Sub Species	Ursus americanus americanus (American black bear)	Ursus americanus cinnamomum (cinnamon bear)	Ursus americanus emmonsii (glacier bear)	Ursus americanus floridanus (Florida black bear)	Ursus americanus kermodei (Kermode bear)	Ursus americanus luteolus (Louisiana black bear)	And about 14 other disputed subspecies		

Adaptation and Behavior

Seasonal cold and forest habitat have shaped the black bear's physical features and behavior. The thick, shaggy, double-layered coat protects it from biting wind, snow, and rain. Its strong forelimbs and short, curved claws are ideal for scaling trees, which cubs do with ease from the moment they leave the den. Similarly, the bear's relatively small, agile body enables it to move freely through leafy boughs.

Coat of many colors

Black bears come in more than one shade or "color phase." The black phase prevails in the east, while the brown, cinnamon, honey, or blond phases are more common in the west. The different colors probably reflect habitat and climate. Black is the perfect camouflage in dense forest, where the bears can melt into the shadows. Cinnamon and honey shades might afford better camouflage in the drier, brighter, more open regions of the southwest. Lighter tones also reflect warmth from the sun, helping to prevent overheating in southern climates. The rare white phase occurs only in coastal British Columbia, most likely as a result of a recessive (weak) gene rather than habitat. The many-colored "black bears" were so named by the early settlers, who first encountered the black phase in the east, where it is most common.

Retiring by nature

By bear standards, *americanus* seems timid, melting into its forest refuge when startled by intruders, and shrinking from its dominant neighbor, the grizzly. Even mothers with cubs often choose flight over fight when surprised or threatened. The safest escape route usually lies up a tree. If forest cover is not close at hand, however, black bears might feel threatened enough to attack, but even then will probably only bluff. By avoiding conflict, black bears have survived civilization far better than the more aggressive grizzly. Being particularly intelligent, adaptable, and tolerant, they live almost unnoticed close to cities and towns.

Hunting and Feeding

Perpetually hungry, bright, and curious, black bears can be tempted by almost anything, from birdseed to hamburgers, from tree sap to toothpaste. Although the bulk of their diet is vegetarian, 15 percent comprises animal, mainly insect, protein.

Easy prey
A hungry spring bear gets its teeth into an elk carcass. In the spring black bears patrol calving meadows and forest glades, where young elk and deer lie hidden and still, unable to outrun a predator. Until the calves and fawns pick up speed, they remain easy prey for the flat-footed bear.

In the spring black bears shuffle sleepily from their winter dens. Many look scrawny after their fast, and need to fatten up quickly. Gravitating toward sunny slopes, fertile floodplains, and wetland meadows, the bears scrub around for succulent shoots and emerging plants, such as horsetail sedges, wild celery, blue joint grass, and juicy skunk cabbage. In shaded valleys and forest glades, overwintered berries or iced-over carrion might remain from the previous fall. A favorite is the high-energy tree sap that lies beneath tree bark, which the bears rip off with teeth and claws.

Vital spring protein
The floodplains also harbor nesting birds, fish, and salamanders, which provide vital protein for the depleted bears. Small mice and birds'

Types of food

Vegetarian fare of sedge, grass, berries, and nuts comprises the bulk of the black bear's diet, but it also enjoys grubs, rodents, and carrion. Where spring elk calves and whitetail fawns or summer spawning salmon are plentiful, black bears can become more carnivorous.

Blue joint grass

Bog blueberries

eggs make easy prey and welcome treats, replenishing lost reserves of fat and protein. Where spring moose calves or whitetail fawns are plentiful, black bears can become quite predatory, although they are too slow for the chase. In Alaska's Kenai Peninsula, for example, black bears kill up to 35 percent of the region's spring moose calves; they also prey on snowshoe hares, mice, voles, and birds. But for many bears, ants, grubs, and bees comprise the bulk of the animal protein in their diet. Favorites are tent caterpillars and bumblebee grubs. When caterpillars are plentiful, black bears will happily devour 2500 a day.

Summer bounty

As spring turns into summer, the bears forage for buds, catkins, and flower roots, although they are ill equipped for digging, preferring to pick fruit from shrubs and trees. During the summer berry season the bears can at last start building up their bulk and energy stores in preparation for the winter sleep. Luscious, sugar-rich berries grow everywhere, and the choice is vast—huckleberries, cranberries, blueberries, and devil's club berries, the last a particular favorite, being especially rich in sugars that can be easily converted into fat. The bears also nose around on the forest floor for beetle larvae and ant grubs nesting in fallen logs. Along the coast, if grizzlies are absent, black bears will amble down to the rivers to catch spawning salmon—a richer source of nutrients.

Fall binge

As the days darken, the bears roam far and wide looking for fat- and sugar-rich nuts and fruits to gorge on before the first snow. In the west, whitebark pine nuts are a special favorite. In the northeast, black bears can feast on beechnuts, acorns, and hickory nuts. In the south, where nuts are less plentiful, the

bears fill up on tupelo berries and needle palm instead. To build up fatty stores before the winter sleep, bears can consume up to 20,000 calories a day. Merely to maintain weight on a berry diet a typical black bear must feed for about 12 hours a day, consuming an average of a berry a second. During the fall binge, they gain up to 30 lb (13.5 kg) a week, increasing body weight by 30–40 percent. Fallen game can be another source of high-energy fat and protein, while around farms and towns the bears might raid cornfields, livestock, and garbage. By late fall more than half of a bear's body weight will be fat. At a certain point an internal mechanism is triggered, shutting off its appetite in preparation for the winter sleep.

Berry picking

Standing tall with feet flat on the grass, a black bear pulls over the ripest berry sprigs, steering them toward its mouth with flexible paws. Once within reach, it will extend its upper lip and strain the berries away from the leaves.

Hazelnuts

Honeypot ants

Whitetailed fawn

Life Cycle

Healthy black bears in prime habitats usually breed every two years, giving birth to two or three cubs. How such shy and secretive creatures meet, let alone mate, remains something of a mystery, but scent is thought to play a part. At the start of the season males rub scent on trees along bear thoroughfares, broadcasting their intentions and warding off rivals.

First weeks of life

Sleeping peacefully
The ideal den is just big enough for the bear to turn in, but small enough to retain heat. Wrapped in its mother's warmth, the tiny cub feels snug, despite snow outside.

Keeping warm
Twin cubs play in a dirt den dugout beneath the roots of a large tree. At eight weeks old, weighing 5.5 lb (2.5 kg), the cubs are almost strong enough to generate their own heat.

In spring, with the onset of estrus, breeding females grow restless and travel more frequently through their range, marking their territory with scent and urine in the hope of attracting roaming males. A courting male who picks up the scent of a female on heat will track her closely for two or three weeks, until she accepts his advances. During peak receptivity the couple is inseparable, feeding and bedding together, and mating frequently. Once fertilized, the embryos float free until the fall when they implant on the uterine wall. Meanwhile, the bears embark on a feeding frenzy to fatten up before winter. If the female does not put on enough fat, her embryos will die.

"Shaping up"
The Romans believed that mother bears licked their formless cubs into shape. In fact licking keeps the fur clean and reduces tell-tale scents that could attract hungry wolves and grizzlies.

The deep sleep
In the late fall, northern bears ready their dens before the first snows of October. Southern bears den later—in early November—although in the most southerly parts of their range, where food is available all year round, only pregnant females den. How bears know instinctively when to den is not entirely clear. It is thought that the shift in the angle and degree of sunlight triggers

Master climber
Fresh out of its birthing den, a spring cub gets to grips with its first tree. Tiny cubs master the art of climbing within weeks. Their mother chases them up trees at the slightest whiff of danger, and stands guard at the base before sounding the "all-clear." When not running from danger, cubs delight in chasing and racing each other up and down trees.

chemical changes, prompting them to binge. After the "fall feasting frenzy," bears enter a "walking sleep," when they slow down, eating and drinking little. By now the expectant mother will have chosen a spot for her birthing den. Ever adaptable, black bears use both natural and man-made resources, sometimes even nesting beneath a house or inside a highway culvert. To keep their cubs safe and warm throughout the winter, females pick a dry, secluded spot, such as a hollow tree or log, tucked away in the forest, or a cave with a long, hidden entry tunnel.

Winter birth
Thick snow falls silently outside while the mother slumbers in her warm den. Sometime in January or early February she gives birth to twins or triplets; only partially awake, she seems barely aware of her labor. Newborns measure less than 8 in (20 cm) long—about the size of a chipmunk—and weigh no more than 8–12oz (225–335 g). Like other bear cubs, they are born blind, deaf, and toothless. As the hindlimbs of black bear cubs are particularly weak, newborns drag themselves around on their forelimbs. By sleeping curled on her

Best buddies
Spring cubs peck each other playfully. As their teeth erupt, they chew on anything in sight, but mouthing each other's jaws is a prelude to gentle sparring or play fighting.

side, the mother's six nipples are drawn closer together, making it easier for the cubs to nurse. After five weeks of suckling her rich milk, they grow strong enough to walk. By early spring, when their mother leaves her den, the lively cubs romp along beside her. Life outside the den is perilous for spring cubs, many of whom die within 60 days. Some starve, others fall prey to bald eagles, wolves, grizzlies, or marauding black bears. If threatened, the cubs scamper up trees, while their mother stands guard, warding off attack. If a mother loses her cubs, she will leave the area immediately.

High living
Growing yearlings spend much of their time in the treetops, climbing, sunning, dozing, and playing. As forest dwellers can easily lose sight of each other in the undergrowth, they tend to be more vocal than grizzlies, calling to each other in the treetops. The little bears stay with their mother for up to 18 months, sharing the winter den for a second year. After weaning her litter in the second spring, the mother comes back into estrus, prompting her to throw off her offspring and mate again. Bewildered by their mom's sudden change of heart, juveniles have no choice but to set off into the big, wide forest alone.

Roving adventurers
Littermates might team up and forage together for a season or two, before going their separate ways. Males are more adventurous than females, and travel farther from home—over 60 miles (100 km). Bold and curious, they expose themselves to risk many times, falling foul of poachers and road traffic. Hunger and lack of experience drive them to scavenge around garbage sites and cropfields, where they are often killed as pests. Young males are also harassed by large, dominant male bears intent on stamping out the competition. Females, by contrast, feel no need to trek so far from home, and often overlap with their mother, sometimes inheriting her range when she dies.

Legend and History

Out on the plains where the grizzly roamed, the smaller, less awesome black bear was often dismissed as a lesser bruin, but on its home ground it was welcomed as a spiritual force for good. For the Navajo, the black bear was the guardian of the tribe, a seer and guide that took care of stray children, and left tracks through the forest leading travelers safely home.

T he truth about bears can sometimes be stranger than legend. The Navajo tell of bear mothers adopting human toddlers, nursing and teaching them what to eat and where to sleep. Not surprisingly, the Navajo regard the black bear as a nurturing force, protecting and guiding them through dark forests and dangerous times. In the old days the Navajo were sometimes enslaved by the Mexicans. Some escaped, only to lose their way in border country, until they called on the bear spirit, who left tracks in the wilderness, leading them home.

The wisest of bears

Like the people of the plains, who venerated the grizzly as an ancestral spirit, many forest peoples revered the black bear as kin and ancestor. The Winnebago, for instance, believed that bear spirits were really people in bear disguise; the first "Shaggy Man," a half-human bear, was born of the marriage between a woman and a bear spirit from the sky. The Cherokee had their own take on black bear ancestry—their forefathers, tiring of the daily grind, had traded their hard lives for the carefree lot of bears. Spiritually, the black bear expresses a gentle, thoughtful force,

Dancing the bear
A bear dance conjures and celebrates the bear spirit. In dances honoring the black, rather than the brown, bear dancers enact the more gentle, playful antics of black bears. (*Bear Dance* by George Catlin, c.1850)

reflecting its shy and secretive nature. For the Winnebago, the black bear was the wisest of bears, endowed with foresight and mind reading. When a Winnebago youth encountered the black bear on his vision quest, he welcomed its insight. The Cherokee tell a story that illustrates the bear's helpful wisdom:

"One day a hunter shot an arrow at a bear, but it ran away. The hunter gave chase, shooting one arrow after another. From time to time, the bear stopped and brushed the arrows off his body as though they were pine needles. Finally, the bear turned, shrugged his hairy shoulders, and huffed, 'It's no good; you can't kill me with arrows. Let's go home and have some berries.' The hunter stared in horror and disbelief. The bear, who could read his thoughts, promised that he had nothing to fear, and persuaded him to follow. As the hunter was too hungry to resist, he trailed after the bear to his cave, where they dined on nuts and berries. For the whole winter the hunter lived in the bear's den, until one morning the animal awoke from a dream and sighed, 'Some people are coming to kill me.' The hunter protested, but the bear just shrugged his shoulders and added: 'After my death, don't forget to cover my blood with leaves…and before you leave remember to turn and look back.' Soon after, men with dogs called the bear out of his den. When he emerged, they killed, skinned, and chopped him up. Before following the men with their trophy, the hunter covered the bear's blood with leaves. When he looked back, he saw the bear rise up from the leaves, shake them off, and amble back into the forest."

The sacred hunt

At a more basic level, bear fat and fur provided energy, warmth, and shelter. While some tribes, like the Navajo, venerated the bear too greatly for the chase, others, such as the Cherokee and Koyukon, hunted the bear, but with reverence. The hunt often served as a boy's rite of passage to manhood. For the Koyukon, den hunting in particular was a test of masculinity. To hunt without offending the bear's spirit, the Koyukon observed respectful customs and rites. A hunter always wore clean boots and used traditional weapons, such as a spear rather than a gun. A hunter never spoke openly about the hunt for fear of offending the bear. Boasting was unthinkable, immoderate, and disrespectful. After the hunt, people gathered for a festive "bear party," celebrating the bear's spirit with songs and dances.

Man-eating lions

White settlers viewed black bears in a rather different light. Describing his boyhood in the 1850s, the naturalist John Muir observed wryly that black bears were imagined "as dangerous as man-eating lions and tigers," likely to "pursue any human being that came in their way." The reality, when it ambled through the local town in search of spring fare, turned out to be just a "poor, timid, bashful creature." As the east was settled and its forests cleared for farming, the "bashful creature" shrank into ever remoter regions, or fell by the thousand for its fat and fur.

The first teddy

By contrast, the sporting hunter President Theodore "Teddy" Roosevelt refused to shoot a defenseless cub in 1902, making headlines in the *Washington Post*. The cartoon illustrating Roosevelt's "fair chase" caught the eye of Brooklyn entrepreneur Morris Mitchom, whose wife designed a toy bear. Mitchom asked Roosevelt if he could call the toy "Teddy's Bear." When the president agreed, the teddy was born, ushering in a sleuth of fictitious bears, one of the best-loved being Winnie-the-Pooh. The original Winnie, another orphan cub, was scooped up by Harry Colebourn, a Canadian vet on his way to battle in World War I. Colebourn left Winnie at London Zoo, where she enthralled children with her gentle ways. One child, Christopher Robin, was so taken by Winnie that he named his teddy after her, inspiring his father, the novelist A.A. Milne, to create dreamy, caring Winnie-the-Pooh—a bear after every child's heart.

Black bear appeal

"Drawing the line in Mississippi"
In the popular 1902 cartoon, President "Teddy" Roosevelt sternly refuses to kill a helpless cub. The story inspired toymaker Morris Mitchom to name his new toy bear "Teddy's Bear." When consulted, the president observed, "I don't think my name will mean much to the bear business, but you're welcome to use it."

Forever young
Make-believe teddies reflect cute bear cubs— tiny, toothless, chubby, and cuddly. Child-like features typically trigger caring impulses in people, perhaps explaining the enduring appeal of teddies. Mirroring one facet of real bears, Winnie-the-Pooh, one of the world's best loved fictional bears, is forever on a quest for honey.

Black bearskins
Like Norse *berserkers*, who went to battle wrapped in threatening fur, Queen Elizabeth II's guards don intimidating bearskin caps. At 18 in (45 cm) tall, they are meant to strike fear in the enemy, but also to keep the soldiers dry and warm. Royal bearskins are made from culled or roadkilled bears.

Threats and Conservation

Although thriving in much of Canada and America, where it is valued and protected as a game animal, the black bear faces extinction in Mexico, where the population is small and isolated. A new threat also now looms on the eastern horizon, as the oriental trade in bear parts spreads westward.

Poaching for the illegal bear trade has become an international, multimillion dollar business. Although less vulnerable than their Asian cousins, black bears are also poached for their paws (relished in oriental cuisine) and gallbladders (prized in traditional Chinese medicine). In Canada, where possession of gallbladders is legal in several territories, more than 40,000 black bears might be poached each year. Until possession of bear parts is outlawed, poaching is likely to escalate, particularly if logging roads remain open, giving easy access into remote forests.

Hope for Mexican bears

In Mexico, where the population is isolated and shrinking, the black bear is seriously endangered. There is hope, though, as pilot trials show that bears can be reintroduced to areas where they have been eliminated. In Arkansas, where black bears were all but extinct in the early part of last century, they have been successfully reintroduced and now live in thriving populations.

A bear's life

The black bear's very tolerance of people, and its adaptability to towns and cities, can expose it to conflict. Any trouble between

"Don't feed the bears"
Last century, "begging bears" commonly panhandled park tourists for juicy tit-bits, often causing "bear jams." As bears cannot always tell where candy ends and hands begin, accidents were inevitable. Parks now wisely discourage feeding to prevent bears associating people with food.

bears and humans usually ends badly for the bear. At campsites and garbage dumps, where hungry, often juvenile, bears scavenge for food, they are likely to be shot or shifted far from their range, where they wander aimlessly. To reduce temptation, garbage should be either cleared or enclosed. Conflict can also be curbed by education, encouraging people to tolerate bears.

The bears and the bees

The black bear's passion for honey is legendary. Some bears have even got tangled in telephone lines, mistaking the sound vibrations for the buzz of bees. Where bees are big business and harvested commercially for honey, bears are invariably treated as pests. In bee-rich Georgia, Florida, and parts of Carolina, for instance, beekeepers are licensed to kill bears caught raiding their hives. To steer bears away from honey bees, aversion therapy has been tried with some success. Another tactic that protects both the bees and the bears is electric fencing.

Bear baiting
The practice of bear baiting—luring hungry spring and fall bears to places baited with food, where they can be easily shot—involves no chase and no skill, so strikes many hunters as unfair and unsporting. Unfortunately, bear baiting is gaining popularity in western Canada, where it is legal.

Tempting bears to behave

Every spring, ravenous black bears beat a path to trees oozing with sugar-rich sap. By peeling off the bark to lap up the sap, the bears can wreak havoc on expensive timber trees, such as Douglas fir, western hemlock, and western red cedar. If the bark is stripped right off, the trees die. Even if the bark is only partially stripped, the tree is exposed to fungal infection. Either way, the timber industry suffers multimillion dollar damage. To curb the harm to the harvest, it was common last century to hunt bears each spring, but the trees were still damaged. Even when, in one pilot study, the bear population was reduced to 20 percent, the bears still harmed the trees. The problem seemed insurmountable until a former hunter, who had wearied of killing black bears, developed an ingenious solution. He created a fruit pulp mixture and left it by the trees to tempt the bears away from the tree sap. Remarkably, the mixture seemed to satisfy both the bears and also the timber industry.

Whistler's bears
Thanks to ecologist Arthur DeJong, the Whistler-Blackcomb Ski Resort in British Columbia offers people the chance to see black bears roaming free in their natural habitat. Local biologist Michael Allen collaborates with DeJong as both researcher and tourist guide.

Keeping tabs on cubs
A sleepy winter cub dozes in a weight sling as a biolgist checks its growth rate. Using radio telemetry, researchers working for the Maine Department of Fisheries and Wildlife regularly tag, measure, and check cubs and mothers.

A tight squeeze
Like little cubs, third-grade classmates explore the cramped space of a bear den dug beneath the roots of a giant tree in Whistler's old-growth forest. Bear researcher Michael Allen teaches schoolchildren all about black bears, paving the way for future positive encounters.

How can we help?
- Campaign against the practice of bear baiting.
- Support measures to restore the black bear's habitats: www.bbcc.org.
- Try watching black bears at the Vince Shute Wildlife Sanctuary in Minnesota: www.americanbear.org.
- Lobby politicians to close logging roads.
- Always use bearproof trash-cans and garbage dumps.
- In Asia refuse to try bear "delicacies," such as paw soup.

current status: **Lower risk**

Species Survival Commission

The World Conservation Union

Kermode Bear

CLASS: Mammalia　　**ORDER:** Carnivora　　**FAMILY:** Ursidae　　**GENUS, SPECIES & SUBSPECIES:** *Ursus americanus kermodei*

Somewhere deep in the virgin rainforest of coastal British Columbia, a rare cloud-white bear shifts between the shadows like a phantom. As wild and pristine as its timeless rainforest retreat, the elusive white bear has lived in serene seclusion since the last ice age, rarely glimpsed even by the aboriginal coast people. Its fleeting appearances and ghostly white color inspired its popular nickname, "White Spirit bear." When scientists first saw its snowy pelt in 1900, they thought they had discovered a new species, but later realized that the Kermode bear is instead an isolated subspecies of American black bear, born with a unique gene for white hair. Hailed as the "panda of Canada" by the world's eco-warriors and wildlife advocates, the rare White Spirit bear has become something of a Holy Grail, an icon of pure wildness, as yet untouched by civilization.

> *"In my career as a wilderness guide, I had never before encountered bears with such trust in humans..."*
>
> Charles Russell, *Spirit Bear* (2002)

Key Features

- An isolated coastal subspecies of American black bear, of which 10 percent are born with white hair.

- With just 200–300 currently alive, Canada's White Spirit bears seem as rare as China's giant pandas.

- Kermode bears (*kermodeis*) are named after Francis Kermode, who studied the species in the early 1900s.

In Focus

A little larger than other American black bears, *kermodeis* have the same broad frame, massive shoulders, classic straight back and "Roman" nose. All Kermode bears carry one recessive (weak) gene for white hair, but only those born with a double recessive trait (inherited from both parents) sport a white coat. The distinctive white fur is often mantled with golden hairs.

Dark eyes

Kermode bears can distinguish different colors, as well as varied shades of green and blue, which allows them to spot berries in a mass of greenery. As the bears are nearsighted, they can easily focus on objects close at hand, which helps when catching leaping salmon or scurrying ants.

Extra sensitive nose

The black nose indicates that the white *kermodei* is not albino. If it were, the nose (and eyes) would be pink. Like its ursine cousins, the Kermode bear has a sense of smell keener even than a bloodhound's. By smell alone, it can track mates, identify cubs, find food, and detect danger.

Sturdy legs

Built for strength rather than speed, the bowed legs are powered by thick muscles, ideal for climbing. Like its bear relatives, a *kermodei* has five toes on each foot, with the biggest on the outside, which accentuates its shuffling gait. The strong, curved claws, just 1.5 in (4 cm) long, act as "grappling hooks" when climbing.

Ghostly white fur

The lush coat is often suffused with amber gold, which changes with the season, deepening in the fall. The color probably stems from foraging in waters stained with humic acids (from rotting matter). The same tint appears on the feathers of swans wintering along the coast. In the summer, after the spring molt, the new fur looks snow-white.

Short furry tail

Measuring just 5 in (13 cm), the flap-like tail, protects the anal region. While other animals use their tails to communicate, bears tend to face friend or foe "head on," conveying intent with subtle body language. Although some tree-climbers use their tails for balance, *kermodeis* maintain their footing by gripping with sharp claws and hairless soles.

Furless footpads

The tough and leathery soles are hairless, giving the bear good gripping power, especially useful when climbing trees and wet boulders, or handling berry-laden branches. During the winter the skin sloughs off, but grows anew by spring, when the bear treads painfully on tender footpads.

Vital Statistics

Weight: Male 130–500 lb (60–225 kg); female 90–330 lb (40–150 kg)

Length: Male 4–6.2 ft (1.2–1.9 m)

Height: 2.3–3.3 ft (0.7–1 m) at the shoulder

Color: White coats range from snow-white to ivory, suffused with golden orange across the shoulders and back; black coats vary from raven black to chestnut brown, with pale hair around the muzzle

Sexual maturity: 4–6 years

Gestation period: 6.5–8.5 months, including delayed implantation

Number of young: 1–6, usually 2

Birth interval: 2 years

Typical diet: Sedges and grasses, buds and catkins, wildflowers, apples, berries, and nuts; insects, small rodents, and spawning salmon

Lifespan: Averages 25 years

Did you know?

● On waking, *kermodeis* often scratch their face, chest, and sides for at least 10 minutes, rubbing off ticks and lice.

● Kermode bears usually amble at a leisurely pace, but can sprint at speeds up to 35 mph (55 kph).

● On ancient bear trails, bear tracks can sink more than 1 ft (30 cm) deep into the forest soil.

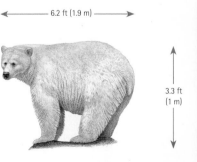

6.2 ft (1.9 m)

3.3 ft (1 m)

Habitat

For over 10,000 years *kermodeis* have dwelt in the luxuriant coastal rainforests of British Columbia, thriving in the highest densities on the secluded islands of Gribbell and Princess Royal. Deep virgin rainforest, interspersed with mossy glades, sheltered canyons, and freshwater streams, offers ideal and abundant resources.

Distribution

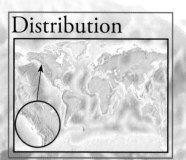

Great Bear Rainforest

Running between the Pacific Ocean and the Coast Mountains, the ancient rainforest provides prime habitat for *kermodeis*, especially on offshore islands, but also along the coastal fringe. On the mainland coast, though, the "white" gene pool is diluted, with only about 1 in 40–100 white births.

Canada

British
Columbia

U.S.A.

Gribbell Island

Although 10 times smaller than Princess Royal Island, covering just 80 square miles (210 square km), Gribbell is nonetheless home to about 50 *kermodeis*, with a high density of white coats—at least 30 percent. The island's small, gentle streams provide happy hunting grounds for the bears.

Princess Royal Island

This remote rocky island offers ideal seasonal resources, ranging from dense forest cover and fertile wetlands, to berry meadows and salmon streams. Providing lush, secluded habitat, the island is home to about 150 *kermodeis*, including 10–20 White Spirit bears, most often glimpsed along the sheltered Laredo inlet.

Pacific Ocean

Drenched in waterlogged rainclouds blowing from the warm Pacific, the coastal rainforest of British Columbia remains humid even in the summer, when enveloped in moist fog. Moderate temperatures rarely drop below freezing in the mild, wet winters, or exceed 80°F (26°C) during the dry summers. Abundant annual rainfall—up to 200 in (508 cm)—sustains the planet's highest biomass (total mass of organisms).

Green groves

Coastal moisture nourishes all things green, from grass and fireweed to ancient conifers, such as western hemlock and red cedar, which grow to record heights and girths along the coast. Red cedar, one of the world's tallest trees, can reach 230 ft (70 m) high, with massive trunks up to 30 ft (9 m) wide. Douglas fir, which can soar even higher—up to 300 ft (92 m) —thrives on drier mountain slopes, while stands of Sitka spruce rise thickly from the shore to the tree line. Draped in soft moss and lichen, evergreen conifers fill the rainforest with fragrant needle leaves that soak up moisture from the summer fogs. Up in the treetops, vast canopies festooned with epiphytic (tree-dwelling) plants create an umbrella effect, sheltering the salmon streams from direct sunlight and seasonal downpours.

Forest cover

Like their continental cousins, coastal *kermodeis* shrink into the shadows at the slightest scent of danger. In the temperate rainforest they never have far to run for cover. Towering Sitka spruces rise close to beaches, riverbanks, and wetlands, where the shy bears can forage in peace within easy reach of cover. The dense understory provides immediate refuge, while tall stands afford escape from marauding grizzlies, which rarely climb. For rest between foraging bouts, *kermodeis* usually flop down in mossy glades under a shady canopy or rocky overhang. As the days shorten and rainstorms lash the coast in the fall, the bears wend their way to warm, dry dens deep in the forest, where they will escape the winter in a sleep-like state until

In fast streams fallen logs break the torrent, creating quiet bathing pools.

spring. Most dens are made in the spacious cavities of giant cedar trunks, but also in snags, stumps, and logs. The ample hollows within tree trunks or logs provide ideal shelter from winter winds and rising waters, as well as from predators, rivals, and hunters. Once settled in its den, the bear curls into a ball on its side, insulated by its plush winter coat. Within days its heartbeat slows down, while its metabolic system processes water and calories—up to 4000 a day—from its fat reserves.

Watering and bathing

The sound of running water can be heard throughout the rainforest. On Princess Island alone, over 27 freshwater salmon streams flow into eddies and estuaries. Elsewhere, along granite creeks and sheltered inlets, swampy bogs and quiet ponds offer ideal bathing pools, where the bears can soak off dirt and mites.

Classification

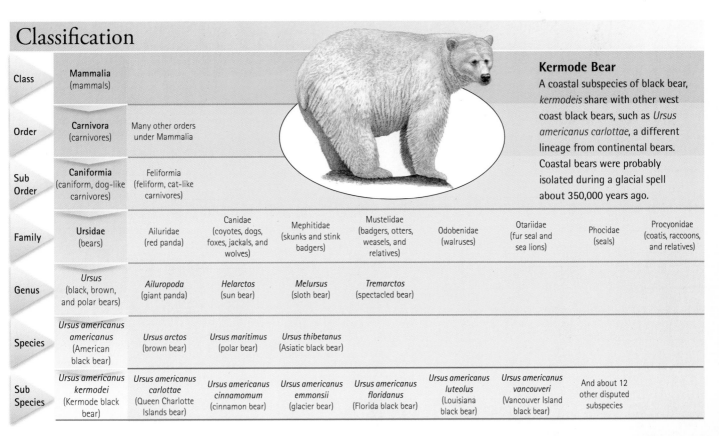

Kermode Bear

A coastal subspecies of black bear, *kermodeis* share with other west coast black bears, such as *Ursus americanus carlottae*, a different lineage from continental bears. Coastal bears were probably isolated during a glacial spell about 350,000 years ago.

Class	Mammalia (mammals)								
Order	Carnivora (carnivores)	Many other orders under Mammalia							
Sub Order	Caniformia (caniform, dog-like carnivores)	Feliformia (feliform, cat-like carnivores)							
Family	Ursidae (bears)	Ailuridae (red panda)	Canidae (coyotes, dogs, foxes, jackals, and wolves)	Mephitidae (skunks and stink badgers)	Mustelidae (badgers, otters, weasels, and relatives)	Odobenidae (walruses)	Otariidae (fur seal and sea lions)	Phocidae (seals)	Procyonidae (coatis, raccoons, and relatives)
Genus	Ursus (black, brown, and polar bears)	Ailuropoda (giant panda)	Helarctos (sun bear)	Melursus (sloth bear)	Tremarctos (spectacled bear)				
Species	Ursus americanus americanus (American black bear)	Ursus arctos (brown bear)	Ursus maritimus (polar bear)	Ursus thibetanus (Asiatic black bear)					
Sub Species	Ursus americanus kermodei (Kermode black bear)	Ursus americanus carlottae (Queen Charlotte Islands bear)	Ursus americanus cinnamomum (cinnamon bear)	Ursus americanus emmonsii (glacier bear)	Ursus americanus floridanus (Florida black bear)	Ursus americanus luteolus (Louisiana black bear)	Ursus americanus vancouveri (Vancouver Island black bear)	And about 12 other disputed subspecies	

Adaptation and Behavior

The Spirit bear's startling white coat has puzzled scientists ever since one of its pelts turned up at the New York Zoological Society in 1900. Some experts speculate that the color evolved as camouflage during the last ice age (2 million–10,000 years ago), but cannot explain why the color persisted after the glaciers had melted.

Coastal and continental cousins

Other experts believe that the recessive "white" gene simply replicated when it was confined to isolated coastal populations, with little alternative "black" gene flow from the mainland. Certainly, "coastal" bears—along the north coast and on the archipelagos of Vancouver, Haida Gwaii (Queen Charlotte), and Princess Royal—seem isolated from their continental cousins. The Coast Mountains, running from Alaska to Vancouver, clearly impede gene flow. Perhaps also continental and coastal lineages split about 350,000 years ago, when an ice sheet possibly pushed inland bears south, while their coastal cousins took refuge on offshore islands. Over time, the island populations probably separated into subspecies (such as *carlottae* on Haida Gwaii, *vancouveri* on Vancouver, and *kermodei* on Princess Royal and Gribbell). Even though the ice sheets melted around 10,000 years ago, coastal bears remained isolated, and the white trait recurred among *kermodeis*, whether or not it served any survival purpose. One benefit, though, seems to be camouflage in white water, enabling white bears to catch more salmon than black bears.

Calling from the treetops

Like other forest dwellers, Spirit bears seem quite vocal. Mothers communicate with their offspring with low grunts and soft growls. Cubs bawl loudly in distress and purr quietly when contented. If badly upset, *kermodeis* moan. When threatened, they lower their heads, flatten their ears, huff, and click their teeth. If aroused to anger, they might swing their heads back and forth, grunt, bellow, snort, and snap their jaws. *Kermodeis* rarely attack, but might bluff-charge if seriously stressed. When bluffing, bears lunge to within a few paces of the intruder, then stop and slap the brush before wandering off.

Hunting and Feeding

With the bounty of the lush rainforest within ambling distance, *kermodeis* almost never go hungry. Enjoying a seasonal mix of sedges, fruits, nuts, fish, and rodents, the bears forage and graze constantly, meandering from wildflower meadows to sedge estuaries, from berry glades to salmon streams.

Salmon for supper

An unlucky salmon hangs limply from the jaws of a ravenous White Spirit bear, rushing back to the bank to devour its catch in peace. During the spawning season salmon provides up to 90 percent of a bear's diet.

As the gusty winter rainstorms die down, the bears amble slowly from their dens and make for sodden river flats, and swollen wetlands, where fresh fields of sprouting sedge offer nutritious spring fare. Grazing for hours, the bears can consume as much as 50–100 lb (23–45 kg) a day. As the spring sun brightens, succulent chocolate lilies, sweet angelica, and other wildflowers blossom, providing extra nourishment. Juicy skunk cabbage and fatty ants nesting in rotten logs also help replenish the bears' depleted reserves. By mid-summer, high-energy berries, Pacific crab apples, and salal fruit ripen in meadows and deltas. The choice of berries is almost limitless. On Princess Royal Island alone, 18 varieties flourish, including bunchberry, salmonberry, huckleberry, blueberry, and crowberry.

Types of food

Kermodeis dine on a mixed diet of green grasses and sedges, berries, and nuts, along with seasonal salmon and the odd mouse or ants' nest. By far the most nutritious ingredient is fish—high in fat and protein—enabling the bears to shore up reserves for their winter sleep.

Skunk cabbage

Chocolate lilies

Salmon runs

After gorging on thousands of sweet berries, the bears turn to the rocky river creeks in late summer to catch the first spawning salmon. From July to November Pacific salmon return from the ocean to swim upriver to the freshwater spawning beds where they first hatched. It is an exhausting upstream journey, battling against the river's current rushing out to sea. Battered by their uphill struggle, spawners make easy prey for hungry bears and wolves lying in wait along the river canyons. Initially, the first salmon of the season fall prey before they spawn, but as the season wears on, most salmon are caught after spawning. Once "spawned out," the adult fish die, leaving their eggs to hatch in the spring. On breaking out of their egg sacs, the young salmon "fry" swim downstream to the open sea, where they dwell for a few years until big enough to battle upstream, repeating the whole cycle again.

On the offshore islands of Gribbell, Princess Royal, Roderick, Swindle, and Pooley, the bears need never tire of salmon, with a choice of five or six varieties—sockeye, coho, chum, steelhead, pink (the most abundant), and chinook (the largest), which can weigh up to 125 lb (55 kg). At the height of the runs, the bears gorge from dawn to dusk, building up layers of fat, and growing thick coats for the winter sleep. Consuming up to 20,000 calories a day, they can gain more than 60 lb (27 kg) in a few weeks, but will lose 30–40 percent of their body weight during the long sleep.

Tried and tested tactics

Kermodeis are natural swimmers, and seem to enjoy "snorkeling" underwater to spy salmon hugging the riverbanks, where the current flows more gently. At the start of the season the bears mass on slippery granite banks by frothy cascades, where salmon slow down to

leap the rapids. As the shiny fish flash by, some bears reach out and swipe with one paw; others perch precariously with open jaws and snap, crablike, as the fish fly by. In small eddies and gentle streams the milling fish make easy prey, and a bear might catch and devour half a dozen in an hour. Only the fatty brains, skin, and eggs are eaten, the remnants left for savengers. When shoals are plentiful, any male fish (devoid of oil-rich eggs) is simply chucked back into the river. If too satiated to finish a meal, some bears stash their catch under a brush pile, where the rotting fish nourishes insects and fertilizes the soil.

Poised to pounce

A resourceful White Spirit bear dives head first between slippery granite boulders to reach the salmon milling in the waters below. The striking amber stain across the bear's white back is caused by humic acids present in the river (created by rotting humus or organic matter).

Spawning sockeye salmon

Bunchberries

Columbian ground squirrel

Life Cycle

As wildflower blossom drifts across spring meadows, courting males pick up the scent of breeding females and track them to secluded arbors, where they become acquainted before mating. As *kermodei* mothers breed about every two years—rather more frequently than either brown or polar bears—male competition for breeding rights is much less intensive.

Like mother, like daughter
Looking like a pale reflection of her big brown mother, the delicate white cub mirrors her mother's every move as she forages for succulent sedges on a southerly slope. Both black (or brown) and white *kermodeis* can give birth to either dark or white cubs in the same litter. Twins of different colors seem to bond as closely as other twins.

Sometime in May or June, breeding females enter estrus, which lasts for about three weeks, when they attract, meet, and mate with one or more successful males. When in estrus, a female's scent acts like a magnet, drawing roving males from afar—just by sniffing a female's footprints, a courting male can track her to ground. After mating repeatedly to stimulate ovulation, both males and females go their separate ways, intent on feasting through the summer and fall to pile on enough fat for the winter sleep. The fertilized egg, meanwhile, initially floats free for a spell of arrested growth (delayed implantation), until the late fall, when it implants on the uterine wall and develops throughout the winter, while the expectant mother lies safe and warm in her den.

Denning sense
Picking the right birthing den is crucial for the survival of both mother and cub. A stable and secluded shelter will protect the young family from winter storms, river floods, and hungry predators, such as wolves or eagles. Although inland females show enormous versatility in their choice of den—ranging from caves to brush piles—coastal mothers need not wander far to find the ideal nest. Along the coast, birthing dens are usually built on gentle

Den hunting

Sniffing for danger
A female raises her nose to test the wind for any whiff of danger near her home. Within the den, her sense of smell grows less acute, although she still identifies her cubs by smell rather than appearance.

Spruce home
The cavities between the giant roots of a spruce or cedar tree provide perfect dens for nursing mothers. Warm, dry, and roomy, they offer ample shelter for a growing family.

Little snow white
Fresh out of its winter den, a kittenish spring cub sports a pristine white coat, licked clean by its attentive mother, who scans the horizon for danger. With small home ranges of around 8 square miles (21 square km), *kermodei* mothers can become quite territorial, giving short shrift to intruders.

slopes in the hollow trunks, or beneath the massive roots, of giant trees. Favored stands are western red and yellow cedar. Both offer warm, dry, spacious chambers, measuring around 10–15 ft (3–4.5 m) wide. Inside, the floor is comfortably lined with soft, insulating matting, sometimes 3 in (8 cm) thick, composed of twigs, leaves, woody debris, and springy moss.

Sleepy birth
While sea storms lash the coastal rainforest, and rising waters flood the creeks and canyons, the white bear slumbers peacefully, barely waking to give birth sometime in late January to a litter of two or three cubs. Although twins are more common than either singletons or triplets, older and heavier mothers sometimes produce larger litters. When born, each little bear measures up to 8 in (20 cm) long—about the size of a chipmunk—and weighs less than 12 oz (340 g), no more than a can of soda. Neonates (newborns) are born with blue-gray eyes, tightly shut, which open within a month, and turn brown within 4–6 months. Although sparsely furred at birth, the cubs keep warm by curling up on their mother's thick winter coat. Within moments of birth, they drag themselves toward her warm nipples, and suckle peacefully. Like their ursine relatives, *kermodei* mothers produce a daily supply of rich, creamy milk, full of bodybuilding nutrients. Within weeks, the neonates have piled on fat and grown lively. By the time they leave the den in the spring, they will weigh 5–10 lb (2.25–4.5 kg).

Cub curiosity
The lamb-like yearling shows innate curiosity, turning inquisitively toward the click of the camera, with ears cocked and nose lifted to the wind.

A bright new world
Out in the spring sunshine the little bears romp about in flower fields, somersault down grassy slopes, and flop around in swampy bogs. Almost immediately they try climbing—chasing each other up and down tall cedar trunks—gripping on with tiny, curved claws. Tree cover is the safest escape route from both marauding grizzlies and wolves, which prey on vulnerable cubs. Always on the lookout for danger, the mother gives a deep woof if anxious, warning her cubs to scamper up the nearest tree. If frightened, the little bears murmur and whimper like children in distress. Mostly, they are carefree and fearless, exploring the bright new world outside the den with boundless curiosity—sniffing flowers, chasing birds and butterflies, and swiping at tufts of grass. While their mother forages and fishes, the cubs watch attentively, mimicking her every move with more or less success. By the time they are six or eight months old, they no longer need to suckle, but stick close to their mother through the next winter, denning again in the hollow trunk of a mighty cedar.

Striking out
Developing faster than their brown or polar bear cousins, *kermodei* yearlings seem ready to go it alone at around 18 months, when their mother chases them off so that she can breed again. Littermates often wander around together for a couple of years, learning by trial and error. While females invariably settle close to their mother or grandmother, male yearlings feel compelled to explore farther afield. As older dominant males resent any budding rivals on their patch, young males disperse widely into unknown terrain, and experience the toughest lessons of life, until they grow big and strong enough to stand their ground on their own home range.

Legend and History

Emerging silently from a cleft in the canyon rock—ghostly white against the glistening granite—the Spirit bear seems almost surreal, like a black bear's phantom double, a photo negative, or an optical illusion. Disappearing into the shadows as magically as it appeared, the apparition lives up to its nickname, and legendary role, as spirit guardian of the forest.

Up and down the rocky coast, the Tsimshian tribes in the north and the Kwakiutl in the south have always revered the White Spirit bear, welcoming the ghostly visitor to their shores. While scientists still wonder why the bear is white, the Tsimshian tell a story that explains it all:

Raven promises
"In distant time, earth slept through the long, silent winter, blanketed in snow. The world sparkled ice-white for as far as the eye could see, from the stars in the night sky to the snowflakes floating silently to earth. After light years of time, the sun drew closer to earth, melting the snow. Earth stirred as the clouds turned golden, and leafy greenery flowed through her fields and forests. Raven, who had created the world, flew down from the heavenly sky to perch on a flame-red cedar and watch the planet glow with the colors of the rainbow as flowers opened and fruits ripened. Knowing that soon people would wander through the mossy green forests, Raven decided to create a memento of the timeless peace before earth awoke and people grew strong on her bounty. Swooping through the fragrant rainforest of Princess Royal Island, he turned every tenth bear white and promised: 'The white bears shall live here forever in peace and harmony.'"

Raven's world
The primal vibrance and surging power of the timeless rainforest is captured here by Emily Carr, one of the first British Columbian painters to record the coastal landscape and culture. All along the coast, groves of totem poles carved with animal spirits, such as Raven here, once lined village thoroughfares. (*Skidegate, Graham Island, British Columbia* by Emily Carr, 1928)

White crest of Masala
Over the millennia, the coast people, especially the Tsimshian Git-ga'at, developed an affinity with the Spirit bear, called Masala. To mark the Git-ga'ats' sense of kinship, the coast tribes agreed, over 1000 years ago, that only the Git-ga'ats' hereditary chief, Mahmobem, could bear the white crest of Masala. Even today the chief alone wears the white emblem, and his people feel lucky if they glimpse the Spirit bear. Along with his tribe, Mahmobem remains a vigilant defender of Masala. When the trapper Al Oeming tried in the 1960s to catch a white bear for his zoo, the Git-ga'at ran him off their land.

The hunter and the white bear
The kinship felt with the Spirit bear runs through many coast legends, where people sometimes turn into bears or vice versa:

"When hunting in the fall, a brave caught sight of a snow-white she-bear flitting between the trees. He chased her up a steep mountain, but on the misty summit she stepped into the clouds and disappeared. Undeterred, the hunter raced on, bounding across thundery cloudfields, until he saw the bear in the distance enter a mist-shrouded longhouse. When the hunter peeked through a hole in the door, he glimpsed a woman shaking off her white bearskin. Catching sight of the hunter, she laughed, flung on her bearskin and rushed outside to pull him out of the clouds. The hunter fell in love with the laughing girl, who turned out to be the daughter of a great chief."

Bear parties

Farther down the coast, the Kwakiutl also paid homage to the phantom bear. The Kwakiutl were famous for their elaborate potlatches (ceremonial feasts), when ranked nobility handed out gifts to loyal commoners. Although the Kwakiutl's flamboyant potlatches were curbed by British colonialists in the 19th century, the tribe's fine sense of style manifested in "bear parties" celebrating the bounty of the hunt. Bear fat, flesh, and fur provided vital sustenance and shelter; fur blankets and robes served also as barter, potlatch gifts, and status symbols—only chiefs wore bearskin hides. Like other tribespeople, the Kwakiutl conjured and placated the hunted bear with time-honored rites that expressed the respect and reverence they felt, not just for a living being and kindred soul, but for a powerful animal spirit. On slaying the first bear of the season, the hunter would carry the warm carcass into the village, calling, "I have a visitor!" When everyone had assembled in the hunter's longhouse, the bear would be pampered like an honored guest. Finely "dressed" with a ring of cedar bark about its neck and eagle down on its head, it was served with a plate from the feast. One by one, people advanced and held its paws. During the celebration the Kwakiutl sang a conciliatory "mourning song," begging the beast to forgive the "poor" hunter for taking its life. When the song was chanted with flair and passion, listeners were moved to tears.

Brief encounters

The startling beauty and rarity of the Spirit bear have enthralled coast people for centuries. Something of its ancient mystique has now spread through the global community of wildlife lovers who, along with the Tsimshian and Kwakiutl, have pledged to save the "panda of Canada," and to defend its home from loggers, poachers, and tourists. One of the White Spirit bear's most appealing traits is its "pure wildness." Dwelling deep in impenetrable island forests, it has barely glimpsed humans. Brief encounters reveal an unusually gentle, trusting, inquisitive nature. In his *Spirit Bear* (2002), Charles Russell portrays an intriguing creature of childlike innocence, unspoilt by contact with people. While keen on any sincere interest in the rare bear, Russell fears that publicity might draw trophy hunters and poachers. Excessive tourism, similarly, could crowd the islands and rob the Spirit bear of its seclusion and innocence. Only time will tell whether the Raven's promise will withstand the pressures of the modern world.

Spirit inspiration

A flair for fishing
Gliding up and down the waterways in finely carved canoes, the coast peoples fished, traded in furs, settled scores, and raided local tribes. Whenever fishing, fighting, or in danger, they called on the Spirit bear's special powers and protection.

Ceremonial lodge
At "bear parties" to celebrate a successful hunt, the slain bear would be seated in a place of honor, usually at the back of the room. During the feast it would be served with treats, and propitiated with moving "mourning songs."

A "new species"?
When American naturalist William Hornaday first saw some white bearskins in 1900, he thought he had discovered a new species. Keen to inspect a live specimen, he solicited the help of local curator Francis Kermode, and named the "new bear" in his honor. By 1928, however, scientists realized that the *kermodei* was a coastal subspecies, with a rare white "phase" (color), rather than a new species.

Threats and Conservation

Historically, epic campaigns have been waged and won to keep persistent loggers and hunters off the Spirit bear's priceless and irreplaceable rainforest homestead. As the fame of the "panda of Canada" spreads, however, trophy hunting, poaching, and intrusive tourism now threaten to swamp its archipelago paradise.

The Spirit bear's historic homeland, abounding in prized red cedar and hemlock, has always attracted loggers who, by the 1980s, had already diminished much rainforest along the coast, and on the islands of Gribbell, Roderick, Pooley, and Princess Royal. Alarmed by the rate of destruction, the Valhalla Wilderness Society spearheaded a coalition of First Nations, wildlife experts, and eco-activists, who campaigned to save the rainforest, not only for the Spirit bear, but for the salmon, wolves, sea lions, deer, and grizzlies. After long talks with the campaigners, the government agreed in February 2006 to protect 4.5 million acres (18,000 square km) of the Great Bear Rainforest, including 520,000 acres (2080 square km) of prime *kermodei* habitat—the Spirit Bear Conservancy—mainly on Princess Royal Island. A mosaic of island and mainland habitats, the new conservancy includes over 50 salmon streams, and countless sheltered inlets and fertile estuaries. In the words of wildlife expert Wayne McCrory, "Once protected, this remote rainforest archipelago will be cherished by generations to come as a world-class natural treasure."

Up, up and away
The rattle of helicopter blades shatters the calm as sawn timber is airlifted clear of the rainforest. An ecological alternative to clearfelling, "selective logging" removes just commercial timber, leaving other trees standing. In similar vein, specialized aircraft, such as the helicopter here, can both saw and airlift timber without the need for destructive logging roads.

Fears of "swamping" the gene pool
Despite the milestone achievement, some parts of *kermodei* habitat remain vulnerable, including the 200,000 acre (800 square km) Green River watershed wilderness, where logging began in late 2006. Destruction of the Green habitat might force black bears to migrate to protected *kermodei* habitats, possibly "swamping" (diluting) the white gene pool. Campaigns are now afoot to protect the Green watershed, as well as other vulnerable regions, particularly Gribbell Island.

Trophy hunting
Since 1965, it has been illegal to hunt white *kermodeis*. Paradoxically, it remains legal to kill black individuals, even though they too carry one recessive gene that could, if united with that of another carrier, generate white offspring. As the fame of the Spirit bear grows, trophy hunters and poachers will undoubtedly gravitate to its island retreats. Fortunately, Masala's local protectors—the coast peoples—remain ever vigilant.

Clearfelling on Gribbell Island
Clearcut logging, which fells all trees in the region, leaves piles of wastage in its wake, and opens up the naturally secluded rainforest to poachers. A less destructive and disruptive alternative would be selective logging.

Glimpsing the White Spirit bear

The Spirit bear's ancient rainforest retreat could become ancient history unless the coast peoples and wildlife activists can stem the flood of tourists and trophy hunters closing in on the popular bear. Although just a handful of charter boat operators currently run summer tours from the mainland ports of Prince Rupert and Hardy, the coast people fear that more could soon follow. While the local Git-ga'at welcome small "pocket" cruise boats, ferrying fewer than 250 passengers, they discourage larger vessels. British Columbian biologist Tony Hamilton also warns: "Unmanaged bear-watching can have substantial negative impact on bears, driving them off their feeding stations." The alternative, espoused by the Git-ga'at, involves low-impact eco-tourism, which opens a window on the wonders of wilderness without ever letting the watchers intrude. Following the rules developed at the renowned McNeil River State Game Sanctuary in Alaska, Git-ga'at guides lead watchers to the best bear spots, where the elusive

creatures can be glimpsed from viewing platforms. People remain put, while the animals come and go. On Princess Royal Island too the local Tsimshian Kitasoo of Klemtu have developed bear-watching from King Pacific Lodge, an ultra eco-friendly, 17-room barge resort anchored offshore.

Eco-watching
Moored off Barnard Harbor, King Pacific Lodge offers eco-friendly bear-viewing on Princess Royal Island. Run by the Kitasoo people, the tours are based on ecological principles.

Breakthrough in conservation
The magical world of the Great Bear Rainforest has remained undisturbed for over 10,000 years. Thanks to the sustained efforts of eco-activists and coast peoples, the natural sanctuary can now remain undisturbed indefinitely, as it was granted governmental protection in 2006.

How can we help?

● Petition government leaders to protect *kermodei* habitat.

● Join the Sierra Club (www.sierraclub.ca/bc) in its campaign to save the critical Green River watershed.

● Help the Western Canada Wilderness Committee (www.wildernesscommittee.org) to protect *kermodei* habitat.

● Support the Rainforest Conservation Society (www.raincoast.org), which sponsors research to restore rainforest ecosystems.

current status: **Lower risk**

SSC
Species Survival Commission

IUCN
The World Conservation Union

Eurasian

Brown Bear

CLASS: Mammalia   **ORDER:** Carnivora   **FAMILY:** Ursidae   **GENUS, SPECIES & SUBSPECIES:** *Ursus arctos arctos*

The oldest of the world's brown bears, "Old Grandfather," as he is called by the local Lapps, settled down to graze on the windswept plains of Old Eurasia over a million years ago. The original brown "bruin" of legend roamed far and wide, ranging from the sunny slopes of the Pyrenees to the frozen steppes of Siberia. Some Siberian brown bears even wandered farther afield—across the Bering land bridge that once linked Siberia and Alaska. The forebears of today's grizzlies, they fanned out across the Great Plains and colonized North America. Back in the Old World, the Eurasian brown bear gradually shrank from its ancestral strongholds—the sad result of centuries of conflict with people—but thrives today in Russia and Scandinavia. Perfectly adapted to life in the remote mountains, forests, and tundra that it inhabits, the magnificent brown bear roams widely, developing an intimate knowledge of its home range and adapting its diet to suit the changing seasons. Contrary to popular belief, brown bears are seldom dangerous, despite their brute strength, and are slowly becoming objects of fascination for bear-watchers.

Europe's largest carnivore eats anything from berries to moose.

Key Features

● Immensely powerful, with a massive muzzle, rippling shoulder muscles, and long, strong claws.

● A natural loner that wanders a huge area, rarely socializing except to breed.

● Thriving populations in Russia and Scandinavia, though numbers are declining elsewhere.

In Focus

The Eurasian brown bear is one of the biggest bears—only polar bears and the Kodiak bears of Alaska are larger. Like all bears, it has a sturdy frame, with a heavy skull, broad snout, and thickset neck. Full-grown males are on average one and a half times the size of females.

Deep-set eyes

The eyes are deep-set and face forward down each side of the snout, providing stereoscopic (binocular) vision, which helps this bear to judge distances accurately. Its long-distance vision, however, is not especially good. A reflective layer at the back of the eyeball enhances its night vision.

Versatile teeth

The bear has 42 teeth, including two large canines. The canine teeth lack the sharp cutting blades of specialist predators, such as the tiger, reflecting the brown bear's more varied diet.

Paws and claws

The powerful curved claws are up to 4 in (10 cm) long and used mostly for digging. Unlike the claws of big cats, they are not retractable, so have blunt edges and show up clearly in the bear's tracks.

Being small and rounded, the ears are often hidden by the bear's thick winter coat. The hearing is poor, so this bear tends to be startled by nearby noises or passers-by.

Vital Statistics

Weight: Male 310–880 lb (140–400 kg); female 210–450 lb (95–205 kg)

Length: 5.5–9.2 ft (1.7–2.8 m)

Height: 3–5 ft (0.9–1.5 m) at the shoulder

Color: Dark chocolate, sometimes black, with paler areas on the head and neck

Sexual maturity: 4–6 years

Gestation period: 6–8.5 months, including delayed implantation

Number of young: 1–4

Birth interval: 2–4 years

Typical diet: Mainly berries, nuts, bulbs, and tubers in summer and fall; roots, grasses, herbs, fungi, bark, insects, fish, carrion, and garbage eaten all year, supplemented with mammal prey up to the size of moose calves

Lifespan: Up to 30 years in the wild and 50 years in captivity

Did you know?

● The heaviest brown bears in Europe or Asia are male Kamchatka bears of eastern Russia, some of which reach over 1320 lb (600 kg).

● An adult brown bear can run at almost 30 mph (48 kph) and has the endurance to outrun a horse across rough terrain.

● As many as three-quarters of all brown bears are thought to harbor parasitic roundworms, probably acquired by eating infected fish.

Fur coat

Dense and thick in winter, the coat is molted in late spring to reveal shorter and darker growth. The overall color is deep brown, occasionally black, often with "blond" areas on the head and neck. Bears from Russia's Kamchatka Peninsula are extremely pale.

|← 9.2 ft (2.8 m) →|

5 ft (1.5 m)

Habitat

Eurasian brown bears are found in a wide variety of landscapes across their huge range, from dense forest to windswept tundra and rocky coasts. But, except for the sparsely populated Arctic, they are absent from lowland areas, having been driven out by centuries of human persecution.

Distribution

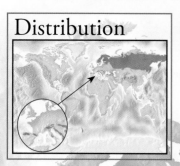

Kamchatka, Russia
This part of eastern Russia supports the densest population of brown bears on the planet—an estimated 12,000 individuals in 1995–6. Big groups of bears gather at Kamchatka's river mouths during the salmon spawning season.

Russia

Spain

Japan

China

Pacific Ocean

Indian Ocean

Pyrenees, Spain
A threatened population of 12–16 brown bears clings to survival in the pine forests and high summer pastures of the Spanish Pyrenees, but they have vanished from the French side of the mountains.

Hokkaido Island, Japan
Japan's heavily forested northern-most island is home to about 3000 brown bears, known locally as *higuma*. These are very large and have distinctive pale fur on the shoulders.

Today the range of the Eurasian brown bear extends from northeastern Norway, through Scandinavia and the northern half of Asia to the easternmost fringes of Siberia. It has a patchy distribution in central and eastern Europe, with strongholds in the Carpathian Mountains of Slovakia and Romania, and in the Rila-Rhodope Mountains of Bulgaria. There are isolated, declining populations of brown bears in Austria, central Italy, Bosnia-Herzegovina, Macedonia, Greece, the Black Sea region of Turkey, and the Cantabrian Mountains of northern Spain.

Northern wilderness

The Eurasian brown bear's heartland is the vast swathe of coniferous forest and bogs that runs for 5000 miles (8000 km) from Finland's border with Russia to the Pacific Ocean. Largely wilderness, this remote area is home to an estimated 140,000 brown bears, with the highest concentrations being found along the Pacific coast and in European Russia (there are thought to be about 37,000 bears in western Russia). The inaccessibility of the terrain, and the bears' elusive habits, make an accurate census almost impossible, but Russia's bear population probably outnumbers that in the whole of Europe (excluding Russia) by a factor of 10 to one.

Southern settlers

To the south of Russia, fragmented populations of brown bears survive in Mongolia's Gobi desert, the Himalayas, and in northern India. These bears are little studied in comparison with their northern counterparts, but may belong to distinctive subspecies (see below). However, the brown bear has long since disappeared from its only African outpost—the Atlas Mountains of North Africa—and likewise became extinct in Syria and Lebanon by the early 1930s.

Bearproof trashcans are designed to deter nocturnal scavenging.

Mixed opportunities

The ideal territory for brown bears is a varied landscape of thick forest (for shelter and denning sites) mixed with several more open habitats, such as moorland, alpine pasture, mountain slopes, and river valleys. These provide maximum feeding opportunities throughout the year. The size of a bear's home range varies considerably, according to whether it lives inland or by the ocean: coasts are such rich feeding grounds that animals living there need to roam far less. On average, one adult bear requires about 12–75 square miles (30–200 square km) near the sea, and 38–380 square miles (100–1000 square km) inland.

Eurasian brown bears tend to avoid human habitation, but in some areas they have learned to take advantage of the year-round food supply from trashcans. In Romania, for example, the residents of the medieval town of Brasov have become accustomed to the sight of bears ambling down their streets at dusk and in the early morning to search for scraps.

Classification

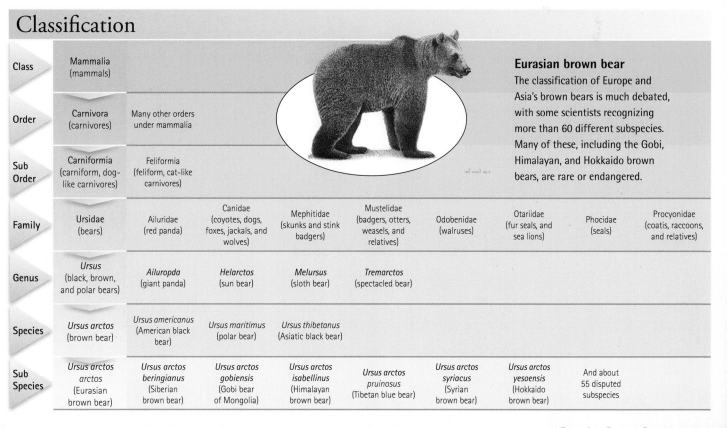

Eurasian brown bear
The classification of Europe and Asia's brown bears is much debated, with some scientists recognizing more than 60 different subspecies. Many of these, including the Gobi, Himalayan, and Hokkaido brown bears, are rare or endangered.

Class	Mammalia (mammals)							
Order	Carnivora (carnivores)	Many other orders under mammalia						
Sub Order	Carniformia (carniform, dog-like carnivores)	Feliformia (feliform, cat-like carnivores)						
Family	Ursidae (bears)	Ailuridae (red panda)	Canidae (coyotes, dogs, foxes, jackals, and wolves)	Mephitidae (skunks and stink badgers)	Mustelidae (badgers, otters, weasels, and relatives)	Odobenidae (walruses)	Otariidae (fur seals, and sea lions)	Phocidae (seals)	Procyonidae (coatis, raccoons, and relatives)
Genus	Ursus (black, brown, and polar bears)	Ailuropda (giant panda)	Helarctos (sun bear)	Melursus (sloth bear)	Tremarctos (spectacled bear)			
Species	Ursus arctos (brown bear)	Ursus americanus (American black bear)	Ursus maritimus (polar bear)	Ursus thibetanus (Asiatic black bear)				
Sub Species	Ursus arctos arctos (Eurasian brown bear)	Ursus arctos beringianus (Siberian brown bear)	Ursus arctos gobiensis (Gobi bear of Mongolia)	Ursus arctos isabellinus (Himalayan brown bear)	Ursus arctos pruinosus (Tibetan blue bear)	Ursus arctos syriacus (Syrian brown bear)	Ursus arctos yesoensis (Hokkaido brown bear)	And about 55 disputed subspecies

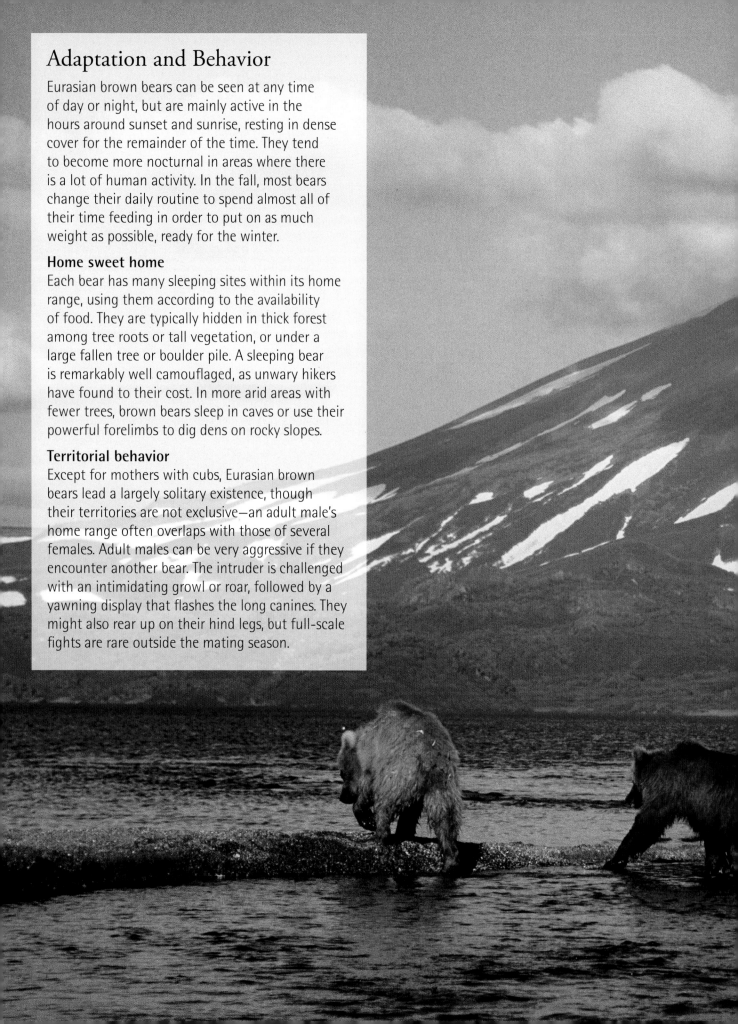

Adaptation and Behavior

Eurasian brown bears can be seen at any time of day or night, but are mainly active in the hours around sunset and sunrise, resting in dense cover for the remainder of the time. They tend to become more nocturnal in areas where there is a lot of human activity. In the fall, most bears change their daily routine to spend almost all of their time feeding in order to put on as much weight as possible, ready for the winter.

Home sweet home
Each bear has many sleeping sites within its home range, using them according to the availability of food. They are typically hidden in thick forest among tree roots or tall vegetation, or under a large fallen tree or boulder pile. A sleeping bear is remarkably well camouflaged, as unwary hikers have found to their cost. In more arid areas with fewer trees, brown bears sleep in caves or use their powerful forelimbs to dig dens on rocky slopes.

Territorial behavior
Except for mothers with cubs, Eurasian brown bears lead a largely solitary existence, though their territories are not exclusive—an adult male's home range often overlaps with those of several females. Adult males can be very aggressive if they encounter another bear. The intruder is challenged with an intimidating growl or roar, followed by a yawning display that flashes the long canines. They might also rear up on their hind legs, but full-scale fights are rare outside the mating season.

Hunting and Feeding

It is often said that brown bears are opportunists, happy to devour just about anything edible. However, research shows that their diet varies widely from place to place, and that they are actually highly selective, choosing different foods at different times of year.

Occasional carnivore
This full-grown bear has caught a wild boar in the forests of Bavaria in southern Germany. Holding the carcass down with its front legs, the bear tears off chunks of meat by shaking its prey from side to side in its powerful jaws.

Eurasian brown bears have an extremely acute sense of smell, which they rely on to find most of their food. Field researchers have demonstrated that they can detect the scent of carrion from a distance of more than 2 miles (3 km). The bears sniff out a wide variety of nutritious underground foods, from truffles to roots, bulbs, and tubers. These hidden feasts are quickly excavated with their long claws, leaving behind telltale earthworks on the forest floor. Smell, rather than sound, is also thought to alert bears to rodents and rabbits in their burrows.

Seasonal variations
Roots and rodent prey are particularly important to brown bears in winter, especially in the north of their range, where snow

Types of food

Eurasian brown bears are omnivorous to a greater extent than most of North America's grizzlies: vegetable matter makes up 80–95 percent of their diet. Rodents, such as voles, lemmings, and mice are dug out of their tunnels, while larger prey includes deer and wild boar.

Bank vole

Cloudberries

blankets the ground for five months of the year. Even so, the bears lose 25–45 percent of their bulk during their long winter dormancy as a result of the fat they must burn in order to fuel their metabolism. When they become fully active again in spring, they start feeding on freshly sprouting grass and the first herbs, such as coltsfoot and butterbur. They pick any sloe berries and rosehips still on bushes from the previous autumn, and strip bark and buds off trees. As the season progresses, new types of food become available. Ants are a major summer food, especially in the Pyrenees, and bears often rip into ant nests to reach the juicy larvae. They will also raid bee and wasp nests, and hunt for wood-boring beetle grubs in rotting tree stumps and logs. Given the opportunity, they will also plunder fields of oats and root crops, such as potatoes.

Fruitful foraging

Late summer and fall is a period of plenty for brown bears, during which they must feed intensively to fatten up in preparation for dormancy. They ignore grass because it is by now high in cellulose, making it tough and difficult to digest. Instead they concentrate on eating fruit, nuts, bulbs, and tubers. Bilberries and cloudberries are favorite foods of bears in Scandinavia and Siberia, while further south in Europe the warmer climate means that plums, apples, and other large fruits are on offer.

Meat on the menu

Meat seldom accounts for more than 20 percent of the Eurasian brown bear's diet, while Japan's bears are almost entirely vegetarian. Even though an adult bear is capable of bringing down prey as large as wild boar, deer, and moose calves, the effort this entails may explain why rodent-sized species are taken far more frequently. Migrating salmon are a

special delicacy for the brown bears of Siberia, which wade into the shallows of rivers to catch the spawning adult fish. In the Kamchatka Peninsula, the spawning season lasts from June to December, and is one of the few occasions when large groups of bears tolerate each other. Siberia's coasts also provide a year-round supply of carrion, washed up on beaches by the tide. A whale carcass is a feast that will feed several bears for days.

Berry feast

Young bears, such as this female Russian cub, are naturally curious, and learn what to eat by watching their mother. They continue suckling throughout the fall and into their second winter, but despite this must still feed intensively to put on extra weight for their winter sleep.

Sweet chestnuts

Crab apples

Roe deer

Life Cycle

Like other bears, Eurasian brown bears are long-lived and their life cycle follows the rhythm of the passing seasons. Females make devoted parents, but males play no part in raising their offspring, and if they do encounter their young in future years, will treat them as rivals.

Newborns

Winter birth
Cubs are born inside their mother's winter den between January and March. They weigh only 10.5–12 oz (300–340 g) at birth.

Spring emergence
The cubs follow their mother out of the den in late March or April, but the timing depends on the weather: if it's too harsh, they remain in the den for longer.

The summer mating season is the only period when male and female Eurasian brown bears spend time together as a pair. It is thought that when females are receptive they leave scent trails to help wandering male bears locate them—an essential adaptation for a wide-ranging species that inhabits the vast Arctic tundra and mountain ranges. It seems to work because bears have been seen to pick up the trail of another bear and follow it for some distance. Sometimes full-scale fights erupt between males when they battle for the right to mate with a receptive female. Such confrontations can result in serious injuries caused by slashing claws, so aggression is usually confined to the mating season and avoided at other times.

When prospective partners eventually meet, their courtship is brief, and its

Sticking close
Female bears make excellent mothers, keeping their cubs close to them for up to four years and ferociously fighting off any creature—bear or otherwise—that dares to present a challenge to their safety.

main purpose is to overcome the bears' natural wariness of each other.

After mating several times over the course of a few days, or sometimes up to two weeks, the female chases her suitor away. Occasionally a female will mate again with a second male, subsequently giving birth to several cubs from different fathers, but this rarely happens since females are not receptive for long enough. Like America's grizzlies, Eurasian brown bears do not mate every year because of the time the cubs take to mature—youngsters usually stay with their mother for 2½–4 years.

Uncertain future
Life outside the den presents various dangers to young bears. Sadly, many brown bear cubs never reach a year old. Some are attacked by adult males, and others die of disease or starvation.

Unpredictable pregnancy
In common with other bears, the female's pregnancy uses a system known as delayed implantation, in which her eggs begin to develop much later than when they are actually fertilized. This causes significant differences in the length of the gestation period, which can last from six months to as long as eight and a half months. If a female is in weak physical condition, her fertilized eggs die. In a successful pregnancy, a litter of 1–4 cubs is produced in late winter, with two or three cubs in a typical litter. The tiny cubs are naked and scarcely able to see or hear, but develop rapidly on their mother's extremely rich milk, which is 33 percent fat, and contains three times as many calories as human breast milk. It is remarkable that a female bear is able to produce milk while she herself is not actually eating or drinking. All of the nutrients and fluids are taken from the reserves laid down in her body during the previous summer and fall.

First steps
On a fine spring day the family finally leaves its den and emerges into the open—the first time that the young have seen the outside world. By now the cubs are strong enough to follow their mother on foot as she urgently searches for food to break her winter fast. The young bears continue suckling for 12 months or so, and the family stays as a tight-knit group for two or three winters, before the female eventually chases them away so that she can mate again. The newly independent bears have acquired all the skills they need to fend for themselves. They reach sexual maturity at about 4–6 years, but are unlikely to breed straight away as they are still relatively inexperienced; they are not physically mature until 10–11 years old.

From birth until death, scent plays a hugely important part in the lives of Eurasian brown bears. In addition to enabling male bears to find mates, and cubs to bond and stay in touch with their mothers, it is the principal way in which these animals organize their territories. Adult bears keep out of each other's way by using a variety of scent signals to advertise their

> *Fully grown male bears are aggressive toward cubs, and kill almost half of all young bears.*

presence. They leave smelly markers at key points around their territory by clawing and scratching trees to remove the bark, scraping the earth, and rubbing their body against tree trunks. One theory is that tree scratching releases aromatic chemicals from under the bark that enhances the bears' own scent.

Learning skills
Throughout the summer the cubs grow stronger and more confident, romping under the watchful gaze of their mother. The moves they practice now will be put to use when they start hunting for themselves.

Legend and History

Racing across the starry sky, the Little Bear (*Ursa minor*) chases after his mother the Great Bear (*Ursa major*) as she roams around the Pole Star. The heavenly bears, like so many Greek legends, owe their presence among the stars to the amorous god Zeus. But even before Zeus immortalized the brown bear mother, she was venerated throughout Old Europe.

Since Paleolithic times, over 30,000 years ago, the people of Old Europe worshiped the brown bear, carving its image on cavern walls by the light of the flickering fire. Like the first hunters of North America, they marveled at the bear's motherly devotion and uncanny resemblance to people, while remaining utterly in awe of its amazing ability to rise each spring, after a deathlike winter sleep. Marvel turned to wonder, and wonder to worship, expressed in cult, legend, and art. The evocative Lady of Vinca, for instance, a bear mother figurine, was created en masse by the Vinca people, *c.*6000 BC. An icon of nurturing, renewing motherhood, each bear-headed goddess nurses a bear-headed child suckling from human breasts.

Legend of the bear mother

The sacred bear mother recurred not only in cult art, but also in an ancient legend that spread throughout the northern hemisphere. At the heart of the legend lies the seduction of a woman by a bear spirit. Forced to live in his cave home, she gives birth to twin sons, bear boys endowed with superhuman strength. In time her brothers track and kill her husband, but not before he has taught his sons the songs and rites that release souls from death and bring luck to the tribe. The bear sons

Festival of the slain bear

Bearing brightly colored gifts for the slain bear, the Ainu of Hokkaido send the "little guest" away to its "master," a mountain god. Before the 1930s, when the ceremony was banned, sacrificial cubs were reared from birth and kept as honored guests, until their ritual killing. (Japanese scroll, c.1870)

grow up strong and handsome. Fearless heroes, they overcome monsters in underground dens, rescue captive princesses, and return victorious with rich spoils from the underworld. The legends and cults of the bear mother, probably thousands of years old, proliferated throughout Old Europe. At first the nurturing, life-renewing mother was celebrated, but in time her heroic sons dominated both cult and legend.

Initiating the she-bears

An early she-bear cult flourished around the Greek goddess Artemis (bear). A "lady of the wild," Artemis pervaded the mountains and fields, guarding the sacred bear and other beasts of the forest. Guardian of growth and renewal, she protected virgin girls, childbearing women, and growing plants, and died each fall to be born again in the spring, much like a bear rising from winter sleep. At her secluded sanctuary in Brauron, near

Athens, virgin girls, or *arktoi* (she-bears), prepared for marriage. Clad in brown robes, they imitated bear cubs, and danced the *arkteuin* (playing the she-bear) during the rite of *arkteia* (bear festival). The Celtic double of Artemis, the bear goddess Artio, was worshiped in Berne (city of bears), now in Switzerland.

The Great Bear in the heavens
The bear mother roamed the heavens too. According to one legend, Callisto was a forest nymph from Arcadia (home of bears), who accompanied Artemis in the chase. Seduced by Zeus, she bore him a son, Arcas (bear). To punish Callisto for the affair, Zeus's jealous wife Hera turned her into a bear. To save Callisto from the hunt, Zeus set her among the stars as the Great Bear. When her son Arcas was killed, Zeus dispatched him to the heavens too, to act as eternal guardian to his mother.

Legends of the bear sons
With the spread of farming, and rise of rival landed chiefdoms, the cult of the bear mother gave way to legends celebrating her intrepid, superstrong sons. One of the first adventurers, the Greek hero Odysseus, descended from bears, while the Anglo-Saxon champion Beowulf (Bear-Wolf), fought with the bear-like strength of 30 men. The Celtic hero Arthur (bear) lies sleeping in an underground tomb, much like a denning bear, biding the time to waken, when the country will return to spring-like joy and festivity. In the cold north, warriors clad in bear shirts (*ber-serkr*) summoned bear courage and roared like bears. In the heat of battle some went berserk, turning into bears. The Lapps and Finns, and Siberian Mansi—all closely related to bears—could just as easily "turn on the bear" whenever the mood moved them.

Summoning "Old Grandfather"
Along with the braves of America, the hunters of Old Europe evolved elaborate rites to invoke, honor, and thank the ancestral bear spirit before and after the hunt. Apart from using archaic weapons, such as spears and axes, hunters spoke in hushed tones, calling the bear by respectful names, such as "Lightfoot" or "Old Grandfather." The Finns and Siberian Ostyaks took care to blame the killing on someone else, preferably the Russians.

Preserved in lineage and fairytale
As farms spread north and forests were cut down, the bear's symbolic power waned. In folktales, such as *The Peasant and the Bear*, the bruin (bear) is played for a fool. Similarly, in *Aesop's Fables*, Bruno is slow and sleepy, although forgiving. Yet it remained fashionable for medieval kings, such as Svend the Dane, to trace their lineage back to the first mythic bear. Elsewhere, in remote parts of Eurasia—among the Siberian Khanty and Japanese Ainu—ancient reverence and rites lingered into the 20th century. Meanwhile, children's fairytales, such as *Beauty and the Beast*, preserved the magical kinship between people and bears. Typically in such "animal-groom" tales, a maiden marries a beast, usually a bear. Gentle and kind, the Beast wins Beauty's love, which breaks the spell that binds him, revealing his true human colors.

Brown bear lore

Summoning the bear
The charismatic eyes of the Siberian brown bear gaze out from a burnished bronze effigy used by shamans to summon the bear spirit during healing or divining rituals. Marveling at its supernatural powers, many tribes regarded the bear as the shaman of the animal world. (Bronze, Siberia, 8th century)

Callisto beguiled by Zeus
The philandering Greek god Zeus disarms the forest nymph Callisto, who bears him a son, Arcas, before she is turned into a bear by Zeus's jealous wife Hera. (*Callisto and Jupiter* by Peter Paul Rubens, 1613)

"Someone's been sitting in my chair!"
Dressed in their Sunday best, the three "good bears" return home to discover a young trespasser, Goldilocks, sleeping in Baby Bear's comfortable bed upstairs. The 19th-century fairytale *Goldilocks and the Three Bears* was innovative in its portrayal of homely, almost suburban bears, and paved the way for future fictitious house-trained bears.

Threats and Conservation

With a growing human population demanding ever more bear habitat, and hunting an ongoing problem, the Eurasian brown bear is in serious trouble in some parts of its range. If present trends do not change, several of its populations will soon cease to exist.

Until recently, there were healthy numbers of the Eurasian brown bear throughout much of Russia. A few conservationists have even suggested that this could be an example of an animal that benefits from climate change: Warming in the Arctic will enable coniferous forests to spread northward into what was formerly a treeless zone, thus creating more areas of suitable habitat for them. However, oil and gas exploration and urban expansion are putting increasing pressure on the formerly pristine wilderness of Russia's far north, where bears used to enjoy a relatively safe existence.

Illegal practices

One of the fastest-growing threats to brown bears in Russia is poaching. This is a particular problem in Kamchatka, where poverty has led to the emergence of a well-equipped poaching industry. Bearskins are illegally supplied to the fur trade, and bear body parts, such as the gallbladder, are shipped overland to China for use in traditional oriental medicine. In 2006 the World Wide Fund for Nature (WWF) launched a project to conserve Kamchatka's bears. It aims to eliminate poaching by organizing anti-hunting patrols, setting up protected reserves, and raising awareness of the bears' plight among local people.

Exploitation

In parts of Asia and eastern Europe bear cubs are "trained" as dancing bears. Apart from being cruel, this encourages spectators to see bears as figures of fun rather than as magnificent wild animals worthy of our protection.

Plight of the hunted

Hunting has long taken a heavy toll on Europe's brown bears, which once ranged across the entire continent. The last wild bear in the British Isles was probably killed during the 10th century, though bears were later reintroduced from continental Europe for bear-baiting. Hunting bears for sport is still widespread in Sweden, Slovakia, Romania, and the Balkans, and bears also suffered extensive disturbance and persecution during the Bosnian War of 1992–5. The last French brown bear, a 15-year-old female known as Cannelle, was shot by hunters in 2004. There is no doubt that trophy hunting prevents Europe's depleted bear populations from recovering, and it makes the natural recolonization of areas formerly occupied by bears more unlikely. Oddly, though, Sweden's brown bears are increasing in number, despite pressure from hunting.

Habitat under threat

Plantations of tightly packed, fast-growing pine trees are replacing old-growth forests across Europe, reducing the amount of habitat for bears.

Fear and the future

For some people, a major cause of concern about bears is that they prey on sheep and calves. In the Pyrenees, shepherds blame bears for the death of hundreds of sheep every year, though they probably account for only 1 percent of the total livestock loss. In fact, many instances of bears "killing" sheep involve them simply scavenging sheep carcasses or stillborn lambs. Overcoming the shepherds' fear of bears is a top priority for conservationists in the Pyrenees, while compensation is paid for livestock deaths that do occur.

In the genes

The isolated nature of most European bear populations, such as in the Pyrenees or Italy's Abruzzo National Park, means that inbreeding has weakened the bears' gene pool, which in turn can lead to outbreaks of disease and reduced breeding success. In addition, small bear populations may have a shortage of either adult males or females of breeding age, making it difficult for the bears to find mates. Several reintroduction programs involving different countries are underway to correct this imbalance. For example, bears born in Slovenia have already been released in both the Pyrenees and Italy, and their progress is being monitored using radio-tracking.

Still in peril

The huge Kronotsky State Biosphere Reserve in Russia's Kamchatka peninsula is the largest protected area for Eurasian brown bears, but poaching is a threat even here.

Voluntary rescue work

For over a decade Valentin Pazhetnov has taken vulnerable bear cubs from the wild near his farm in western Russia to protect them during the winter hunting season, when unscrupulous hunters target females in their dens. He releases the cubs the following summer.

How can we help?

● Find out more about Eurasian brown bear research projects on the web and support their work.

● Learn about the fight to save bears in the Spanish Pyrenees, and how you can help, by visiting www.iberianature.com/material/spainbearnews.htm.

● Support environmental campaigns against the poaching of brown bears.

● Go on a bear-watching trip to Sweden, Finland, or Romania, where bear tourism is now firmly established (June to mid-August is the best time).

current status: **Lower risk**

SSC
Species Survival Commission

IUCN
The World Conservation Union

American Grizzly

CLASS: Mammalia   **ORDER:** Carnivora   **FAMILY:** Ursidae   **GENUS, SPECIES & SUBSPECIES:** *Ursus arctos horribilis*

For many, the great American grizzly symbolizes the raw power and awesome beauty of the wild. Its colossal bulk and mythic ferocity inspired fear and fascination wherever it roamed. For the first peoples of the plains, the grizzly was a "real bear" of whom "people should always speak carefully." For the first explorers to cross the continent, the gigantic brown bear was a "most tremendous-looking animal and extremely hard to kill," as thrillingly formidable as the African lion or Bengal tiger. Its very name—*grisly*, from the Old English *grisan* (to shudder)—means "horrendous," much like its Latin name, *horribilis*. Yet the great brown bear was first dubbed "grizzly" not for its alleged ferocity, but for its silvery, grizzled hair, and air of distinction.

> *"A grizzly will only fight if wounded or cornered, or, at least, if he thinks himself cornered."*
>
> Theodore Roosevelt, *Hunting Trips of a Ranchman* (1885)

Key Features

- The largest land carnivore after the polar and Kodiak bears.

- Despite their carnivorous canines and sharp claws, grizzly brown bears eat surprisingly little meat.

- Although stable and fairly common in Canada and Alaska, barely 1500 grizzlies survive in the Lower States.

- Huge and hulking, grizzlies usually lumber along, but can bound across a creek at lightning speed.

In Focus

Massively built, with a sturdy frame and broad "teddy" head, grizzlies are much bulkier than black bears. Their distinctive humped back—a knot of muscle over the shoulders—packs a powerful punch and helps with digging. Grizzlies amble in a ponderous way, with head hung low, as though deep in thought, but are probably just bent on nosing out the next sweet root.

Round, furry ears

Despite having small ears, a grizzly's hearing is sharp. With the aid of its acute sense of smell, it might even pick up the patter of rodents scurrying underground, as it pounces on burrowing prey with uncanny accuracy.

Bright eyes

Although small, the eyes can spot distant movement and recognize shapes over 200 ft (60 m) away. Like other bears, grizzlies see well in low light, as their eyes are reflective, mirroring the glow of the moon.

Powerful jaws

A grizzly's molars are large, with tubular crowns, ideal for crushing and grinding plants, while its long canines can slash efficiently into elk and salmon. With massively powerful jaws, a grizzly can grip and strip the bark off a tree from the ground up.

Moccasin Joe

The uncanny similarity between grizzly and human footprints inspired one of the bear's nicknames, Moccasin Joe. Like other bears, grizzlies stand upright to sniff the air and scan the horizon. When planted flat on snow or mud, their leathery soles release heat through surface blood vessels, leaving clear footprints.

Vital Statistics

Weight: Male 400–1200 lb (180–545 kg), up to 1500 lb (680 kg) along the coast; female 175–550 lb (80–250 kg), up to 750 lb (340 kg) along the coast

Length: 5–9 ft (1.5-2.7 m)

Height: 3–4.9 ft (0.90–1.5 m) at the shoulder

Color: Uniform shades of brown, from honey through auburn to deep chestnut; silver-tipped (grizzled) in the interior

Sexual maturity: 5–7 years

Gestation period: 6.5–8.5 months, including delayed implantation

Number of young: 1–4, most often 2 or 3

Birth interval: 3–4 years

Typical diet: Roots, tubers, bulbs, and forbs; sedges and grasses; berries, nuts, and pine seeds; spawning fish, ground rodents, and calves, both wild and domestic

Grizzled fur

The luxuriant fur changes texture and color with the season and region, being sparse and straggly during the spring molt, but growing dense and glossy by the fall. The hair of inland grizzlies is silver-tipped (grizzled), whereas coastal bears—often known simply as "brown bears"—have paler, less grizzled coats.

Did you know?

● One Californian grizzly of the early 1900s weighed 2350 lb (1066 kg).

● A grizzly can take a running leap up to 15 ft (4.5 m).

● Coastal brown bears in Alaska weigh twice as much as inland grizzlies.

● *Horribilis* can overtake a galloping horse, and reach speeds of 35 mph (56 kph) over short spurts.

Gardening tools

When not worn down by a summer's digging, grizzly foreclaws can grow 4 in (10 cm) long. They are ideal tools for uprooting tubers and bulbs, overturning logs, and unearthing rodent dens. Like badgers, grizzlies shift acres of land, usefully dispersing seed in the process.

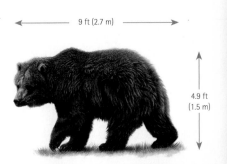

9 ft (2.7 m)

4.9 ft (1.5 m)

Habitat

A creature of grassland slopes and high mountain tundra, the grizzly needs room to roam. Once widespread across the Great Plains, its habitat has now shrunk to fragmented patches in the Lower States, but the bears still range across the windswept tundra and mountains of British Columbia, Canada, and Alaska.

Distribution

Alaska

Canada

U.S.A.

Katmai

Wyoming

Pacific Ocean

The Rockies
When the early explorers Meriwether Lewis and William Clark pushed across the Rockies in the 1800s, they found virgin forests teeming with bears and wolves. Grizzlies still roam the grassy upper slopes and thick forests of fir, spruce, and pine.

Alpine slopes, Wyoming
As a "Species of Concern," the grizzly is heavily protected in Wyoming, where it roams undisturbed through meadows and river valleys. On alpine slopes the bears feast on army cutworm moths that mass in rocky crevices. Although grizzlies also enjoy whitebark pine nuts, the trees have been under attack from mountain pine beetle.

Katmai National Park, Alaska
A remote wilderness famous for its smoking volcanoes, rushing rivers, and diverse wildlife, Katmai offers brown bears ideal and varied habitats, ranging from succulent grasslands to fertile river flats. At Brooks River, as many as 100 bears can gather to catch the sockeye salmon pushing upstream to spawn in Brooks Lake.

Before the arrival of white settlers in the 19th century, grizzlies roamed treeless prairies, with little to disturb their solitary grazing. As creatures of space, they thrive best in stretches of unbroken wilderness. Wherever land has been cleared, whether by flood, fire, storm, or avalanche, grizzlies settle down to graze and breed.

Of browns and grizzlies

Although "grizzly" generally refers to the American rather than the Eurasian brown bear, within America itself "grizzly" can mean the inland rather than coastal "brown bear." Inland grizzlies are usually smaller, with a silver-flecked coat, longer claws, a bigger hump, and more dish-shaped face than their coastal cousins. Lacking a coastal diet of fat-rich salmon, inland bears live in sparser populations with much wider home ranges, reflecting their less abundant resources.

Resting and nesting

When not actively digging for roots, or hunting salmon, the bears like to bask on rocky ledges. In extreme heat they prefer to duck into shady thickets, cool caves, or dirt daybeds scraped out beneath tree roots. To escape the harsh winter and seasonal food shortage, most northern bears den in dirt dugouts on remote hill slopes, sleeping deeply until spring. Hillside dens are easier to dig, and create better heat traps, than ground shelters.

Mudbaths and facial scrubs

As grizzlies easily overheat in their dense, shaggy coats, they relish a cool dip in lakes and creeks, where they sometimes give their faces a good scrub with mossy sods. Wet mudflats and pebbly banks also provide therapeutic scrubbing sites, where the great bears can roll around scratching itches and scraping off ticks.

On black bear patch

Although grizzlies overlap with black bears in much of their range, the two species usually tread separate paths, the grizzly climbing up the mountain slopes and the black bear melting into the forest. As both bears do, however, eat similar plants, they could end up on the same berry patch. A subtle difference

Coastal populations can be four times as dense as inland ones.

in their diets, though, prevents excessive conflict. While both bears rummage for plants above ground, only grizzlies can easily uproot bulbs and forbs with their long claws. Even where the two species do overlap, they tend to forage at varied times, black bears by day and brown bears more actively at night.

Straying on the wild side

Adolescents "going it alone" tend to explore widely before settling into a home range. Young males may wander up to 60 miles (100 km), and often stray into human settlements, where their lack of experience can lead them into conflict with people.

Classification

American grizzly

A subspecies of brown bear, *Ursus arctos horribilis* is descended from the brown bears that first colonized North America *c.*50,000 years ago. Crossing from Siberia to Alaska along the Bering land bridge, they probably traveled in two or more waves, and spread across the Great Plains.

Class	Mammalia (mammals)								
Order	Carnivora (carnivores)	Many other orders							
Sub Order	Caniformia (caniform, dog-like carnivores)	Feliformia (feliform, cat-like carnivores)							
Family	Ursidae (bears)	Ailuridae (red panda)	Canidae (coyotes, dogs, foxes, jackals, and wolves)	Mephitidae (skunks and stink badgers)	Mustelidae (badgers, otters, weasels, and relatives)	Odobenidae (walruses)	Otariidae (fur seals and sea lions)	Phocidae (seals)	Procyonidae (coatis, racoons, and relatives)
Genus	*Ursus* (black, brown, and polar bears)	*Ailuropoda* (giant panda)	*Helarctus* (sun bear)	*Melursus* (sloth bear)	*Tremarctos* (spectacled bear)				
Species	*Ursus arctos* (brown bear)	*Ursus americanus* (American black bear)	*Ursus maritimus* (polar bear)	*Ursus thibetanus* (Asiatic black bear)					
Sub-species	*Ursus arctos horribilis* (American grizzly)	*Ursus arctos arctos* (Eurasian brown bear)	*Ursus arctos middendorffi* (Kodiak bear)	And about 60 disputed subspecies					

Adaptation and Behavior

Massive and hulking, too heavy to hide in trees, the grizzly's body was built for standing its ground on the prairies. Its coat, matching the earth tones of tundra, meadow, and mountain slope, ranges from golden honey to chestnut brown.

Tools for the tundra

The great bear's hump of muscle rippling across its shoulders provides digging power, while its long rake-like claws efficiently scoop out bulbs and burrowing beavers. Digging like badgers, grizzlies can shift cartloads of soil and boulders.

Problem-solvers

Grizzlies seem bright and curious, able to adapt and think problems through. They generally ferret out hidden food, however carefully stashed, and cleverly outsmart hunters by covering their tracks.

When size matters

Although typically solitary, grizzlies mass at rich feeding sites, such as berry patches, garbage dumps, and salmon falls. Wherever bears gather, size matters. The largest tend to dominate, although even alpha males sometimes sidestep a nursing mother, who would not hesitate to tackle the largest male if her cubs were being threatened. In crowds, where personal space is invaded, tensions often mount. Stress levels are signaled by yawns, salivation, laid-back ears, growls, and huffing. Before tempers flare, the less dominant males usually back down, avoiding serious injury.

Tree signals

Like their ursine cousins, grizzlies rub and scratch trees along well-worn bear trails, leaving strong visual and scent markers. Tree signals possibly serve to mark territory and warn off would-be trespassers, while also attracting mates. Male grizzlies intent on getting the message across can tear off a 20 ft (6 m) slab of bark, often breaking their jaw in the process.

Hunting and Feeding

Although far from fussy, grizzlies show a fine sense of timing, and turn up at just the right moment to catch the fattest spawning salmon, nibble the most succulent sedge, and feast on the ripest berries. Despite their carnivorous canines and slashing claws, grizzlies eat a mainly vegetarian diet.

Quite a catch
Sodden from chasing salmon in the rushing water, an Alaskan brown bear grasps its slippery catch firmly between cutting canines. Once safely on the bank, the bear will carefully shear off the fat-rich skin, brain, and eggs.

To fuel their massive bodies, grizzlies consume many calories and roam far in search of high-energy food. As the seasons turn, the bears follow well-worn paths to varied feeding sites, from intertidal flats to avalanche shutes. Drawing on seemingly infallible memory and navigation skills, they home in on newborn calves, buried clams, sprouting bulbs, and nesting ants.

Seasonal menu
Shaking off their winter sleep, scrawny, lethargic bears shuffle out into the bright spring sunshine. After quenching their thirst at mountain streams, they rummage around for anything edible beneath the melting snowpack. Gravitating to sunny slopes and southerly meadows, the bears nudge out glacier lily bulbs, and various "bear roots,"

Types of food

Despite their ferocity and sharp canines, grizzlies eat little meat. The bulk of their diet—up to 80 percent—comprises roots, forbs, and bulbs; sprouting grasses and sedges; ripe berries and nuts. During the fall feasting frenzy, individuals can gain 3–6 lb (1.5–3 kg) a day.

Lily bulb

Bark beetles

such as sweetvetch, along with the first shoots of sedge, which are particularly nutritious, providing 24 percent of the protein needed in a bear's diet. Unexpected windfalls can surface along avalanche shutes, where elk and bison often lie crushed beneath last year's snowfall. With less choice of greens further north, Arctic bears search for overwintered berries and snow-covered carrion, both high in energy. On coastal and river plains the pickings are more plentiful. The sea might wash up stranded whales, molluscs and seaweed, while river flats, drenched with flood waters, provide fertile ground for new growth, such as juicy skunk cabbage and succulent hairgrass. Grasping skunk cabbage between their paws, the bears shear off the outer leaves to feast on the nutritious hearts. As the days lengthen, grizzlies continue to dig up bulbs and roots, but also graze on freshly sprouting plants, such as horsetail tips, high in vital protein.

Summer feasts

By July, a lush variety of new greenery surrounds all but the Arctic grizzlies. In burnt-out forest glades and open meadows, sugar-high berries ripen slowly, while fat-rich ants and termites breed in rotting logs. Where berry patches are large and laden, the great bears overcome their natural reserve and pick fruit together.

As the first salmon push up the creeks to their spawning beds in late summer, the bears mass along the shallows and rapids to catch the plump fish milling in eddies or leaping over the falls. When salmon are plentiful, the great bears delicately pick out the brain, eggs, and skin, leaving the rest for gulls, foxes, and other scavengers. After the last run of salmon in September or October, many grizzlies turn to the mountain slopes, where alpine berries ripen in the fall. Feasting gathers momentum as the fattening bears gorge on late berries and nuts, squirrels, marmots, and insects; where army cutworm moths are plentiful, a bear might devour up to 40,000 a day. At peak feasting, an individual can consume up to 80–90 lb (35–40 kg) a day.

Hunting tactics

Grizzlies are enterprising fishers. Some plunge head first into the stream and snap up a fish from the spawn. Others stand on the bank, poised to swipe at salmon leaping over the falls. In some regions, such as the foothills of Alberta, grizzlies prey on moose and caribou calves, stalking in a zigzag pattern,

Berry bonanza
Reaching for ripening berries, a grizzly uses its claws like fingers, delicately steering a succulent sprig into its mouth. During the berry season, grizzlies can eat as many as 200,000 berries a day.

with nose to the ground, until close enough to charge. At rich feeding sites, such as garbage dumps or beached whales, hungry bears gather en masse. More than 100 grizzlies might jostle for position at a plentiful salmon run, such as McNeil River in Alaska. In any gathering, or "sleuth of bears," a male-dominated hierarchy immediately snaps into place, with alpha males assuming the best positions, while females and youngsters skirt carefully around their "superiors."

Alpine bearberries

Chum salmon

Ground squirrel

Life Cycle

Grizzly mothers are devoted, licking and cuffing their rough cubs into shape with utmost patience. As females nurse and nurture their young for at least three years, only one-third will be free to breed in any one year, forcing males to compete intensively. Dominant males provide good genes, but show little interest in their offspring.

Early days

Birthing dens
Dens dug deep into remote, snowy hillsides provide ideal birth places. At about 7 ft (2 m) wide, they are cramped but cozy.

Snug cub
Nestling comfortably amid its mother's fur, a 10-day-old cub bleats for attention.

In late spring males travel far in search of mates, tracking the scent of females on heat. Once a likely partner is found, the male shadows her until she becomes amenable. At the peak of her cycle, he herds her into an isolated spot for mating. Couples spend up to a week together, when they eat, sleep, and travel as a pair, mating frequently to stimulate ovulation.

After feasting intensively in the summer and fall to pile on fat for the winter sleep, the female prepares her birthing den. Often dug out of slopes with good drainage, some dens have a long entry tunnel leading to a cozy nesting chamber.

Snug in her secluded den, the mother gives birth in midwinter to 1–4 cubs, often twins, weighing just 14 oz (400 g).

Who's for seconds?
Clambering over their mother, three cubs suckle contentedly at her six nipples. Even after they start foraging, the young bears will continue to nurse well into their third year.

Kittenish and minute, newborns are blind and toothless. Although quite helpless, they gravitate to the warmth of their mother's nipples, and suckle as she slumbers. Nourished by her rich, creamy milk, they grow rapidly, piling on fat. By spring, cubs have usually put on 15 lb (7 kg); by autumn, 60–70 lb (27–32 kg).

Emerging from the warm den on to the melting snowpack, mothers and cubs immediately retreat to secluded slopes with good visibility, safe from wolves,

eagles, and marauding males. In the first week, before she shakes off her winter sleep, the mother is lethargic, with little appetite. Her cubs, by contrast, are always hungry, and nurse every 2–3 hours.

Mother love

Grizzly mothers gained an early reputation for ferocity in protecting their young, which are less adept at escaping up trees than black bear cubs. Outside the safety of the den, the cubs are vulnerable despite their mother's round-the-clock care, and the first-year mortality rate is high—30 or 40 percent. Male brown bears pose the greatest threat—attacking newborns in an effort to force the mother to mate. Cubs also face disease, starvation, accidental falls, and drowning. The cubs that make it through the first year have a fighting chance of reaching adulthood, as mortality rates drop sharply in the second year of life before the cubs are fully weaned. By the time they are yearlings, males will have outstripped their sisters in bulk. Over the next couple of years, the little bears will romp around their mother, observing closely her every move, and learning foraging and survival skills.

Tough love

The end of lactation correlates with a shift in the mother's hormones, which prompts her to chase away the cubs she once tended so devotedly. If they linger, she might snap and bite them on the rump until they scamper off, entirely bewildered. Soon afterwards she will go into estrus and mate again.

Teammates

Weaned littermates might pair up for a season or two, foraging and even denning together. But as they grow up, they tend to go their separate ways. While females establish home ranges close to or even overlapping their mother's, males wander far in search of new stamping grounds, ensuring genetic diversity.

Grizzly company

Although often described as solitary, grizzlies do mingle. Females, inevitably, spend much of their life in close-knit family units with a succession of offspring. Littermates share the first few months of life in the intimacy of their mother's den before growing up together over the next three years. Where adult bears gather en masse—at salmon runs, berry patches, and garbage dumps—they socialize politely, communicating with subtle but clear body language. Both cubs and adults enjoy playing and sparring, testing boundaries, and learning social skills.

Roly-poly

Just like babies, growing cubs play with anything within reach—tugging at their feet, clapping their paws, and rolling in the grass. All bright, inquisitive animals play, both alone and with peers. Solitary play, whether sliding down slopes or rolling on the grass, helps hone coordination skills.

Legend and History

The grizzly loomed large in the legends and culture of America's first peoples. More awesome and spiritually empowered than the black bear, it was revered as part-human, part-divine, as guide and healer, as kin and ancestor. The first white settlers regarded the grizzly as neither human nor divine, but a marauding monster to overcome and tame.

The natural world of early tribespeople was charged with supernatural powers—the forests and rivers alive with vibrant spiritual presences that could help or hinder individuals on their path through life. Feeling much at the mercy of natural forces—storm, fire, flood, and famine—tribal people called on supernatural forces, or "power spirits," to steer them through troubled times. Everyone enjoyed the protection and potential of a personal power spirit, sometimes from birth, sometimes revealed at puberty. An eagle power spirit, for example, might impart its foresight and fearlessness.

A double-edged sword
A grizzly spirit, by contrast, being unpredictable and potentially lethal, was regarded as something of a loose canon, too hot for all but the bravest and strongest to handle. For the clan's elite— the chiefs, champion warriors, and shamans (spiritual leaders) —a grizzly power spirit was welcomed. Its potent qualities imparted strength in battle and power in council. On the battlefield, decked out in threatening bearskins and impressive bear claw crowns or necklaces, braves roared with battle rage, invoking the bear's fearless ferocity and brute strength.

Physician of the woods
A gentler, more maternal, nurturing aspect of grizzly power lay in its healing capacity. Many tribes, such as the Sioux, regarded

Grizzly hunting
A posse of Sioux braves with primitive weapons tackles a raging grizzly. Facing an animal four times the weight of a man was a feat of courage, even on horseback. Few encounters ended without the death of at least one brave. (*Native Americans Killing a Bear* by George Catlin, c.1850)

the bear as a foremost doctor, versed in herbal lore, and endowed with the power to cure sickness. Faith in the bear's healing capacity arose from watching how it sealed its wounds with mud, or rubbed cleansing "bear root" on its fur, and picked plants at their most nutritious.

Bear shamans
Regarded as the shamans of the animal world, grizzlies shared much in common with tribal shamans. Both were fierce and gentle, with power to destroy and heal. Both could "shape shift," traveling through time, and between the visible and invisible realms. Both trod a solitary path in pursuit of wisdom. During healing rites, shamans dressed and danced like grizzlies, rattling claws to summon the curative force of the bear spirit.

Bear mother clans
Like medieval kings, some chiefs traced their ancestry back to a mythic beast at the dawn of time. In common with many plains Indians, the Modoc of California claimed descent from the first

bear mother to amble through the ancient forests of primeval earth. The Modoc tell of a time when an earth bear and sky spirit fell in love, and produced beautiful bear children—the first Modoc. The people of a grizzly clan, such as the Modoc, enjoyed the special protection of the great bear spirit, and invoked its formidable powers when in trouble.

Conjuring the grizzly

Hunting such a potent animal spirit with nothing more than a spear was no mean feat, and unthinkable without the animal's blessing. Before, during, and after the hunt, elaborate rites and taboos served to summon, placate, honor, and finally to thank the bear for its sacrifice. The first step involved divining the bear in its den through rites and dreams. Although hunting taboos varied from tribe to tribe, most involved the use of archaic (noble) weapons, such as spears and axes, respectful treatment of the carcass, and elaborate celebrations to honor the slain beast. At the feast, specific parts were reserved for various members of the tribe. The heart, for instance, might be eaten by a young boy to absorb the bear's legendary courage.

Frontier myth of the killer grizzly

When the first explorers crossed the continent in the 1800s, they saw "hundreds" of grizzlies grazing on the Great Plains. In their wake, wagonloads of settlers encountered grizzlies, but did not stop to marvel. Fearing for their lives and livestock, ranchers hired hunters to trap, lasso, and shoot roving bears on sight. With the advent of the repeating rifle in the 1870s, grizzlies fell by their thousands, until by 1900 they had been wiped off the prairies, less than 100 years after the first settlers had arrived.

In California, the "Golden Bear State"—once home to the highest density of grizzlies—popular prize fights between bears and bulls led to the extinction of the golden bear in the early 1920s.

Grizzly Adams

The colorful mountain man John Capen Adams wandered the American west capturing, training, and exhibiting bears. Two cubs that he fostered—Lady Washington and Benjamin Franklin—became his constant traveling companions and servants, keeping him warm at night and bearing his trophies home. A master showman, Adams advertised his Mountain Museum by wandering down the street with tamed bears in tow. Although romanticized as a hero, Adams beat his cubs into submission. Neither a naturalist nor a conservationist, he probably precipitated the extinction of the grizzly in California.

Wilderness icon

As the mighty grizzly loped off the plains, many Americans expressed concern, voiced in cult novels, such as James Oliver Curwood's *The Grizzly King* (1918), in which the bear's sanctuary is violated. Similarly, Ernest Thompson Seton's *King of the Grizzlies* (1899) cast the bear as a tragic giant "…seeking only to be left alone," while in William Faulkner's stark *The Bear* (1935), the grizzly's death foretells the end of wilderness.

Grizzly cults

Grizzly clan crest
Two totem poles guard a family house in British Columbia. The eagle at the top represents the paternal clan. Beneath the eagle, the bear—shown devouring a rival chief—stands for the maternal clan. Bear clans traced their ancestry back to the first mythic bear at the dawn of time. (*Carved Posts at Alert Bay*, Edward S. Curtis, c.1900)

Mark of honor
Only the bravest and strongest earned the right to wear a bear claw crown or necklace (shown here). Imbued with spiritual potency, bear claws imparted courage in battle, power in tribal council, and spiritual insight in shamanic healing or divining rituals.

Grizzly Adams
Battle-scarred from many contests with grizzlies, John Capen "Grizzly" Adams captured and trained both grizzly and black bear cubs. One of his favorites, Benjamin Franklin (shown here), followed Adams with devotion, defending him from a wild grizzly five times his size.

Threats and Conservation

Grizzlies once roamed the western United States from Mexico to the Arctic. Even as recently as 1850, up to 100,000 bears dwelt in the 48 Lower States, but their range shrank, and their numbers fell as settlers rolled in by the wagonload. Now barely 1500 grizzlies survive in the Lower States of the U.S.A.

In both Alaska and Canada, where vast tracts of protected land have been preserved in parks and forests, grizzlies are more widespread. Canada is home to about 25,000, and Alaska to about 33,000. Even in Canada and Alaska, however, the great bear faces threats, sometimes from conflict with humans, but more often from mining or logging programs. In the extreme north, for instance, oil and gas development threaten to fragment bear country.

Bear jams

National parks, in turn, bring their own problems by closing the distance between people and grizzlies. All bears, but especially the solitary brown bear, prefer to avoid contact with people. During the summer tourist season when crowds fill the parks, bear-related injuries increase, mainly at campsite picnics and along backcountry hiking trails. In most negative encounters, bears generally lose out, usually being dispatched elsewhere. Transplanting nuisance bears does not always solve the problem,

Teddy bears' picnic
Tantalizingly smelly garbage tempts a mother and her cubs to rip through the flimsy plastic liner. Once bears become used to easy handouts, they quickly come back for more, pushing into backyards and communal garbage dumps.

as they invariably return to the site of trouble, or wander aimlessly in unknown terrain, unable to fend for themselves. Hungry, disoriented, and tetchy, translocated bears eventually stray into someone's backyard, only to find themselves transplanted again, or shot.

As bears cannot resist easily accessible garbage, an effective solution would be to replace all campsite dumps with incinerators and bearproof trashcans. A more interventionist, and controversial tactic would be to lure bears away from campsites by providing them with easy meals (such as elk carcasses) at alternative feeding sites in remote back country.

Conflict control

Deterrents, such as rubber bullets or red pepper spray, can also help steer bears away from campsite picnics, where most trouble arises. A more long-term solution—successfully tested in British Columbia and Alaska—would be to shift hiking trails and campsites to less secluded spots, minimizing the chance of negative bear encounters.

Grizzly under pressure
Even in Alaska's expansive Denali National Park, bears share their range with tourists, and risk their lives on the highway.

Bear zones, bear rules

Created exclusively for bear rather than human occupation, bear zones offer the best refuge from human encroachment. In national parks bear zones have sometimes expanded into full-blown sanctuaries. One of the most famous is the McNeil River State Game Sanctuary in Alaska, where controlled numbers of supervised tourists can watch "bears being bears," but only under strict rules that prevent the bears ever associating people with food. McNeil River bears have grown habituated to people, but regard them apparently without alarm, possibly, as the warden suggests, as "innocuous features of the landscape." Hugely popular, bear-viewing programs help expand people's minds and dispel fears.

Looking to the future

Where grizzly habitat has already been fragmented, as in the Rockies, activists are campaigning to prevent further fracturing. Elsewhere, one of the best long-term hopes lies in expanding

protected preserves, especially where tourism provides an added incentive. British Columbia, for instance, led the way at the turn of the millennium by more than doubling its protected preserves, including White Grizzly-Goat Range Wilderness, Granby and Tatshenshini, and Khutzeymateen.

Karelian bear dogs
A Russian breed not unlike collies, Karelian dogs are trained to shepherd bears away from human settlements, minimizing conflict.

How can we help?

● Support organizations that purchase or protect critical habitat, such as the Vital Ground Foundation: www.vitalground.org.

● Find out how conservation organizations are promoting wilderness at World Wildlife Fund Canada: www.wwf.ca.

● Join campaigns to protect the grizzly: www.greatbear.org.

● Explore ecotourism at Trail of the Great Bear: www.trailofthegreatbear.com.

● Try bear-watching online at www.nps.gov/glac.

Photographers' delight
At the McNeil River State Game Sanctuary, thanks to restricted numbers of viewers, structured viewing, and strict rules of conduct, bears have become habituated to close human presence. Viewers are limited to 10 at a time, and always accompanied by expert wildlife guides.

current status: **Threatened in the 48 Lower States**

SSC
Species Survival Commission

IUCN
The World Conservation Union

Kodiak Bear

CLASS: Mammalia   **ORDER:** Carnivora   **FAMILY:** Ursidae   **GENUS, SPECIES & SUBSPECIES:** *Ursus arctos middendorffi*

On the Kodiak archipelago in the Gulf of Alaska a giant race of brown bears has roamed free for over 12,000 years. Living in splendid isolation, genetically cut off from Alaskan brown bears on the mainland, Kodiak bears followed their own evolutionary path, feasting on fat-rich salmon and luscious greenery, and growing to mythic proportions—almost twice the height of the average man. Like the fabulous creatures in a medieval bestiary, Kodiak's honey-colored bears reign supreme on their lush island paradise. Although threatened briefly last century by commercial hunters and defensive ranchers, Kodiak bears now lead a charmed life within the safety of the Kodiak National Wildlife Refuge, which encompasses two-thirds of the "Great Bear Island."

> *"Kodiak...the name conjures up images of mystery, grandeur, and power. At the heart of that mystique is the mighty Kodiak bear."*
>
> Larry van Daele, *The History of Bears on the Kodiak Archipelago* (2003)

Key Features

- Twice the weight of its inland cousin, the American grizzly, the Kodiak bear ranks among the world's largest, second only to the polar bear.

- Although massive and muscular, *Ursus arctos middendorffi* moves with surprising speed and grace.

- Kodiak bears live in the most dense brown bear populations, with 0.7 bears per square mile (2.6 square km).

In Focus

Kodiak bears are colossal, towering almost twice the height of a black bear, and weighing as much as a compact car. With immensely long, trowel-like claws and powerful shoulder muscles, they can dig up tracts of land the size of soccer fields in search of roots or burrowing rodents.

Brown eyes

Set wide on the head and facing forward, Kodiak eyes are usually a shade of brown. Although seemingly small on its massive head, the bear's eyes allow it to spot distant movement and distinguish color and activity at all levels of light, even at night.

Long muzzle

Although faintly dog-like in appearance, the bear's nose—like that of its ursine cousins—is four or five times more sensitive than a dog's. Whether pressed close to the tundra or raised high to the wind, its nose can detect the faintest whiff of friend or foe.

Crunching bite

Kodiak bears are more carnivorous than black bears, but do not bite to kill like polar bears. Instead, when catching fish or rodents, they grip their prey between pointed canines and crunch down with powerful jaw muscles. For crushing and grinding plants, the broad, flat cheek teeth and mobile jawbone hinge are ideal.

Golden guard hair

The dense, double-layered coat provides all the warmth needed during cold Alaskan winters: An outer layer of long, glossy "guard" hair protects the thick, fluffy underpelt. Often a soft honey gold, Kodiak guard hair can turn coppery in the afternoon sunlight, and range from cinnamon to rich auburn, depending on the season.

Sturdy "shoes"

The bear's immense hind paws, about the size of dinner plates, help spread its colossal weight. The footpads, which are covered with tough, rough, durable skin, serve as sturdy, self-renewing shoes.

Fine tools

Kodiak bears wield their rake-like claws with amazing dexterity—swiftly skinning a slippery salmon, deftly unscrewing a honey jar, or carefully snipping off pine nuts. The foreclaws can grow up to 5 in (13 cm) long; usually black, they whiten with age.

Vital Statistics

Weight: Male 750–1500 lb (340–680 kg); female 350–750 lb (160–340 kg)

Length: 6.5–9 ft (2–2.7 m)

Height: 3–5 ft (0.90–1.5 m) at the shoulder

Color: Honey brown, ranging from tan to creamy gold.

Sexual maturity: 5–7 years

Gestation period: 6 months, including delayed implantation

Number of young: 1–3, most often 2

Birth interval: 4 years

Typical diet: Salmon, rodents, and elk or deer young; sedges and grasses; forbs, roots, and bulbs; wild berries and nuts; carrion

Lifespan: 20 years, but can reach 30

Did you know?

● One captive overfed male weighed 2400 lb (1090 kg), with a fat layer of 9 in (23 cm).

● The longest-living Kodiak bear reached the age of 35.

● The gigantic Kodiak bear is 10 times heavier than the world's smallest bear, the sun bear.

● Apart from polar bears, Kodiak and coastal brown bears suffer most from the roundworm *trichonelle*, caught from infected salmon.

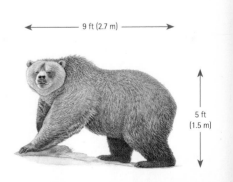

9 ft (2.7 m)

5 ft (1.5 m)

Habitat

Whether bathing in cool mountain streams, rolling in tidal mudbaths, or bedding down in alpine dugouts, Kodiak bears enjoy every comfort in their archipelago home. Resources are so abundant, particularly on Kodiak Island, that the bears do not need to roam as widely as brown bears in poorer habitats.

Distribution

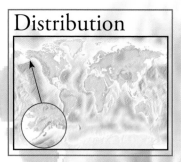

Alaska

Kodiak archipelago

Shuyak Island
Although Shuyak is relatively flat, with thick spruce forests blanketing much of the island, its rugged coastline offers a maze of deep bays and inlets, where bears can forage for buried clams, fresh sedge, and spawning salmon. At higher levels, remote hilly slopes and alder thickets provide natural cover for daybeds and dens.

Gulf of Alaska

Kodiak—Alaska's "emerald isle"
The largest island in the archipelago, Kodiak is the second biggest in the U.S.A., after Big Island in Hawaii. During the summer the emerald isle is carpeted in greenery, from coastal sedge and fireweed meadows to spruce woodlands and alpine tundra, providing ideal resources for the bears.

Pacific Ocean

Afognak Island
Afognak is an island of contrasts, ranging from steep cliffs to broad tidal flats. In the spring the bears forage on grassy slopes and muskegs (bogs), moving down to tidal flats and creeks for the summer salmon runs. Shrubs and Sitka spruce provide ample shelter, while rugged alpine slopes offer cover for anxious mothers.

Ranging from lush coastal flats to high alpine tundra, the Kodiak archipelago offers prime habitat for brown bears, with acres of undisturbed wilderness in which to roam. Thick spruce forest, remote mountain slopes, salmon-rich streams, and fertile grasslands provide the bears with the four vital ingredients of ideal habitat—ample shelter and space, flowing water, and plentiful food. With such abundant resources, Kodiak bears thrive in some of the densest brown bear populations in the world. Although densities vary seasonally, the highest occur on Kodiak Island around Karluk Lake and Kiliuda Bay, where bears number between 210 and 400 per 385 square miles (1000 square km).

Chilling out

Over 300 streams flow through the archipelago, providing the local wildlife with plentiful sources for drinking and, almost as importantly, for cooling down. The Kodiak bear's natural bulk, thick layer of fat, and dense fur coat keep it warm through wind and storm, but can lead to overheating in summer months or after strenuous exercise, such as chasing salmon. As bears lack sweat glands, cooling down is not as easy as with some mammals. To chill out, Kodiak bears roll on alpine snowbanks or river mudflats, or bathe in shallow streams.

Crashing out

The diverse habitat on the archipelago provides varied cover for daybeds and dens. Kodiak bears typically create several daybeds along familiar trails, providing instant shelter for rest and refuge by day or night. Whether stressed, sleepy, soaked, or hot, the bears can easily duck into a cozy daybed. Alder thickets, which make ideal shelters, abound at shore and subalpine levels on Kodiak Island and southwest Afognak Island. Elsewhere, on Shuyak Island, much of Afognak and northeast Kodiak, hilltop dugouts, or spruce forest with undergrowth of devil's club, afford alternative cover. Inside a dirt dugout or brush shelter, matted underbush or chewed-up roots provide soft,

Although a bear can cross the island in a week, few bother, as resources close by are so abundant.

dry bedding. In common with their mainland relatives, many Kodiak bears den during the cold season when temperatures drop below freezing and food is scarce. For winter denning, the hills and hummocks provide steep slopes with good drainage. If the ground is too friable to dig out a secure den, the bears create shelters beneath the stable roots of alder or spruce.

Kodiak neighbors

Kodiak bears share their lush home with over 250 diverse species of fish, birds, and mammals, as well as 600 breeding pairs of bald eagles. Offering possibly the best brown bear habitat in the world, the archipelago sustains one of the densest populations of brown bears, which grow to record proportions.

Classification

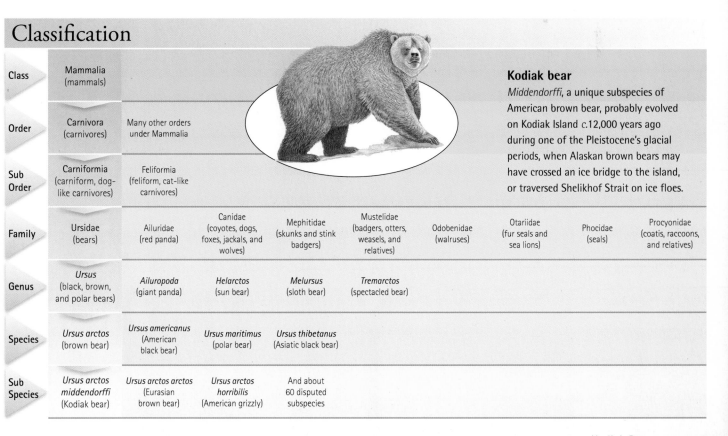

Class	Mammalia (mammals)								
Order	Carnivora (carnivores)	Many other orders under Mammalia							
Sub Order	Carniformia (carniform, dog-like carnivores)	Feliformia (feliform, cat-like carnivores)							
Family	Ursidae (bears)	Ailuridae (red panda)	Canidae (coyotes, dogs, foxes, jackals, and wolves)	Mephitidae (skunks and stink badgers)	Mustelidae (badgers, otters, weasels, and relatives)	Odobenidae (walruses)	Otariidae (fur seals and sea lions)	Phocidae (seals)	Procyonidae (coatis, raccoons, and relatives)
Genus	Ursus (black, brown, and polar bears)	Ailuropoda (giant panda)	Helarctos (sun bear)	Melursus (sloth bear)	Tremarctos (spectacled bear)				
Species	Ursus arctos (brown bear)	Ursus americanus (American black bear)	Ursus maritimus (polar bear)	Ursus thibetanus (Asiatic black bear)					
Sub Species	Ursus arctos middendorffi (Kodiak bear)	Ursus arctos arctos (Eurasian brown bear)	Ursus arctos horribilis (American grizzly)	And about 60 disputed subspecies					

Kodiak bear
Middendorffi, a unique subspecies of American brown bear, probably evolved on Kodiak Island c.12,000 years ago during one of the Pleistocene's glacial periods, when Alaskan brown bears may have crossed an ice bridge to the island, or traversed Shelikhof Strait on ice floes.

Adaptation and Behavior

Although natural loners, Kodiak bears rub along together at mass feeding sites, such as berry patches, salmon runs, and shores with beached whales. To minimize conflict the big bears express their feelings and assert their dominance through clear vocal calls and subtle body postures. If a bear feels another is overstepping the mark, it might flash its teeth in a threat display. By making its status and intention clear, direct confrontation can be avoided. Although Kodiak bears do not defend their territory, each has its own home range. Male ranges are usually four times the size of female ones, not only because a male's larger body demands more foraging ground, but because males aim to overlap the ranges of several breeding females.

Encounters with humans
Normally shy and peaceable, Kodiak bears only turn on people if afraid or provoked—perhaps startled at close quarters, or disturbed at a feast. While structured viewing programs seem to have little adverse impact on bears, unregulated viewing near vital feeding grounds does seem to invade their space.

Reading the signals
People can read a Kodiak bear's mood from its body language. If relaxed, it will carry on unperturbed, whether feeding, resting, or nursing. If nervous or inquisitive, it will move off its trail, pace around, rise on its hindlegs to get a better view, and perhaps break into a run. If agitated, the bear will start woofing, walk stiff-legged, salivate, and moan or growl. Seriously angry bears pop their jaws, bounce on their front legs, and slap brush before charging. The rush might or might not be a bluff.

Fast learners
Kodiak bears are quick to pick up on a new source of food, be it picnic garbage or hunters' game. During a deer-hunting surge in 1987, the bears reacted to hunters' gunshots as though they were "dinner bells," and turned up for a free serving of deer.

Hunting and Feeding

Despite an abundant source of spring fawns, summer-spawning salmon, and burrowing rodents, Kodiak bears remain essentially omnivores, typically spending more time munching juicy kelp and sedge, succulent roots, forbs, and sweet berries than any other food.

Missed!
A slippery salmon dodges two surprised bears hovering hopefully by the falls. At the peak of the salmon runs big males balance precariously by the riffles to swipe leaping fish with their paws.

Kodiak bears display an uncanny ability to show up at the right place and time for the best bear fare, be it coastal sedge in the spring, river salmon in the summer, or alpine berries in the fall. For the vital animal protein in their diet, they chase not only spawning salmon, but also burrowing rodents, such as ground squirrels, and Roosevelt elk calves or Sitka black-tailed fawns. Whenever possible, however, they opt for easy prey, such as washed-up walrus or whale, which provides copious fat and protein.

Kodiak connoisseurs
At all times through the seasons, Kodiak bears select the most nutritious parts of the animal or plant to maximize their weight gain. Grass and forbs are eaten only at their most

Types of food

Sprouting sedges, grasses, and seaweed are favorites in spring, followed in the summer by sweet berries, devil's club, and alpine grasses, then chinook, chum, sockeye, and pink salmon. In the fall, bears gorge on late berries, roots, nuts, rodents, and late spawning coho salmon.

Kelp

Chinook salmon

digestible and protein-rich—when growing rapidly in spring and early summer. Berries are picked at their ripest, in the summer and fall, when the sugar content is highest. When salmon is plentiful, just the fatty skin, brains, and eggs are eaten. Only juveniles, or ravenous mothers emerging from their winter fast, devour the whole fish. When feeding on deer, elk, and cattle, the internal organs are picked out first before the less nutritious flesh.

Sedge and kelp salad

In spring the bears graze on grasses and forbs sprouting on sunny slopes and in open meadows. Springtime plants are supplemented by newborn fawns or frozen carrion left over from the winter. Some bears amble down to the beach to munch kelp and slurp up nutritious beach lice (organisms that thrive in kelp beds). As spring turns to summer, many bears forage along river estuaries, nosing out sedge ripening in the fertile flats. By mid-June, when salmon enter the streams, most bears migrate to the falls. Some remain on alpine slopes, chewing sedge and picking ripening berries. The choice of berries is endless, including huckleberries, red-berried elder, blueberries, and devil's club, a particular favorite.

Salmon menu

When it comes to salmon, Kodiak bears are spoilt for choice from a selection of five varieties during the summer spawning season. After chinook, the largest and first of the season, the bears turn to chum, sockeye, and pink salmon, followed by late spawning coho in the fall. In the high season, around August, Kodiak bears can easily consume over 80 lb (36 kg) a day. As more berry crops ripen in mid-August, many bears shift to a diet of elderberries and salmonberries. Others mix fish and berries. In the fall all Kodiak bears

turn to a mixed diet of late berries, salmon, roots, and burrowing voles. As the days darken, the feasting frenzy gathers momentum, and the bears gorge by day and night to lay up enough fatty reserves for the long winter sleep.

Fishing and foraging tactics

Much like grizzlies, Kodiak bears use their claws to dig up roots, their lips to pick fruit, and their ingenuity to catch spawning salmon. As their size slows them down when hunting land mammals, such as elk, the bears prey on the young and sick. After successful foraging at dawn and dusk, they rest at midday and night.

Slick fisher

A laid-back bear reaches lazily into the river shallows. With an abundant source of salmon on Kodiak Island, catching supper requires minimal effort.

Bog cranberrry

Snowshoe hare

Kodiak grasses

Life Cycle

Gathering at ripening berry patches, prospective mates size up the local talent before the breeding season peaks in the summer. As only one in three females is free of cubs each year, alpha males sometimes battle fiercely for mating rights, the winner driving off rivals before herding his chosen one into a secluded glade.

Winter birth

Dirt dugout
Dens are scooped out of dry, stable soil, usually on a remote slope with good drainage. Snow provides an extra layer of insulation.

Sleepyhead
A den cub snuggles into its mother's plush fur. Even at four weeks old, the baby's claws are long enough to comb through its mother's dense pelt to reach her nipples.

Courtship starts not long after the bears leave their dens in late spring or summer. Stimulated by female estrus, males grow restless, agitated, and persistent, sometimes chasing and panting after a desirable mate all day long. Rising levels of male arousal spark off contests between rivals, ranging from brief dominance displays to protracted fights and injury. Once the victor has dispatched all rivals, the couple stays together for a few days or weeks, mating frequently to stimulate ovulation. As soon as the egg is fertilized and divides a few times, it enters a state of suspended animation until the fall, when it finally implants on the female's uterine wall and begins to grow again.

Winter denning
On Kodiak Island, where the winter can sometimes be mild, with little snow

Bathtime
Feisty twins take turns pushing each other around in the mud, while their mother searches patiently for clams in the intertidal flats. Young and old, bears love rolling around in cool, pebbly mud, rubbing away old ticks and itches.

and abundant food, adult males might not bother to den. Regardless of how mild it may be, pregnant females tend to den by early November, preparing the ground in late October. Birthing dens are dug in well-drained areas, often on high, secluded slopes. Females frequently return to the same denning site. After a gestation period of around six months, mothers give birth sometime in February to two or three small, sparsely furred, and highly dependent cubs. Weighing less than 1 lb (450 g), about as big as a large hamster, they are blind, deaf, and toothless. While their mother sleeps,

Rough and tumble
Sparring playfully, first-year cubs learn new tricks and tactics that will come in handy later in life when forced to fight real battles with rivals. Mouthing gently, they chew at each other's jaws, but rarely draw blood.

Orphaned cubs console each other with frequent hugs, and are sometimes adopted by another nursing bear.

the cubs suckle, purring contentedly, and develop rapidly on her high-fat milk. Within a few weeks, they grow more active, playing with littermates, exploring the cramped den, and clambering all over their mother while she slumbers.

A cub's life
Out in the warm spring sunshine, mothers wisely lead their cubs farther up secluded slopes to hide from marauding males, who typically prey on young bears in an effort to force their mother to breed again. Scooping the fluffy cubs up by the scruff of their necks, their mother sets them gently on the melting snow, while she hungrily snatches at sprouting grass. The cubs learn much from watching their mother, but also from trial and error. Despite her vigilance, over 25 percent die in the first year, whether from cold, accidents, predatory wolves and bald eagles, or marauding males. If cubs are orphaned, they stick close together for longer than usual, and remain wary of trying anything new, or venturing far from their birthplace.

As spring turns to summer and the little bears grow strong, they follow their mother down the mountain to graze on roots and fast-growing grasses and forbs. To suckle, they clamber on to her stomach and chest as she lies back in the grass. The cubs will stick close to their mother for another two or three

years, nursing, foraging, and denning. By the time third-year cubs emerge from the winter den, they will look almost as big as their mother. Once lactation ends, usually in the third year, a shift in the mother's hormones changes her mood. No longer tolerant of her offspring's playful antics, she snaps, cuffs, and bites their rumps until they run away, utterly confused. Out on their own, adolescents have the toughest time, struggling to find enough to eat, often lacking any real grasp of danger. Only 50 percent of cubs survive to adulthood. The ones that make it can start their own families at about five or seven, but most do not breed until they are more mature—around seven or nine.

Etiquette in Kodiak society
Kodiak bears, especially dominant males, are natural loners, preferring to rove free, but they gather at salmon runs and beached whales, when young cubs learn fast how to behave in society. Large males pick the best spots for fishing and expect the rest of the clan to fall in line. If any cub puts a foot wrong, a swift cuff from his mother will soon put him straight. If tension mounts between rival males, strict codes of conduct and subtle dominance displays prevent open conflict and serious injuries.

Spruce and scrubbed
A yearling grooms its paws, combing through dirt and debris with its long claws. As Kodiak bears dig up mounds of soil to get to succulent roots and burrowing rodents, their claws can get clogged with sticky mud and stones.

Legend and History

The original Alutiiq people of Kodiak regarded *taquka'aq* the bear with a mixture of fascination and fear. Like their cousins the Arctic Inuit and Alaskan Yup'ik, they credited bears with extraordinary powers. It is no wonder, as *taquka'aq* mysteriously disappeared underground each winter, only to emerge miraculously each spring. He knew where and when the flowers would open, and where the salmon would run.

Even before the Alutiiq settled on the island around 1200, the first peoples of Kodiak left rock carvings and fetishes immortalizing the bear over 2500 years ago. For the Alutiiq, bears were always "very different from other animals because bears were once people." Like tribal shamans, bears could change shape and travel to other times and dimensions, where they could read thoughts, forecast the weather, and foretell the future. Even today, the elders remember a time when "people talked to bears because bears understand."

Kodiak bear ceremonies

If bears were all-powerful, all-knowing, part-human souls, how could they ever be hunted without inciting the bear spirit's anger, or causing the hunter remorse? Only by elaborate rituals of appeasement and thanksgiving before and after the hunt. During masked dances and ceremonies, the bear was conjured, honored, placated, and celebrated. Mask-making, an ancient Alutiiq craft, played a vital role in ritual. Carved in wood and bark, whistling masks served to summon animal and ancestral

Alutiiq homestead

An Alutiiq family gathers around a traditional skin tent. Inside, people snuggled around a slate hearth fire and sandstone oil lamp. The skin covering, often from a bear, was usually tanned red. Sod houses replaced skin tents early on, but hunting and fishing families continued to camp in makeshift shelters. Lone travelers improvised too by bedding down on spruce branches, covered with the massive hide of a Kodiak bear.

spirits. After the ceremony, the masks were broken to release the conjured soul. For boys on the verge of manhood, hunting the giant Kodiak bear was a rite of passage and feat of bravery. On the eve of his first hunt, a boy cleansed himself in a sweat bath while an elder chanted. After killing his first Kodiak bear with spear and arrow, the youth put his hand down its throat to dispel his fear, and absorb the bear's courage and strength. The hunt culminated with a ceremonial feast, when the slain beast was honored with songs and gifts. In a ritual still practiced by some Alaskans today, the bear's bones were returned to the hunting ground as a sign of respect, and to release its soul.

Bear harvest

Although the Alutiiq relied on the sea for daily sustenance, they harvested several bears a year for the fat-rich meat and warm fur. Every part of the animal had a use. Hides were turned into bedding, clothing, and shelter, while sinews were wrought into binding thread. The intestines, once dried and stretched, made the best waterproof *parkas*. Bacculae (penis bones) and long limb bones were fashioned into tools. Teeth and claws served as adornments and amulets, infused with the bear's "power spirit," which acted much like a guardian spirit, imparting its particular gifts—of courage, strength, and hunting skill.

Russian trappers

Alutiiq supremacy ended after the island was discovered by the Russians during the Bering expedition of 1741. Kodiak was soon flooded with waves of *promishleniki* (independent trappers) and fur traders after rich pickings. By 1784, the Russian entrepreneur Grigory Shelikhof had founded a thriving settlement at Three Saints Bay. As farms and homesteads spread into bear country, however, clashes became inevitable. To curb the conflict, Russian dogs were trained to steer bears away from cattle, a habit still practiced in modern Russia, where Karelian dogs herd "nuisance" bears away from towns and livestock.

The first wave of Russian trappers were much more interested in sea otter pelts than bearskins, which were generally regarded as "minor furs." It was not until otters declined in the early 19th century that the number of Kodiak bear hides peaked at around 268 a year between 1821 and 1842.

American fair chase

After the U.S.A. bought Alaska in 1867, the bear harvest increased, although the Americans, like the Russians, showed little interest in bear meat. Soldiers posted at the American fort observed: "Brown bears of great size are sometimes killed. The natives eat these when they can get them, but the flesh is rank and disagreeable, as the animal, like the native, lives mostly on fish and shellfish." Pelt harvest, however, escalated, reaching an average of 548 a year by 1880. The American settlers also tried salmon fishing, moving into bear terrain. When commercial fishing expanded and canneries proliferated in the 1880s, any bears caught fishing were routinely shot as pests. Matters worsened in the 1890s when the annual salmon harvest peaked at 3.4 million, depriving bears of a staple source of protein.

When, at the end of the century, trophy hunters came after the "largest bear in the world," they found too few left to hunt with honor. Appalled by the loss of Kodiak bears, the sporting Boone & Crockett Club, led by Theodore "Teddy" Roosevelt, lobbied for wildlife regulations, and in 1900 helped push through the Lacey Act, which laid the groundwork for future legal protection of American wildlife. After commercial hunting was abolished in 1925, the bear population recovered dramatically, prompting ranchers to complain that "pest bears" had increased fivefold. Eventually, with the help of President Franklin Roosevelt, the Kodiak National Wildlife Refuge was created for bears and other wildlife in 1941.

Kodiak sagas

Russian boom time
Ships laden with precious fur glide out of Kodiak's busy harbor at the peak of the Russian fur trade in the 18th century. The Russians settled on Kodiak in 1784, piercing the skyline with their Russian Orthodox domes, and leaving a legacy of words and customs.

Bart appeal
The giant Kodiak bear Bart starred in many films, including *The Bear* (1989), based on James Curwood's novel *The Grizzly King* (1916). Bart also acted as "spokesbear" for the Vital Ground Foundation, which has saved wildlife habitat in the Rockies and on Kodiak Island. Bart was trained from birth by Doug Seus, seen here.

Kodiak kayak
Alutiiq model fishermen paddle a three-hole kayak covered in hide, probably sewn with bear sinew. Model boats served to teach boys the basics of fishing. The model paddlers wear waterproof *parkas*, often made from dried bear intestines. Their distinctive wooden hats were created from spruce root. The first Alutiiq settlers probably traveled from Alaska to Kodiak Island in similar boats.

Threats and Conservation

Although Kodiak bears seem healthy and stable, potential risks lie in their genetic isolation and low reproductive rate, which could, theoretically, undermine their long-term survival. More worrying is the steady increase in human activity and pressures on bear habitat.

Living in a closed population, with little genetic diversity, Kodiak bears are potentially at risk from the side effects of genetic isolation. Isolated populations have small gene pools with low genetic diversity, which can undermine the biological fitness, fertility, and ultimate survival of a species. But isolation does not seem to have harmed the population on the Kodiak archipelago, which remains stable and thriving. To date, the count of bears, at around 3000, remains as high as it has ever been. Even though the archipelago is isolated and relatively small, it offers a wide variety of prime habitats and resources.

Little cause for concern

Over the past 100 years, increased ranching, logging, power development, and tourism have altered pristine countryside, but the bears do not seem to have been badly affected. Roads have been restricted to the northeast coast and the immediate vicinity of villages, rather than invading the backcountry. Although the Terror Lake hydroelectric project could disrupt inland bears, so far, due to careful planning, it has shown little negative impact. Similarly, on Afognak Island, where commercial logging has, over the past 25 years, altered bear habitat, no major adverse effects have been reported. Grasses and berries still grow in abundance, and the salmon runs remain healthy.

"Grab and go"
All bears are drawn to "fast food" garbage. But if they become dependent, they push fearlessly into human territory, raiding backyards and kitchens. When things get out of hand, nuisance bears are shifted or shot.

Regulated hunting
Overhunting became a serious problem early last century, when the bear population was threatened by commercial and trophy hunters. Although the abolition of commercial harvesting in 1925 prevented further loss, sports hunters remain drawn to the island, spending huge sums—$4.5 million in 2004 —to hunt on Kodiak. To regulate sports hunting, a restricted annual hunt is closely monitored by the Alaska Department of Fish and Game and the U.S. Fish and Wildlife Service.

Future strategies
As interest in the famous bears increases, seasonal pressures will undoubtedly mount. Luckily, two-thirds of Kodiak Island is protected by the Kodiak National Wildlife Refuge. The islanders too are determined to protect the bears and their pristine habitat. Together, the Refuge, islanders, and the Alaska Department of Fish and Game hope to design the "best brown bear conservation and management strategy in the world."

Oily clean-up
A villager sponges up sludge-like oil "mousse" washed ashore from a spillage off Alaska. Oil has contaminated the wildlife of the archipelago since the 1800s when oil first became a popular fuel for powering boats.

Living in bear country

The fame of Kodiak's "gentle giants" has spread beyond Alaska, increasing popular demand for watching and hunting the bears. Although some interest seems incidental to other pursuits, such as hiking and fishing, many tourists come just for the bears. Bear-viewing helps expand people's knowledge and appreciation of wildlife. The starring bears, in their turn, show increased tolerance of human presence, without any apparent harm to either species. The key is bear "habituation" (getting used to people), without any association with food. To promote positive bear-watching, Kodiak's experts guide hunters and tourists.

Bear conflicts escalated unexpectedly in the summer of 1999, when local people and deer-hunters reported recurrent rogue bear behavior. Eight nuisance bears foraging near towns had to be put down. The reason for the raids lay in a berry shortage caused by severe winter frost. Missing their berry fare, the bears rampaged through crop fields, attacked livestock, and foraged in backyards for garbage. When the cause of the unruly behavior was understood, Kodiak people found solutions. Litter

laws were enforced, and bearproof dumpsters installed; electric fencing around the community landfill was reinforced, and garbage buried more frequently. Hunters, villagers, and visitors were educated, and conflicts gradually subsided. Kodiak people have learned to live with the bears in their backyards and backcountry. Although encounters between people and bears are common on the archipelago, only one person has been killed by a bear in the past 70 years.

Safe refuge

The lush green landscape of Kodiak Island provides prime habitat for Kodiak bears. The Kodiak National Wildlife Refuge, set up to protect brown bears and other wildlife, now covers 1.9 million acres (7600 square km).

How can we help?

● Find out more about Kodiak bears and their habitat at www.fws.gov/Refuges.

● Support the Vital Ground Foundation, a land trust that protects habitat for wildlife, and has already procured habitat on Kodiak Island: www.vitalground.org.

● When in bear land, follow backcountry basics—Be Bear Safe: www.fws.gov/Refuges.

● Find out how the Kodiak Brown Bear Trust has helped restore bear habitat: www.safariclubfoundation.org.

current status: **Healthy and stable**

Species Survival Commission   The World Conservation Union

Protected salmon

An Alutiiq fisherman harvests salmon on Olga Bay, off Kodiak Island. Salmon fishing is carefully managed to prevent overharvesting and to ensure a sustained yield for both bears and humans.

Polar Bear

CLASS: Mammalia   **ORDER:** Carnivora   **FAMILY:** Ursidae   **GENUS & SPECIES:** *Ursus maritimus*

Shuffling nonchalantly through wailing winds and biting blizzards, the great ice bear roams relentlessly across the frozen wastes of the circumpolar Arctic. The Inuit call him Pisingtoog, "the great wanderer," and no wonder, as he travels on an endless quest for prey, seeking the blubber-rich seals that swim beneath the polar pack ice. The only bear to survive and even thrive on sea ice, Pisingtoog follows the movements of the shifting drift ice that spreads out across the ocean each winter, then melts and shrinks back to shore each summer. Riding the drifting ice floes, the great white bear can wander far from home, sometimes as far as the Japanese island of Hokkaido.

Polar bears living along the edge of the polar basin might never set foot on dry land.

Key Features

- The world's largest land carnivore, and the top predator in the Arctic ecosystem.

- *Ursus maritimus* (the sea bear) lives and hunts on sea ice and water.

- Metabolically unique, polar bears can "shut down" and fast whenever food is scarce.

- Polar bears retain virtually all their body heat, even at subzero temperatures.

In Focus

Ursus maritimus is easily the world's largest bear, matched only by some of the biggest Alaskan Kodiak bears. Although massive in build, polar bears are less chunky than American grizzlies—more elongated and streamlined—with sloping shoulders, a narrow, pointed head, sleek profile, and an aquiline nose.

Small furry ears

The relatively small, streamlined ears lie flat and closed when the bear swims under water. Their size reflects "Allen's Rule" (formulated by the biologist Joel Allen in 1877) that the farther north an animal lives, the smaller its extremities, minimizing heat loss.

Underwater sight

With large eyes and outstanding vision, *maritimus* can see through blinding blizzards and glaring sunlight. Under water a nictitating membrane (translucent inner eyelid) protects the eye, while allowing clear underwater vision—the bear can spot shellfish lying on the seabed.

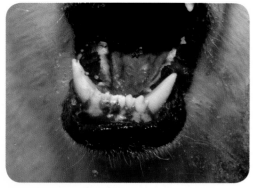

Jagged teeth

A polar bear's cheek molars are much more jagged than those of other bears. Its canines are larger and sharper too, allowing the bear to grip a seal's head in its jaws, and stab it to death before shearing off the fat-rich skin and blubber. Lacking flat grinding teeth, polar bears tend to gulp their prey down in chunks.

Paddling paws

A polar bear's forepaws are huge—up to I ft (30 cm) wide. In the water polar bears paddle with their forepaws, using their hindlegs as a steering rudder. Out on the friable snow, the massive forepaws work like snowshoes, spreading the bear's weight to stop it from sinking.

Vital Statistics

Weight: Male 880–1760 lb (400–800 kg); female 440–770 lb (200–350 kg)

Length: 6.5–9 ft (2–2.7 m)

Height: 3–5.3 ft (0.90–1.6 m) at the shoulder

Color: Arctic white, but reflects the light, so ranges from creamy yellow to pale ice blue

Sexual maturity: 5–6 years

Gestation period: 8 months, including delayed implantation

Number of young: 1 or, more usually, 2

Birth interval: 3–4 years

Typical diet: Mostly ringed seals, but also other seals and marine mammals; seabirds and carrion; algae and kelp when meat is scarce

Lifespan: Male 15–20; female 25–30

Fantastic fur

The polar bear's seemingly snow-white coat is actually translucent. Each hair reflects the surrounding light, giving the fur a golden cast at sunset and a bluish tinge at night. The hollow, waterproof hairs help keep the bear afloat in water.

Did you know?

● A record-breaking male stood 12 ft (3.65 m) tall on its hindlegs, and weighed 2210 lb (1000 kg).

● Migrating with the seasonal drift ice, some bears travel up to 20,000 square miles (51,800 square km) a year.

● A polar bear can flip a 500 lb (225 kg) seal out of the water with one paw.

● The largest polar bears can be two or three times the size of black bears.

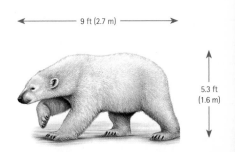

9 ft (2.7 m)

5.3 ft (1.6 m)

Ice-pick claws

Polar bear claws are short and needle-sharp, ideal for grasping wriggling prey, such as slippery seals. On sea ice and frozen tundra, the sharp claw points act like pick-axes, giving the bear a firm grip on steep icy slopes.

Habitat

The only bear to thrive on sea ice, *Ursus maritimus* is, as its name implies, essentially a "sea bear." Supremely adapted to life in the icebound Arctic, it roams the frozen seas and shores of all five Arctic nations—Russia, Norway, Greenland, Canada, and the U.S.A.

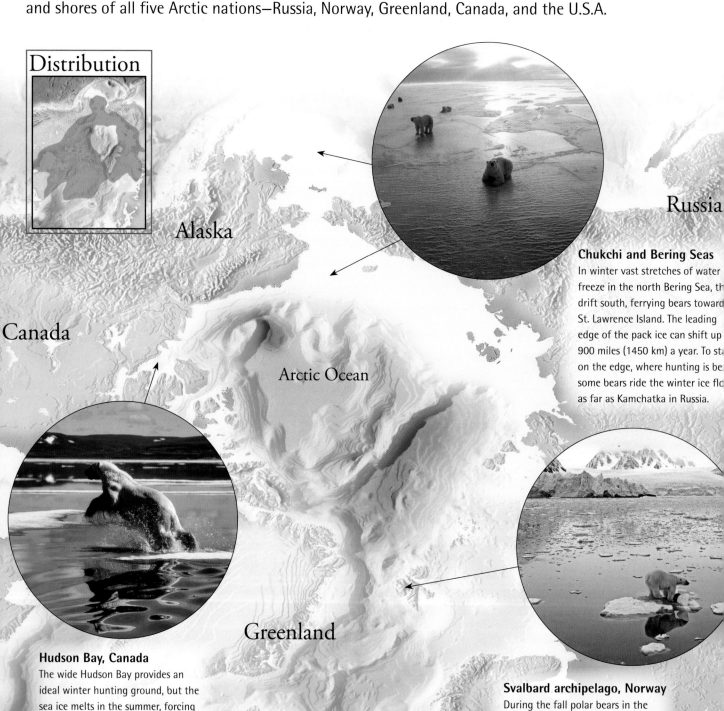

Distribution

Alaska

Russia

Canada

Arctic Ocean

Greenland

Norway

Chukchi and Bering Seas
In winter vast stretches of water freeze in the north Bering Sea, th drift south, ferrying bears toward St. Lawrence Island. The leading edge of the pack ice can shift up 900 miles (1450 km) a year. To sta on the edge, where hunting is be some bears ride the winter ice flo as far as Kamchatka in Russia.

Hudson Bay, Canada
The wide Hudson Bay provides an ideal winter hunting ground, but the sea ice melts in the summer, forcing the bears ashore, where they live on stored fat until the fall. By late summer, the polar bears start trekking up to the bay's northwest coast, where they mass along the shore waiting for freeze-up.

Svalbard archipelago, Norway
During the fall polar bears in the Greenland and Barents Seas ride ice floes drifting south toward the Svalbard archipelago, where they hunt along the shore. Sometimes in the spring large fields of ice stick to the coast, stranding the bears on shore, where they can wreak havoc if they stray near houses.

Although polar bear footprints have been seen close to the North Pole, the bears rarely live on the polar ice cap itself. Instead, they stick to the leading edge of the pack ice, where shore-fast ice and shifting sea ice meet. It is a vibrant, fertile zone, where ice and water intermingle, freezing and melting to create pools or "polynyas" of open water, and long cracks or "leads" running parallel to the shore. Stirred by winds and currents, both leads and polynyas abound in wintering and migrating sea life, which provides food for polar bears and other Arctic predators, such as foxes and seabirds.

Seasonal migration

The pack ice shifts with the seasons and currents, expanding south in the winter and shrinking north in the summer. In some areas, such as the Bering or Greenland Seas, polar bears migrate south and north with the seasonal ice in pursuit of their primary prey, ringed seals. In more southerly spots, such as James Bay and Hudson Bay, the ice melts completely in summer, forcing the bears ashore, where they linger in large packs until the winter freeze-up in November. In Alaska some bears migrate east and west, which might reflect seasonal changes in the shifting pattern of ice and water.

Polar nomads?

A polar bear's travels around the Arctic Pole were, until recently, thought to be entirely random. Scientists now understand that while polar bears do travel far in search of seals, and ride the seasonal drift ice across the Arctic seas, they show a "seasonal fidelity" to certain regions. A bear that winters on Bering Sea ice, for instance, will return each winter to the same frozen sea.

As polar bears seem to stick to certain spots, scientists have now identified 19 self-contained populations that rarely interbreed.

Seaside resorts

Where bears are forced to spend summer ashore, they endure warmer weather by lazing around in cool peat pits or summer dens dug through the tundra to permafrost. Dominant male bears choose the best spots close to the beach on capes and headlands. Females with cubs remain farther inland. Young males and single females fan out still farther from the ocean.

Polar bears leap and play in the water like dolphins, and seem to like rocking little icebergs.

Bunkered in

Although only pregnant females den throughout the Arctic winter, both males and females take refuge in shelters during blizzards, when temperatures can drop to –30°F (–34°C). Snow offers ready shelter during winter snowstorms, when bears dig out shallow pits and turn their backs to the wind. Snow also provides daybeds for rest, and wonderful bathtubs for cubs, and for washing off grease and blood after gorging on seal blubber.

Classification

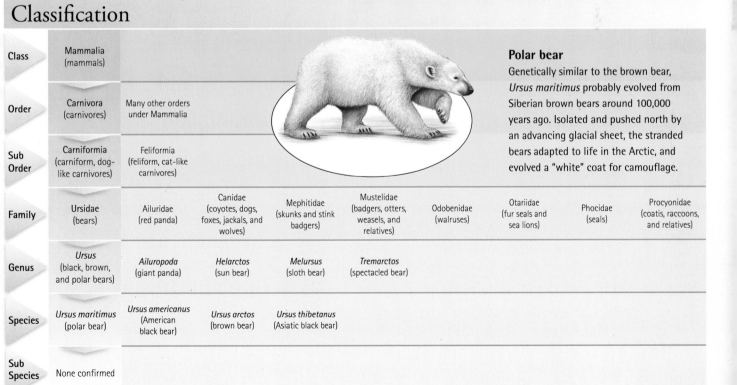

Class	Mammalia (mammals)								
Order	Carnivora (carnivores)	Many other orders under Mammalia							
Sub Order	Carniformia (carniform, dog-like carnivores)	Feliformia (feliform, cat-like carnivores)							
Family	Ursidae (bears)	Ailuridae (red panda)	Canidae (coyotes, dogs, foxes, jackals, and wolves)	Mephitidae (skunks and stink badgers)	Mustelidae (badgers, otters, weasels, and relatives)	Odobenidae (walruses)	Otariidae (fur seals and sea lions)	Phocidae (seals)	Procyonidae (coatis, raccoons, and relatives)
Genus	Ursus (black, brown, and polar bears)	Ailuropoda (giant panda)	Helarctos (sun bear)	Melursus (sloth bear)	Tremarctos (spectacled bear)				
Species	Ursus maritimus (polar bear)	Ursus americanus (American black bear)	Ursus arctos (brown bear)	Ursus thibetanus (Asiatic black bear)					
Sub Species	None confirmed								

Polar bear
Genetically similar to the brown bear, *Ursus maritimus* probably evolved from Siberian brown bears around 100,000 years ago. Isolated and pushed north by an advancing glacial sheet, the stranded bears adapted to life in the Arctic, and evolved a "white" coat for camouflage.

Adaptation and Behavior

Like the seals it stalks, the sea bear glides through the water, buoyed up by a layer of blubber. Using its paddle-like paws as flippers and its hindlegs as rudders, it can swim nonstop for up to 60 miles (95 km) at a rate of 6 mph (10 kph). For crossing frozen seascapes, polar bears have evolved huge splayed feet with suction soles, ice-pick claws, and snowshoe paws. On particularly thin ice the bear will lie on its belly, spreading its weight.

Chilling out

Maritimus has no trouble keeping warm. Its problem is keeping cool. The very features that enable it to thrive on the ice sometimes lead to overheating. Its dense underpelt is covered by transparent and hollow guard hairs that transmit the sun's rays instantly to the heat-absorbing black skin beneath. The thick layer of fat and mass of blubber on its rump also serve to keep the bear warm in subzero cold. So efficient is its heating system that the slightest rise in temperature—in the summer or when running—can cause serious overheating. To cool down, bears roll in the snow or plunge into icy waters offshore.

Quenching thirst

With little fresh water on the pack ice, polar bears seldom drink. Instead, their body metabolizes water from its plentiful store of fats. As water is usually needed to flush out urea—a poisonous by-product of proteins—polar bears simply avoid eating protein, feasting instead on the fat of seals and other blubber-rich prey.

Not a party animal

Although polar bears seem solitary and isolated creatures, wandering through bleak, empty icescapes for thousands of miles, they do nonetheless form ties. Mothers and cubs live in close-knit units for at least three years, while males form strong sparring friendships that can endure as long.

Hunting and Feeding

Polar bears are truly carnivorous and predatory, enjoying a meaty diet of blubber-rich seals, along with the occasional walrus or whale. To remain fit, a polar bear must kill a seal every five or six days. With a huge stomach, it can gorge if needed, assimilating up to 20 percent of its weight in a single meal.

Seal for supper
A ravenous polar bear bites into a plump ringed seal, gulping down its high-energy fat. When seal pups are plentiful in the spring, bears can load up to 150 lb (70 kg) of fat-rich blubber in one sitting.

To maintain their bulk and generate enough energy to survive in subzero cold, polar bears need to consume about 4 lb (2 kg) of fat a day. Ringed seals, especially rich in fat, make up the bulk of a bear's diet, although it also preys on bearded and harp seals. Polar bears attack through the seals' breathing holes in the ice, or through an open-water lead at the edge of the pack ice.

Deadly tactics
Crouched low, sometimes splayed out on its belly beside a seal's breathing hole, a polar bear can wait as still and silent as an iceberg for up to 14 hours, until the seal pops its nose through the thin ice to breathe. In a flash, the bear clamps the seal's head in its powerful jaws and yanks it through the ice hole, before smashing it to death on the pack ice.

Types of prey

Polar bears prefer ringed seals, especially pups, but also prey on young walrus and beluga whale, occasionally on narwhal, crabs, shellfish, and seabirds. When meat is scarce, they forage for kelp or sedges. Near towns bears rummage through rotten garbage.

Arctic seabird

Harp seal pup

Easy prey

Seal pups are a spring-time favorite, as they are easier to catch than vigilant adults. Although the snow-white pups, called "dovecoats," are virtually invisible, and hidden in snow-covered lairs, polar bears can smell them 1 mile (1.6 km) away, and 3 ft (1 m) beneath the snow. Following its twitching nose, a bear slinks up to the seal's lair and waits silently. When it detects the exact position of a pup, it rears up on its hindlegs and crashes down with its front paws, smashing through the lair roof. If the bear fails to break through at first, it will try jumping on the lair again, although by then the lucky pup will have made its escape.

Silent stalking

In the summer seals heave themselves out of the shore leads and bask in the sun on the sparkling ice. To surprise its prey, the polar bear creeps up silently, moving against the wind and keeping a low profile. Its habit of crouching below the horizon, casting no shadow, inspired one of its Inuit nicknames, Nanuk (without shadow). But seals are wise to the canny ways of bears, and doze only briefly, opening their eyes every 20 or 30 seconds to scan the horizon for danger. Each time the seal nods off, the polar bear inches forward until close enough to pounce. Polar bears also ambush seals lazing on the pack ice by swimming under water, then exploding out of the sea just beneath the startled seal. Seabirds hovering too close to the water can also be surprised by a bear leaping 8 ft (2.5 m) in the air. Despite such deadly tactics, fewer than 15 percent of the bear's hunts are successful.

Discerning eaters

As polar bears can assimilate 97 percent of the fat they take in, they need eat only the fatty blubber and skin of a seal. Only a ravenous

bear or a mother emerging from her den will devour the flesh. Even hungry bears discard the seal's hair and bone, as they are indigestible and reduce the absorption of nutrients. Whatever remains of the kill will be eagerly scavenged by gulls, foxes, and juvenile bears.

Polar bears also prey on bearded and harp seals, young walrus, musk oxen, ground squirrels, lemmings, waterfowl, and even beluga or narwhal, though rarely. If live meat is hard to catch during the ice-free summers of their southern range, polar bears will feed on carrion, birds' eggs, or even kelp and sedge.

At Hudson Bay, where sea ice melts for about four months each year, the bears subsist on stored fat supplemented with grass, berries, and algae, along with any human garbage.

Freeze!

A polar bear peers intently into the obscure depths of the cold waters lapping against its iceberg. With super eyesight, *maritimus* can spot the shadowy ripple of a seal swimming beneath the swirling waters. Poised to pounce, with just its claws gripping the ice, a polar bear can remain as frozen as the Arctic landscape for 14 hours.

Ringed seal pup

Beluga whale

Tundra willow

Life Cycle

Temporarily abandoning their solitary existence to breed, courting males compete intensively for mates, as there is usually a shortage of breeding females. Most are too busy nursing cubs, allowing only about one in three to mate each season. Contests for breeding rights are fierce, leaving rivals with broken canines and smashed jaws.

A moment's peace
Even in sleep, a mother shelters her cubs from the icy wind. After playful hours with the twins, she nods off briefly, but will be on her feet at the slightest scent of danger. Cubs are particularly vulnerable to wolves and male polar bears, who sometimes kill young bears in an effort to force their mother to mate and breed again.

During the breeding season males travel far in search of mates. Once a willing partner is found, the male herds her away from rival suitors. The couple mate repeatedly on the pack ice, staying close together for at least a week. As with most other bears, frequent mating is needed to induce ovulation. Once pregnant, the female starts storing fat for the winter sleep. She will gain at least 200 lb (90 kg) before entering her birthing den in the fall. Pregnant females generally leave the sea ice and come ashore to den between September and November, while the rest of the clan remains active on the pack ice throughout the winter hunting season.

Snow dens
Mothers generally dig dens near the coast on south-facing snow banks, where the sun will be strongest when the cubs emerge in springtime. In colder spots, such as the Beaufort Sea, some bears might need to dig dens in snow drifts on multiyear (permanent) ice floes. By contrast, in the warmer southern Hudson Bay, dens are sometimes dug into frozen peat banks. Mothers often return to the same dens each year. Some denning sites, such as Wrangel Island off Russia's northeast coast, attract hundreds

First months of life

Cub's eye view
A cub's first sight of the bright, sunlit tundra is glimpsed at the end of a long, protective tunnel dug out of snow. Dens often contain more than one room for cubs to romp in.

Peas in a pod
Snuggling close for warmth and comfort, twin cubs bond while their mother slumbers. Restless and feisty, they soon start scooping out extra tunnels and play pits.

Who's going first?
Inquisitive triplets sniff the spring air and peer out at the bright new world beyond the warmth of their birth den. Their mother wisely dug her den on a sunny slope.

Litter natter
Before setting out for the sea ice, littermates spend hours rolling and romping in the snow by their den, keeping warm and developing muscles.

annually. Typical dens are entered through a long tunnel that opens out into an oval chamber, often leading to two, or even three, smaller rooms for the cubs to romp in. The main chamber averages 6 x 10 ft (2 x 3 m) and 4 ft (1.2 m) high. The insulation of snow dens is so effective that temperatures within can be 60°F (15°C) higher than outside. At the same time, the roof of the snow den remains thin enough for oxygen to pass through the snow crystals, allowing the family to breathe.

Mid-winter birth
Ensconsed within her warm, soft *igloovikus* (den), as the Inuit call it, the mother bear drifts in and out of sleep, living off her fat stores. Sometime in December or January she gives birth, usually to twins, weighing around 1.5 lb (680 g), with fine, almost invisible down. Although larger than other bear cubs, they are still small—about the size of a hamster—blind, deaf, and quite helpless. After struggling through their mother's thick fur to reach her warm nipples, the cubs suckle contentedly on her creamy milk, which contains 46 percent fat and tastes like cod liver oil. After one month the cubs can crawl; after six weeks they can open their eyes; and at 10 weeks, when they weigh about 25 lb (11 kg), they can keep their balance. When the cubs emerge from the den in March or April, they weigh up to 30 lb (14 kg). Before setting out for the pack ice, the cubs play in the snow by the den for a week or so, adjusting to the cold and piling on fat, until they are strong enough to travel

Breaking the ice
Two polar pals sniff and circle each other, bowing and bobbing, with eyes lowered and heads wagging—inviting play. Silently they rise and wrestle in slow motion, gently shoving, tugging, hugging, and rolling over in the snow, with huge paws flaying in the air. Despite their awesome power, fangs, and claws, sparring buddies never hurt each other. Little is known about such friendships, which can last for weeks or even years.

across the frozen tundra and brave the sea ice with their mother. The journey to the shore can be slow, with stops for naps along the way. Sometimes the cubs ride on their mother's back. Having lived on her reserves for seven or eight months, she is scrawny and ravenous. As soon as she makes a seal kill, she will consume the rich blubber and skin for energy.

Lessons of life
Although by August the cubs usually weigh over 100 lb (45 kg), they remain dependent on their mother, nursing six or seven times a day, until they are nearly two, and probably denning with her for another two or even three winters. Over the next 28 months the budding bears will learn to hunt and survive on the ice by watching their mother's every move. She will teach them how to toboggan down rough glaciers and tumbled pack ice. The hardest year for growing cubs is the first, when 20 or 40 percent die from starvation or freezing. Even after weaning, life remains tough during the first few years when youngsters must adapt to life on their own. Bereft of their attentive mother, they usually drift about uncertainly. Littermates often pair up for a year or two, increasing their chance of survival.

As most bears in the wild do not live much beyond 20, many females will have no more than five litters in their lifetime. Males often die younger, as mating contests take their toll.

Chuffing and purring
Polar bears communicate with varied vocal calls: angry hisses and growls, agitated moans and contented purring. Chuffing—expelling air in brief bursts—means different things at different times. During courtship it expresses excitement; between a mother and cub, it acts like a tap on the shoulder. When a bear is upset, chuffing might precede the roar before the rush.

Legend and History

For the Inuit, the "invisible" white bear Nanuk appears almost magically out of the wind-driven snow, and casts no shadow on the shining ice as he crouches low beside a seal's breathing hole. Marveling at Nanuk's hunting craft and ability to ride the perilous pack ice, the Inuit watched his every move, until they could hunt and live on the ice almost as well as the ice bear himself.

The polar bear played a pivotal role in the lives of the Arctic Inuit, serving as a model for hunting, traveling, and thriving on the hazardous pack ice. Its awesome predatory and navigation skills inspired its evocative nicknames, Nanuk (without shadow) and Pisingtoog (great wanderer). If one follows Pisingtoog, the Inuit believe, one can learn a lot. With so much to teach, the polar bear was often chosen by the tribal shaman (spiritual guide) for his *tornaq* (guardian). When the legendary shaman Angakoq made his fabled trip to the moon, he was never without his spirit bear companion.

Along with the first peoples of the plains and forests, the Inuit believed that the spirits of men and bears were inextricably linked. Stripped of its fur, a polar bear's slim body looks uncannily human. She-bears suckle and cuff their cubs like human mothers. Young males cavort around, shoving and butting each other like overgrown teenagers. A sense of kinship runs through all Inuit legends: When polar bears walk into an igloo, they take off their furry coats and turn into people; when they go out into the driving snow, they put on their furs and turn back into bears again.

Willem Barents's crew capture a polar bear
Ever inquisitive, the first polar bear spotted by Dutch explorers in 1596 immediately tried to clamber aboard the small boat, threatening to capsize it. (From *Diarium Nauticum...*, engraved by Gerrit de Veer, 1596)

True hunters

"Almost a man," and almost as powerful as Sedna, goddess of the sea, the polar bear inspired unparalleled awe among the Inuit, prompting elaborate rites and taboos to attract its blessings and deflect its wrath. To propitiate Nanuk, hunters obeyed strict codes of conduct. If a bear were wounded, it had to be tracked down and killed to release its soul. After the kill, hunters would not hunt for at least four days, allowing the beast's soul to return to its family. In the meantime, the hunt would be celebrated, and the bear honored with songs, prayers, and gifts for its journey home. Abiding by their strict codes, the Inuit successfully harvested the polar bear for over 1000 years, using its hide for clothing and bedding, its meat for food, its bones and teeth for tools or amulets. Even today, wearing polar-hide pants is a badge of honor, the sign of a true hunter.

Polaris burns brightly

Sparkling in the northern sky, Polaris, the Pole Star, shines brightly at the heart of the Little Bear and Great Bear constellations. The Inuit tell how the Great Bear arose in the sky:

"One day an Inuit woman caught in a snowstorm took refuge in an igloo full of bear people. Whenever they left for the hunt, the people threw on beautiful snow-white bearskins and turned into bears. When they returned, they shook off their furry hides and became human again. The woman lived with the bear people for some time, until, yearning for her husband, she tore herself away. Although the bear people begged her to keep their hideaway secret, her inquisitive husband made her tell. Angry at her betrayal, the bear people tracked her down. One broke into her igloo and bit her to death. As he was turning away, the husband's dogs hurled themselves at him. Dogs and bear wrestled wildly, with sparks flying. Suddenly they burned bright and spiraled upward into the night sky like swirling stars. The dogs still chase the bear every night in the northern sky."

Star appeal

The rarity and pristine beauty of the ice bear have made it a star attraction in animal shows since ancient times. As far back as *c.*260 BC, Ptolemy II, King of Egypt, kept a polar bear. As explorers penetrated the Arctic, the startling white bear became a coveted prize for emperors. In the 9th century Norsemen risked life and limb to capture one—pelt or live. In the budding medieval kingdoms of Norway, Denmark, England, Germany, and Damascus, princes paid princely prices to flaunt a captive polar bear as the ultimate status symbol.

With increased trade and travel in the 19th and 20th centuries, a wider audience could glimpse the white bear at traveling animal shows. Willy Hagenbeck, nephew of the famous bear tamer Carl, entertained huge crowds with his troupe of 70 polar bears. Equipped with no more than a whip and wooden truncheon, Willy steered his fearsome charges around the ring as easily as a dog herds sheep. Gutsy and glitzy lady trainers added glamor during the 1950s and '60s. Munich's Lilo Schäfer, dressed as an ice princess in fluffy blue fur and white satin, stepped lithely into a cageful of savage ice bears, emerging unruffled and unmolested. In the 1960s petite Ursula Böttcher, "brilliant baroness of the bears," toured throughout Europe and the U.S.A., enthralling the crowds with her troupe of polar beauties. A particular thrill at the end of the show was her legendary "death kiss." Today conservationists frown on bear taming. Caged polar bears, however kindly treated, show quiet despair by pacing and neglecting their young.

Ice dancing

The modern and more humane way to observe polar bears is to travel to Alaska, or Churchill in Canada, where hundreds of bears languish along the shore each fall, waiting for freeze-up. With nothing to do and nothing to eat, the bears crash out on the snow, or cavort around with their buddies. Hundreds of tourists stare wide-eyed as young males stand up to spar, circling each other in graceful minuets on the ice.

Polar inspiration

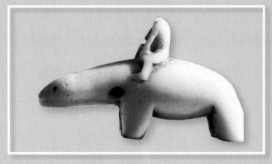

Stuff of dreams
Although the Inuit never ride polar bears, they must have seen cubs hitch a lift on their mother's back, and probably imagined the fabled shaman Angakoq flying to the moon on his polar bear spirit guide.

Waiting on the ice
Hunting like Nanuk, the Inuit wait motionless beside a seal's breathing hole. The seated hunter warms his feet on a patch of polar bear fur. (*Seal Hunting* by Gallino Gallo, *c.*1800)

Carl Hagenbeck's open-air zoo, Hamburg
Animal trainer Carl Hagenbeck strokes a tame walrus in his "natural" zoo, overlooked by peaceful polar bears basking on an ice rockery. Moved by pity, Carl pioneered "nonviolent" bear taming. Although his methods were humane in his day, activists now frown on any training. (*Carl Hagenbeck in His Zoo* by Lovis Corinth, 1911)

Threats and Conservation

Although pushed close to extinction by trophy hunting in the 1970s, the ice bear recovered. The threats it now faces are less tangible, but no less real: pollutant poisoning, persistent poaching, and—by far the gravest and least predictable danger—global warming, which threatens to dissolve the ice bear's very world.

The ice bear's ground is melting beneath its feet. Sea ice now breaks up earlier in the spring and freezes later in the fall, leaving polar bears less time to hunt on the ice. For bears in southern regions, such as Canada's Hudson Bay, where the sea ice melts entirely during the summer, a shorter hunting season reduces the vital time needed to store fat for the summer fast. Canadian researchers have found that for each week lost from the hunting season in Hudson Bay, female polar bears step ashore 22 lb (10 kg) lighter. With less fat, they are less able to rear healthy cubs. Mothers are now nursing cubs an extra year before weaning. Most worrying, the western Hudson Bay population has dropped from 1200 to fewer than 950 bears within the past decade. Other effects of climate change include increased rainfall in winter, which can cause dens to collapse, exposing cubs to the elements. The trend, also, in stronger winds and ice drift, seen over the past 50 years, is expected to increase the stress and energy levels of polar bears on the ice. Scientists predict that if global warming continues, all summer sea ice could disappear by 2100, along with the polar bear.

An ice mess—persistent pollutants

Although the Arctic seems pristine and untouched by civilization, man-made pollutants, borne by winds and currents, have contaminated the Arctic atmosphere. High levels of heavy metals found in both seals and polar bears affect brain

Meltdown
Arctic sea ice seems to be melting three time faster than estimated, while air temperatures have risen by about 41°F (5°C) over the last 100 years.

Fatal attraction
The white bears turn black after feasting on rotting garbage. Fearless and curious, they will try anything, from rubber tyres to lethal batteries. Until garbage dumps are enclosed, they remain a source of danger.

development and reproduction. Even worse, the fat and organs of many Arctic animals have been infected with "persistent organic pollutants" (POPs), a toxic brew of long-lasting contaminants, industrial chemicals, and pesticides. As one animal eats another, the pollutants intensify up the food chain, until they reach the polar bear, who gulps down a concentrated dose of toxins. Studies show that a build-up of POPs in polar bears depletes vitamin A and thyroid hormone levels, both of which affect growth, development, reproduction, and resistance to disease. When the pollutants poison a bear's milk, her cubs die. Although POPs have now been outlawed in many countries, enforcement cannot be relaxed.

Oil issues

Oil spills also pose serious health risks to polar bears. Oiled fur reduces warmth, while ingested oil—from licking oily fur or eating oiled prey—can kill a bear. In fact, oil development iself threatens polar bears. Expectant mothers, already undermined by shortened feeding seasons, seem stressed by seismic blasting and continuous oil and gas drilling near their dens.

Save the Arctic, save the polar bear

Once an icon of Arctic survival and independence, the polar bear now symbolizes the fragility and interdependence of all life. With temperatures rising faster than expected, nations are collaborating to limit global warming. The polar bear's best hope, says bear biologist Ian Stirling, lies in its popularity. People care enough about Nanuk to "think green" and save the Arctic.

Polar bear capital of the world

Spreading the ice bear's popularity, the deepwater town of Churchill offers prime viewing in the summer, when bears mass along the coast waiting for freeze-up. Churchill lies in the direct path of migrating bears, attracting tourists—and trouble. Fasting bears, drawn by garbage, are not afraid to raid hotels or attack tourists who stray near their dens. Rather than shoot the troublemakers, the town came up with an innovative solution—a polar bear jail, where nuisance bears can be held during the ice-free summer. Watered,

but not fed, the fasting bears live on fat reserves until freeze-up, when they are tranquilized and airlifted across the frozen sea. The jail has proved a huge success, as has the Polar Bear Alert program and hotline, which help prevent panic shootings when hungry bears stray into town. With the recent invention, also, of the safe tundra buggy, tourists can now roam alongside the bear in its icy habitat.

Liftoff!
Tourists watch the annual airlift of Churchill's nuisance bears, which have spent the summer dozing in the local bear jail. With freeze-up in the fall, the bears are released over the frozen bay, where they can hunt seal all winter.

How can we help?

● Think green! Even small changes can make a difference if each of us helps. Calculate your carbon footprint at www. liveneutral.org.

● Join groups campaigning for the polar bear, such as Polar Bears International: www. polarbearsinternational.org.

● Adopt a polar bear and help save its home: https://support. wwf.org.uk.

● Petition governments to save habitat for polar bears.

● To help stem global warming, adopt an acre of rainforest: www.nature.org.

current status: **Vulnerable**

Tagged and tattooed
Spring cubs peek curiously over their tranquilized mother, as biologists assess her general health. Research is vital in the race to stem the harmful effects of pollution and global warming. Each year scientists tag, tattoo, measure, weigh, and check polar bears for levels of fat and contaminants.

Asiatic Black Bear

CLASS: Mammalia   **ORDER:** Carnivora   **FAMILY:** Ursidae   **GENUS & SPECIES:** *Ursus thibetanus*

As dark and mysterious as the Himalayan night, *Ursus thibetanus*, the beautiful black "bear of Tibet," roams far more widely than its scientific name suggests—ranging from the luminous snowdrifts of the Himalayas to the steamy, scented stillness of the tropical jungle. At one time it was thought to be sufficiently different from other bears to be placed in its own genus, *Selenarctos* (after Selene, Greek goddess of the moon), but as knowledge of the timid and elusive bear expanded, it was grouped with its cousins in the genus *Ursus*.

The striking white crescent on the bear's chest, evoking the crescent moon, inspired its popular name "moon bear."

Key Features

● A close cousin of the American black bear—similar in size and diet.

● A nocturnal loner, spends much of its time in trees, eating and sleeping.

● Omnivorous, but meat forms only a small part of its diet.

● Dens for the winter in northern parts of its range, but further south might migrate to avoid hibernation altogether.

Asiatic Black Bear 169

In Focus

As their name suggests, Asiatic black bears are most often jet-black in color, but they may very rarely be a shade of brown. Common to all of them is a thick mane of long fur around the neck and shoulders, a pale-colored muzzle, and a distinctive crescent of light-colored hair that runs across the chest. Males are generally larger than females, and both are at their heaviest in the fall, prior to hibernation.

Beady eyes

The eyes are brown and relatively small, with round pupils. It is thought that *thibetanus* can see in partial color and, like other bears, with a form of telescopic vision. A nictitating membrane (transparent inner eyelid) protects the eye and keeps it moist.

Powerful teeth

Although the incisors and canine teeth are smaller than in some bears, the molars are longer, and there are more premolars. As teeth are vital for feeding and self-defense, a bear will usually have its full complement of 42 by the age of two and a half.

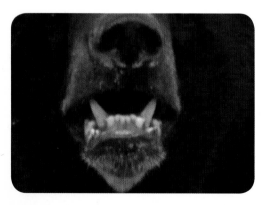

Rounded ears

Set wide on the head, the distinctive ears of the Asiatic black bear are larger and less pointed than those of its American cousin. Its hearing is also believed to be very acute, picking up sounds at frequencies as high as 30kHz, far beyond the human limit of 20kHz.

Adaptable coat

Bears living at higher altitudes or in cool northern latitudes have a dense layer of underwool beneath the fur, which keeps them warm. In more southern, tropical regions, the bears have shorter, thinner coats with less of an underpelt.

Generous paws

At 7–8 in (18–20 cm) long, the back paws are unusually large. Each paw has five pads or toes, which are essential for gripping. The soles are hairless, though a fringe of hairs separates the pads. While the bear is in its winter den, the skin of the footpads is sloughed off and replaced with new skin.

Strong claws

The front claws are curved and slightly longer than those on the hind paws—2 in (5 cm) in length—but they are strong and ideally adapted for climbing. Being able to shin up trees enables this bear to compete for fruit with ground-based rivals, such as brown bears and wild pigs.

Vital Statistics

Weight: Male 132–440 lb (60–200 kg); female 88–310 lb (40–140 kg)

Length: Male 3.9–6.2 ft (1.2–1.9 m); female 4–5 ft (1.2–1.5 m)

Height: 2.3–3.3 ft (0.7–1 m) at the shoulder

Color: Often jet-black, but very rarely brown, with a pale, crescent-shaped mark on the chest

Sexual maturity: 3 years

Gestation period: 7–8 months including delayed implantation

Number of young: Usually 2, sometimes 1

Birth interval: 2–3 years

Typical diet: Mainly fruit, berries, seeds, nuts, and grasses; occasional fish, birds, and rodents, plus carrion

Lifespan: Around 25 years in the wild; up to 37 years in captivity

Did you know?

● On emerging from their winter sleep, Russian black bears eat birch sap, a laxative that helps to expel the remnants of their last winter meal.

● *Ursus thibetanus* sometimes builds tree nests up to 65 ft (20 m) above the ground.

● In the spring, when some bears strip trees for sap, they can debark 40 in a single night.

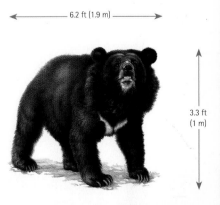

← 6.2 ft (1.9 m) →

3.3 ft (1 m)

Habitat

Asiatic black bears have a wide distribution, being found right across Asia, from Afghanistan to Burma and Vietnam, and into northeastern China, southeastern Russia, Taiwan, and Japan. They like virtually any type of hilly or mountainous forest, ranging from coniferous alpine woods to tropical rainforests.

Distribution

Japanese broadleaf forests
The Japanese black bear (*Ursus thibetanus japonicus*) is present on three of Japan's four main islands—Honshu, Kyushu, and Shikoku. Here it lives in a variety of forest habitats, including areas of broadleaf trees, such as beech and oak, and dwarf bamboo thickets.

Russia

China

Japan

India

Pacific Ocean

Indian Ocean

Indian Himalayas
On scrubby hill slopes in northern India, among the outer Himalayas, there are few large trees, so denning often takes place in rock caves and cavities. Bears may move into a natural cave, or may instead enlarge a cavity to suit their needs. The small but muscular black bears have been seen to move large boulders and logs in their quest to create a den.

Taiwan bamboo forests
On the heavily populated island of Taiwan, the Formosan black bear (as it is called there) finds refuge in the bamboo forests of the island's national parks. Here it constructs bowl-shaped ground nests made from grass. These are about 2 ft (60 cm) wide inside, and 1 ft (30 cm) deep.

Originally found from Iran to Southeast Asia, including Japan and Taiwan, today the Asiatic black bear has a much reduced and fragmented distribution. It usually lives in hilly or mountainous forested areas up to about 10,000 ft (3000 m), particularly tropical rainforest, temperate broadleafed forests, and tropical monsoon and dry forests, making its home in trees, caves, or on the ground in hollows or rock crevices. However, habitat destruction might be forcing many bears to spend longer periods of time at lower altitudes and nearer to areas of human activity as these places offer them an ample supply of food. This is particularly tempting as the Asiatic bear must consume vast quantities during the summer months in order to lay down enough fat to survive during its winter sleep. Inevitably, though, this brings it into conflict with humans, and can result in bears being killed as pests.

Many Asiatic black bears migrate according to the season, spending warmer months at high altitudes, and descending during colder months to lower levels. Within their preferred habitats these solitary creatures roam home ranges of varying size, from 2.5–14 square miles (6.5–36.5 square km). Despite some overlap, home ranges help reduce competition for vital resources, such as food, space, water, and shelter.

Preparing for the winter

In most parts of its range the Asiatic black bear goes into a winter sleep during the late fall. Only in a few areas, such as in Pakistan, is there adequate food and a climate mild enough for the animal to remain active all year round. In other places it starts to look for a den site as winter approaches. Depending on what is available, it will sleep about 15 ft (4.5 m) above the ground in a hollow tree, or make a circular den 1.5 ft (50 cm) wide and 6 ft (2 m) deep on the sunny, southern side of a steep mountain slope and line it with a thick mat of grass, herbs, leaves, and branches.

Asiatic black bears have been known to swim across lakes rather than walk around them.

The demands of hibernation

During the bear's winter sleep the heartbeat initially drops from 98 beats per minute to 40–45, slowing by around December to 8–10 beats per minute during deep hibernation. At the same time oxygen intake reduces by about 50 percent. The body temperature, however, drops by only 5.4–12.6°F (3–7°C). The result is that females retain enough body heat to keep their young warm over the winter, and can also rouse quickly if anything untoward happens. The period of sleep varies depending on the location, weather, and temperature. In Siberia, for example, the bear will sleep for 4–5 months from November, while in Japan it will sleep for 5–6 months; in the Himalayas, however, it sleeps only during the coldest months, emerging occasionally.

Classification

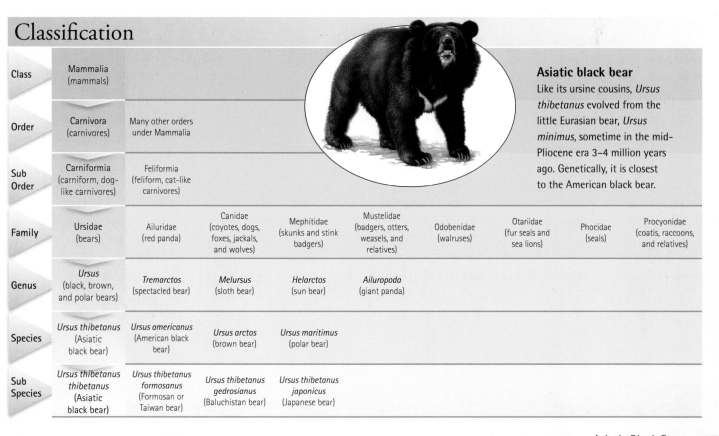

Asiatic black bear
Like its ursine cousins, *Ursus thibetanus* evolved from the little Eurasian bear, *Ursus minimus*, sometime in the mid-Pliocene era 3–4 million years ago. Genetically, it is closest to the American black bear.

Class	Mammalia (mammals)								
Order	Carnivora (carnivores)	Many other orders under Mammalia							
Sub Order	Carniformia (carniform, dog-like carnivores)	Feliformia (feliform, cat-like carnivores)							
Family	Ursidae (bears)	Ailuridae (red panda)	Canidae (coyotes, dogs, foxes, jackals, and wolves)	Mephitidae (skunks and stink badgers)	Mustelidae (badgers, otters, weasels, and relatives)	Odobenidae (walruses)	Otariidae (fur seals and sea lions)	Phocidae (seals)	Procyonidae (coatis, raccoons, and relatives)
Genus	Ursus (black, brown, and polar bears)	Tremarctos (spectacled bear)	Melursus (sloth bear)	Helarctos (sun bear)	Ailuropoda (giant panda)				
Species	Ursus thibetanus (Asiatic black bear)	Ursus americanus (American black bear)	Ursus arctos (brown bear)	Ursus maritimus (polar bear)					
Sub Species	Ursus thibetanus thibetanus (Asiatic black bear)	Ursus thibetanus formosanus (Formosan or Taiwan bear)	Ursus thibetanus gedrosianus (Baluchistan bear)	Ursus thibetanus japonicus (Japanese bear)					

Adaptation and Behavior

Thibetanus displays all the adaptations and behaviors that are typical of the bear family. As an omnivore, it eats opportunistically, changing its diet through the year to maximize its deposition of fat, which sustains it through its winter sleep.

Expert climber

Like its American cousin, *Ursus americanus*, the Asiatic black bear is one of the more tree-loving ursids. As a result, it has strong forelimbs for climbing, with long, powerful claws for gripping. Once it has climbed into a nut tree, it uses its dextrous forepaws to make a feeding platform (known as a *kuma dama*—"bear shelf"—in Japanese) by bending back nearby branches. The finished structure looks like a scruffy, oversized bird's nest, and here the bear sits, consuming all the nuts within reach. It may then sleep in the tree, as resting in the shade of leafy boughs conserves body heat.

Getting comfortable

Down on the forest floor the bears will forage for other favorite foodstuffs, stopping occasionally to rest in a surprisingly human fashion, by sitting with their back against a tree. Even more curiously, when the ground is wet or muddy, the bears have been known to select several large, broad leaves and carefully lay them down to sit on.

Deterring predators

Humans and tigers, with which much of its range overlaps, are the only enemies of this bear. The ruff of longer, thicker fur around its neck helps to exaggerate its size and may provide protection from predation, as a tiger grabbing the animal by the neck would simply get a mouthful of fur. Rearing up and exposing the white crescent on its chest may also be a startling display designed to deter tigers, but an alternative suggestion is that it may act as a signal to other bears in the dim light of the forest.

Hunting and Feeding

While Asiatic black bears are naturally omnivorous, meat makes up only a small part of their diet. Being scavengers who will eat almost anything, their usual fare comprises fruit, roots, fungi, and tubers, as well as grubs and insects such as bees, wasps, and ants.

Varied diet

Always happy to feast on sweet berries and fruit, Asiatic black bears are virtually vegetarian in Japan, where their passion for sugary tree sap can enrage local farmers. Elsewhere, in Tibet and India, the bears are just as partial to meat, picking up the scent of a dead carcass from many miles away.

The bears' diet changes with the seasons. In spring they forage for grasses, sedges, herbs, buds, nuts, and bamboo shoots. In summer, berries and insects become the favored foods, while in the fall, nuts and berries, including acorns and beechnuts, provide vital winter fat and protein. In the wild, Asiatic black bears typically forage alone. However, during the breeding season pairs can be seen hunting and gathering together.

Nimble fingers

The bears are extremely dextrous, and can peel nuts, pick berries, and extract pine nuts from cones. They have even learned to take the lids from jars and manipulate other small man-made objects. They climb trees easily and frequently, and will break branches to reach fruit and berries. The bears will also rip through the trunk of a tree to reach a source of honey, and will dig up wasps' nests. When

Types of food

In early spring, bears survive on new shoots, and nuts shed from trees the previous year. By summer they turn to ripening berries, and other soft fruits, as well as a variety of insects and grasses. In the fall they return to nuts, feasting on the new crop to build up fat reserves for the winter.

Acorns

Hydrangeas

food sources are scarce, Asiatic black bears will strip the bark off trees and eat the sapwood, which does not endear them to logging companies.

A taste for meat

Although largely herbivorous, Asiatic black bears are also fond of meat. They have the strength to kill a large animal, breaking its neck with a single blow, and can carry carcasses over long distances. An easier option for the bear is to feast on the slain prey of other carnivores, such as the Siberian tiger. However, if the tiger catches a bear in the act, the thief will be swiftly killed and eaten itself.

Sadly, with so much of their natural habitat now destroyed, Asiatic black bears are being forced to live in ever closer proximity to humans. As a result, they have modified their sources of prey and may focus on farm livestock, including sheep, goats, and even buffalo. Hungry bears also raid cultivated seed and fruit crops, such as maize, sorghum, dates, and pineapple. Inevitably, Asiatic black bears are unpopular with farmers and are often killed while trying to feed on crops. For this reason they have been known to change their sleeping patterns in order to avoid human encounters.

Unlimited appetite

When sleeping bears are roused by rising temperatures in the spring, most of them are underweight, having lived off stored fat during their winter sleep. Desperate to eat and restore their vigor, they feed on anything they can find. As fall approaches again, the bears gorge for much longer periods, and often during the night too, as they must lay down enough fat for the winter. At this time they can eat continually without feeling full.

Eating imperative
When the pressure is on in the late summer and fall to lay down fat reserves in preparation for the winter sleep, the Asiatic black bear will go to almost any lengths—or heights—to access tasty, nutritious foodstuffs.

Berries

Termites

Grasses

Life Cycle

Most of what we know about reproduction in the Asiatic black bear has been learned by observing captive animals. Both sexes mature at about 3–4 years, and the young are born helpless and blind during early winter. They remain with their mother for up to three years, so females are sometimes seen with cubs and young from a previous year.

Natural dens

Born aloft
Tree dens might look scrappy and insecure, but they are warm, safe, secluded shelters for giving birth, nursing, and nurturing the tiny, dependent cubs.

Cozy cave
A natural cave is an ideal denning site because it will remain safe, warm, and dry during the critical first months of a cub's life, and be a family refuge for several years after.

Births may be related to climatic temperature: In Siberia, mating takes place in June or July, and births occur in February, whereas in Pakistan, mating occurs in October, and births coincide with the start of the hot weather in April or May. The gestation period lasts from 7–8 months, and may be shorter in more tropical areas.

Mating patterns
In captivity the mating pattern is promiscuous. There is a hierarchy among adult male bears, with those above six years of age spending more days mating than younger ones. The heavier, more dominant males are more likely to mate than smaller ones that weigh less than 175 lb (80 kg). Females mate over periods of 12–35 days, and,

Sibling support
Littermates, like these four-month-old Japanese black bear cubs, spend all their time together during the first years of life. Whether playing, sparring, or hunting, they are always learning—preparing for when they strike out on their own.

like many other bears, implantation of the embryo is delayed until the fall.

Helpless newborns
Theoretically, female Asiatic black bears could produce one litter of cubs per year, but they do not usually do so, instead breeding every 2–3 years. Cubs are born in a cave, hollow tree, or in thick undergrowth in winter or early spring—usually only two cubs per litter, though single cubs are born on occasion. Like many small mammals,

Hang on!
Climbing trees comes as naturally—and easily—to young bears as breathing, but sometimes they misjudge their own ability and get stuck. This intrepid cub eventually managed to get safely back to earth.

Asiatic black bear cubs are blind and helpless at birth, and a newborn cub will weigh only 8–10.5 oz (225–300 g). Their survival is extremely precarious at this stage of life, and they risk predation by other animals, such as the tiger, so they depend totally upon their mother to protect them. One reason why all bear cubs are born so small is because, unlike many other mammals, the mother does not eat during the gestation period. Instead of eating, proteins in the mother's body break down into glucose to provide nourishment for her developing offspring. As the cub receives so few nutrients before birth, it is born in a premature state. But young Asiatic black bears grow very rapidly during the first few months of life, largely thanks to the high fat content of their mother's milk—believed to be 33 percent, as opposed to just 4 percent in human milk. As soon as they can see, which can be earlier than their American cousins, as early as 10 days after birth, they become increasingly lively, inquisitive, and vocal, crying loudly if unhappy.

First foraging trips
By the time they reach 3–4 weeks old, the cubs' eyes are fully open, and they first accompany their mother out of the den at 8–10 weeks. To help them stay safe on these tentative expeditions, young bear cubs make very distinctive crying calls that the mother will recognize. They are not fully weaned until they are 3–4 months old, and they will stay with their fiercely protective mother, learning survival and other skills until they are two or three years old. Sadly, cubs unfortunate enough to be orphaned stand little chance of survival even long after they

Mock battles
Young bears learn the importance of body language through play. A bear that wants to submit to another will move away, sit, or lie down, while a dominant bear will walk or run toward a rival.

have been weaned. Since a mother will often pair off to mate before her cubs have left her, it is not uncommon for her to be accompanied by two litters. This sense of motherly duty is not all-consuming however—if cubs get too boisterous, she has little hesitation in giving them a cuff that will send them sprawling.

A cub who has not yet learned to walk can quickly climb a tree, and slide down it equally fast, tail first.

Playful siblings
When not scrambling up trees, tumbling around on the ground, or clambering over their mother, the cubs play with each other, engaging in mock wrestling matches. In fact, play fights between siblings are an important part of growing up, as they teach the cubs skills that they will eventually need when they finally set out on their own to explore the big wide world.

Legend and History

Dwelling among the magical, mist-shrouded Himalayas, the moon bear itself often seems veiled in mystery and paradox. Could it be the elusive yeti that prowls the snowfields of Kashmir and Tibet? Is the rare "golden moon bear" a new color phase, or even an undiscovered species? Is the moon bear's legendary healing power real or imaginary?

From ancient times, moon bears had the ear of gods and emperors. An early Chou emperor (*c*.1122 BC) dreamed that a bear entered his bedchamber, settled himself comfortably in a chair, and foretold crucial matters of state. The legendary Yellow Emperor enlisted legions of warrior bears for the imperial guard, much like the Indian prince Rama. Nearby, on the borders of Manchuria, Tangun, first king of Korea, claimed descent from a bear mother and sky god. His parentage might seem a little unusual, but simply mirrors the legendary lineage of the American bear clans and royal houses of Scandinavia. Tangun's family history unfolds in the heavens:

Tangun, the legend

"Among the stars dwelt the heavenly king Hwanin with his family and celestial court. The king's son Hwanung looked down on earth and, much intrigued by the busy lives of the people, longed to join them. The king granted the boy's wish, sending him to earth with a retinue of 3000. The heavenly prince alighted on Mount T'aebaeksan under the sandalwood tree, where he founded his Sacred City, which he ruled with wisdom, initiating a reign of justice and plenty. In a nearby cave a bear and a tiger also yearned to be human. Hwanung heard their prayers and tested their resolve. Giving each 20 cloves and some mugwort, he instructed them to remain in the

Duel of honor

Armed only with his sword and courage, the samurai Kamei Rokuro faces a raging moon bear in mortal combat, watched by the warlord Minamoto Yoshitsune. After proving himself, Kamei enlisted as one of Yoshitsune's "retainers," bound in honor, like a feudal knight, to serve his liege lord. (*Kamei Rokuro and the Black Bear in the Snow* by Utagawa Kuniyoshi, 1849)

dark for 100 days. After a while, the tiger grew frisky, yawned, stretched its tail, and loped off into the sunlight. But the bear curled up quietly for 21 days, when she miraculously turned into a beautiful woman. Overjoyed, she soon longed for a child. Hwanung, moved by her prayers, breathed on her and fathered his son Tangun. The people rejoiced at the birth of the prince, who reigned as the first king of Choson, 'Land of Morning Calm' (now called Korea), from the memorable year 2333 BC."

The "Buddhist Madonna's" emissary

In Buddhist lands the moon bear came to be regarded as the special emissary of the healing goddess of mercy, Kuan-yin. A household name in Asia, the popular, all-listening "Buddhist Madonna" personifies compassion and wisdom, guarding and guiding the human race, lighting the way to *nirvana* (heaven).

Belief in the healing power of bears seems universal, based in part on watching bears treat themselves with natural cures.

The brown bear, for instance, rubs insect-repellant "bear root" on its fur. In a tragic twist of the old belief, modern moon bears are poached for their parts and milked for their bile, enduring nightmarish lives of torment. An old Japanese legend, with a touch of Zen wisdom, offers an alternative cure:

Hair of the bear

"After the Great War, a battle-weary soldier wends his way uphill to his forest home. His wife, who had given up hope of ever seeing him again, flies down through the bamboo trees to greet her lost husband. After pulling him indoors, she rushes around baking treats. He seems distracted, barely touches his lunch, and wanders outside to kick at tufts of grass. His wife plies him with delicacies for days, but he pushes them away, and broods in the woods. In despair, she consults the local shaman, who promises a cure, but confesses that she is out of bear hair, and asks the wife to fetch one strand from the moon bear on the mountain.

The wife travels for days, pushing up through thickening snow until she reaches the bear's rocky den. Leaving juicy fruit at the mouth of the cave, she waits until, drawn by the sweet scent, the bear emerges and guzzles up the treat. She repeats the ploy all week, moving closer every time, until the last day, when she waits with trepidation by the den. After wolfing the berries down, the bear sniffs around her feet. She talks to him like an old friend, telling of her plight and begging for a silver hair. When at last he stops prowling and listens to her melodious voice, he inches nearer, halting just a few paces in front of her, and shyly bares his chest. She reaches out fearlessly and plucks a hair. The bear holds her eyes for a second, nods, turns to lick up any dregs of fruit, and wanders back to his den. The wife rushes home to the shaman, who fingers the hair by the light of the fire, then thrusts it into the flames, where it sizzles. The wife stares in horror, but the shaman consoles her. 'It was good hair, but the hair is not the cure.' The shaman holds her finger out and points to the moon. 'Do you see the moon?' The wife stares at the shaman's finger, and nods. The shaman smiles and wags her finger, 'The finger is not the moon. Don't mistake the signpost for the road. Remember how you found a way up the mountain? Remember how you trusted the bear? Remember what you felt in your heart—that is the cure.'"

Unresolved mysteries—legends without end

For centuries, explorers have glimpsed a shadowy, man-like creature shifting between snowdrifts on the Himalayas. Known locally as meti or yeti (rock bear), the shaggy "big-foot" was thought to be a relict man-ape, but recent tests of hair suggest it might just be a bear, either the rare snow bear (*Ursus arctos isabellinus*), or the moon bear. The jury is still out, though, as many remain doubtful that the Tibetans could fail to recognize their own bear, even if shrouded in snow. Meanwhile, in unexplored mountain forests, the elusive "golden moon bear" baffles scientists. Covered in glowing golden hair, it was at first thought to be a new subspecies, but the evidence remains tantalizingly inconclusive. Some now believe that it might be just a color phase, while others speculate that it could be an entirely new bear—or even, perhaps, the timeless yeti.

Moon bear myths

King of the Koreans

Tangun, the legendary founder of Old Choson (Korea), claimed divine descent from a bear mother and sky father. The halo in his state portrait here highlights Tangun's divine status, while the leafy cape hints at his magical birth by the sacred sandalwood tree. When Tangun abdicated, at the grand age of 1908, he became a *san-sin* (mountain god). His birthday (Opening of Heaven Day) is still a holiday for children.

Chinese bear cult

Since ancient times, moon bears were celebrated in Chinese art and ritual. Shamans donned bearskins and masks to summon the bear spirit for healing and divining rites, while early courtiers flaunted bear insignia on their robes. Even as late as Jin times (c.265–420), bears were celebrated in bronze and stoneware.

Light of compassion

Moved by the tears of the world, the Buddhist goddess of mercy Kuan-yin heals the sick and lights the way to *nirvana* (heaven). According to legend, she graced her emissary, the moon bear, with her emblem, the crescent moon, which symbolizes her spiritual radiance—pervading and embracing all things with its luminance.

Threats and Conservation

As is so often the case with bears, the Asiatic black bear's most deadly predator is man. While overhunting and habitat destruction have left them vulnerable and endangered in many regions, it is the apparently insatiable appetite of some cultures for their body parts that represents the biggest threat.

Asiatic black bears do not make a habit of attacking humans, and, if left to their own devices, will go to great lengths to avoid people wherever possible. The exception is when they are wounded, surprised, or trying to protect their young. Sadly, fragmentation and loss of habitat have forced bears into more frequent contact with humans in recent years, occasioning more opportunities for confrontation, and leading some to consider them an aggressive species.

Habitat destruction

Uncontrolled harvesting, deforestation, and urban development have encroached on the bears' habitat to such an extent that the animals might be forced to survive at lower altitudes in greater proximity to man. In this environment they are tempted to take advantage of "easy meals" by raiding fields of crops, and have now become a threat to farmers' livelihoods in some areas. As a result of this behavior, they are at greater risk of being hunted, poached, or shot.

Genetic isolation

A consequence of habitat destruction is that bears no longer migrate and share territory to the extent that they once used to, so genetic differences are beginning to show within separate bear populations, such as in Japan and Korea. Genetic isolation is a problem because it reduces genetic diversity and can compromise health within the species.

Unnecessary abuse
Caged Asiatic black bears suffer greatly when their bile (inset) is extracted. This awful practice is indefensible on any grounds, as a cheap, synthetic substitute for bear bile acid (ursodeoxycholic acid) has been developed.

Cruel delicacies
Apart from bile, other bear products—meat, skin, fur, bone, and fat—are also prized in different countries around the world. Bear paws, for example, are considered a delicacy in Korea, Japan, and China, where they may be roasted or used to make soup.

Bile extraction

The cruelest threat to the survival of wild bears comes from the market for bear bile and gallbladder products, which are sold legally in China and Thailand as remedies for impotence, heart disease, and liver complaints. The methods used for bile extraction are horrific and inhumane. Dozens of bears are kept in "farms," trapped in cages often so small that they can't move. Their bile ducts are punctured with crude and often dirty tubes that enable the farmers to "milk" their bile twice a day. The extracted fluid is then dried and sold in the form of dark brown crystals. After extraction the distressed bears often curl up into a ball and hold their paws to their stomach, gnash their teeth, and bite the bars of their cage.

Rescue and recovery

Unfortunately, there are no up-to-date or reliable population figures for the Asiatic black bear. Although listed as "Vulnerable" on the IUCN's Red List of threatened animals, and legally protected everywhere it lives—with the exception of Japan—protection remains extremely difficult to enforce, and conservation in impoverished countries is slow to become a priority.

Positive action

The good news is that some countries are taking an active interest in the bears. In Sichuan province in China, the World Society for the Protection of Animals (WSPA) is supporting the first survey of the bears to see how poaching for body parts is affecting their numbers. By interviewing local people and mapping claw marks on trees, they are hoping to create an accurate range map for the bears that can be used for future population monitoring, and to highlight areas in which conservation efforts should be focused.

Peace at last

Bears that have been rescued from bile farms carry ghastly physical and emotional scars from their time in captivity, but various charities exist to help them recover. Here a black bear plays at the Moon Bear Rescue Center in Chengdu, China. Established in 2002, the center has saved hundreds of bears and is cooperating with local governments to eliminate bear farming in China.

Legalized farming

In recent years China legalized bear farming to protect the remaining wild bear population, but many experts feel that this has backfired because there is now a parallel black market in the body parts of wild bears. The International Fund for Animal Welfare (IFAW) is currently working to eliminate bear bile farming altogether.

Delicate operation

Bears rescued from farms often require treatment for injuries they have sustained during bile extraction. Here zoo workers in Shenyang, northeastern China, prepare a rescued black bear for surgery.

How can we help?

● Make a donation to the WSPA, which campaigns to bring an end to the inhumane industry of bear bile farming.

● Log on to the International Fund for Animal Welfare (www.ifaw.org) to find out more about their efforts to eliminate bear bile farming and promote research into alternatives for use in traditional medicines.

● Support the charity Animals Asia (www.animalsasia.org), which is pressing the Chinese government to ban bear farming outright before the 2008 Olympics in Beijing.

current status: **Vulnerable**

SSC
Species Survival Commission

IUCN
The World Conservation Union

Bibliography

General

Bieder, Robert E. *Bear*. Reaktion Books, 2005.

Brown, Garry. *The Great Bear Almanac*. The Lyons Press, 1996.

Domico, Terry. *Bears of the World*. Facts on File, 1988.

Macdonald, David W., ed. *The Encyclopedia of Mammals*. Oxford University Press, 2006.

McAllister, Ian and Karen. *The Great Bear Rainforest: Canada's Forgotten Coast*. Harbour Publishing, 1997.

Payton, Brian. *In Bear Country: A Global Journey in Vanishing Wilderness*. Old Street Publishing, 2007.

Sherwonit, Bill. *Alaska's Bears: Grizzlies, Black Bears and Polar Bear*. Alaska Northwest Books, 1998.

Stirling, Ian, ed. *Bears: Majestic Creatures of the Wild*. Harper Collins Pubrs., 1993.

Thomas, Keltie. *Bear Rescue: Changing the Future for Endangered Wildlife*, Firefly Books, 2006.

Van Tighem, Kevin. *Bears*. Altitude Publishing, 1999.

Ward, Paul and Kynaston, Suzanne. *Bears of the World*. Facts on File, 2003.

Giant panda

Angel, Heather. *Giant Pandas*. Evans Mitchell Books, 2006.

Gould, Stephen Jay. *The Panda's Thumb: More Reflections in Natural History*. Penguin Books, 1992.

Pan, Wenshi and Lu, Zhi. "The Giant Panda," in Ian Stirling, ed. *Bears: Majestic Creatures of the Wild*. Harper Collins Pubrs., 1993, pp. 140–51.

Schaller, George B. *et al*. *The Giant Pandas of Wolong*. University of Chicago Press, 1985.

Schaller, George B. *The Last Panda*. University of Chicago Press, 1993.

Sun bear

Augeri, David M. "On the biogeographic ecology of the Malayan sun bear," PhD thesis, Cambridge University, 2005.

Fitzgerald, Christoper S. and Paul R. Krausman. *Helarctos malayanus*. *Mammalian Species* 696: 1–5 (July 2002).

Fredriksson, Gabriella M. "Predation on sun bears by reticulated python in east Kalimantan Indonesian Borneo." *The Raffles Bulletin of Zoology* 53(1): 165–68 (2005).

Normuya, Fayuki *et al*. "Notes on oil palm plantation use and seasonal spatial relationships of sun bears in Sabah, Malaysia." *Ursus* 15(2): 227–31 (2004).

Servheen, Christopher. "The Malayan Sun Bear," in Ian Stirling, ed. *Bears: Majestic Creatures of the Wild*. Harper Collins Pubrs., 1993, pp. 124–27.

Wong, Siew Te. "The ecology of Malayan sun bears (*Helarctos malayanus*) in the lowland tropical rainforest of Sabah, Malaysian Borneo. MSc thesis, University of Montana, 2002.

Wong, Siew Te, Christopher Servheen, and Laurentius Ambu. "Food habits of Malayan sun bears in lowland tropical forests of Borneo." *Ursus* 13: 127–36 (2002).

Sloth bear

Bargali, H. S. *et al*. "Characteristics of sloth bear attacks and human casualties in North Bilaspur Forest Division, Chhattisgarh, India." *Ursus* 16(2): 263–67 (2005).

Bargali, H. S. *et al*. "Feeding ecology of sloth bears in a disturbed area in central India." *Ursus* 15 (2): 212–17 (2004).

Kandasamy, Y., *et al*. "Evaluating Panna National Park with special reference to ecology of the sloth bear (*Melursus ursinus*)." Final project report, Wildlife Institute of India (Sep 2005).

Kandasamy, C. G. Rice, and A.J.T. Johnsingh. "Sloth Bear (*Melursus ursinus*)," in A.J.T. Johnsingh, and N. Manjrekar, ed., *Mammals of South Asia* (in press). Universities Press, Hyderabad.

Seidensticker, John. "The Sloth Bear," in Ian Stirling, ed. *Bears: Majestic Creatures of the Wild*. Harper Collins Pubrs., 1993, pp.128–33.

Spectacled bear

Fry, Stephen. *Rescuing the Spectacled Bear: A Peruvian Diary* Hutchinson, 2002.

Lord, Rexford D. *Mammals of South America*. The Johns Hopkins University Press, 2007.

Weinhardt, Diana. "The Spectacled Bear," in Ian Stirling, ed. *Bears: Majestic Creatures of the Wild*. Harper Collins Pubrs., 1993, pp. 134–39

American black and Kermode bears

Bergdahl, James *et al*. "Conservation assesment and reserve proposal for British Columbia's white black bears (*Ursus americanus kermodei*). Abstract for a presentation at the 7th Western North American Black Bear Workshop (2000).

Blood, D.A. "The white-phase Kermode bear, with particular reference to Princess Royal Island, British Columbia." Report (May 1997).

Byun, S.A. *et al*. "North American black bear mtDNA phylogeography: implications for morphology and the Haida Gwaii glacial refugium controversy." *Evolution* 51 (5): 1647–53 (Oct 1997).

Lariviere, Serge. *Ursus americanus. Mammalian Species* 647: 1–11.

Lucas, Eric. "Canada's spirit bears gain perilous popularity." *National Georgraphic News* (July 25, 2003).

"Potential for gene swamping in Kermode bears on Princess Royal Island." Scientific Panel Workshop Summer Report, Vancouver, British Columbia (Feb 15, 2007).

Russell, Charles. *Spirit Bear: Encounters with the White Bear of the Western Rainforest*. Key Porter Books, 1997.

Schooler, Lynn. *The Blue Bear*. Arrow Books, 2002.

Taylor, Dave. *Black Bears: A Natural History*. Fitzhenry and Whiteside, 2006.

Tess, Grandma. *White Spirit Bear*. Hancock House Pubrs., 2000.

Brown bears

Bunnell, Fred L. and Robert K. McCann. "The brown or grizzly bear," in Ian Stirling, ed. *Bears: Majestic Creatures of the Wild*. Harper Collins, 1993, pp. 88–97.

Holzworth, John M. *The Wild Grizzlies of Alaska*. The Knickerbocker Press, 1930.

Sparks, John. *Realms of the Russian Bear: A Natural History of Russia and the Central Asian Republics*. BBC Books, 1992.

Van Daele, Larry. *The History of the Bears on the Kodiak Archipelago*. Alaska Natural History Association, 2003.

Wakeman, Dan and Wendy Shymanski. *Fortress of the Grizzlies: The Khutzeymateen Grizzly Bear Sanctuary*. Heritage House, 2003.

Walker, Tom. *The Way of the Grizzly: The Bears of Alaska's Famed McNeil River*. Voyageur Press, 1998.

Wood, Jason. *Kodiak Kings*. Nodin Press, 2006.

Polar bear

Milse, Thorsten. *Little Polar Bears*. CJ Bucher Verlag, 2006.

Norris, Stefan *et al*. *Polar bears at Risk*. World Wildlife Fund Status Report, 2002.

Rich, T. and A. Rouse. *Polar Bears*, Evans Mitchell Books, 2006.

Rosing, Norbert. *The World of the Polar Bear*. A & C Black, 2007.

Stirling, Ian. *Polar Bears*. University of Michigan Press, 1998.

Stirling, Ian. "The Polar Bear," in Ian Stirling, ed. *Bears: Majestic Creatures of the Wild*. Harper Collins Pubrs., 1993, pp. 98–107.

Asiatic black bear

Kinloch, Colonel. *Travel, Exploration and Sports in the Himalayas*. Bhavana Books, 1885.

Mills, J.A., Simba Chan and Akiko Ishihara *The Bear Facts: The East Asian Market for Bear Gall Bladder*. TRAFFIC, 1995.

Montgomery, Sy. *Search for the Golden Moon Bear: Science and Adventure in Pursuit of a New Species*. Simon & Schuster, 2002.

Reid, Donald G. "The Asiatic black bear, " in Ian Stirling, ed. *Bears: Majestic Creatures of the Wild*. Harper Collins Pubrs., 1993, pp. 118–23.

Reid, D., M. Jiang, Q. Teng, Z. Qin, J. Hu. "Ecology of the Asiatic black bear *Ursus Thibetanus* in Sichuan China." *Mammalia*, 55 (2): 221–37 (1991).

Legend and history

Barbeau, Marius. "Bear mother." *The Journal of American Folklore* 59: 231 (Jan-Mch 1945).

Boas, Franz. "Current beliefs of the Kwakiutl indians." *The Journal of American Folklore* 45: 176 (Apr-Jun 1932).

Brunner, Bernd Bears: *A Brief History*. Yale University Press, 2007.

Eliade, Mircea. *Shamanism: Archaic Techniques of Ecstasy*. Princeton University Press, 1964.

Eliade, Mircea. *The Sacred and the Profane: The Nature of Religion*. Harcourt Inc, 1987.

Hagar, Stansbury. "The celestial bear." *The Journal of American Folklore* 13 (49): 92–103 (Apr-Jun 1900).

Hallowell, A. Irving. "Bear Ceremonialism in the Northern Hemisphere." *American Anthropologist* 28(1): 1–175 (Jan-Mch 1926).

Hatt, Robert T. "A thirteenth-century Tibetan reliquary. An iconographic and physical analysis." *Artibus Asiae*, 42 (2–3): 175–220 (1980).

Janhunen, Juha "Tracing the bear myth in northeast Asia." *Acta Slavica Lapponica* 20: 1–24 (2003).

Masco, Joseph. "It is a strict law that bids us dance:" Cosmologies, colonialism, death, and ritual authority in the Kwakwaka' wakw potlach, 1849–1922." *Comparative Studies, Society and Hisotry* 37 (1): 41–75 (Jan 1995).

McCullough, Helen Craig. "A tale of mutsu." *Harvard Journal of Asiatic Studies* 25: 178–211 (1964-5).

Mckenzie, Donald A. *Myths of China and Japan*. The Gresham Publishing Co. Ltd., 1923.

McKie, Ronald. *The Company of Animals*. Angus and Robertson, 1965.

Morison, Mrs O. "Tsimshian proverbs." *The Journal of American Folklore* 2: 7 (Oct-Dec 1889): 285–6.

Muir, John. *Travels in Alaska*. The Modern Library, 2001.

Nelson, Richard K. *Make Prayers to the Raven: A Koyukon View of the Northern Forest*. University of Chicago Press, 1983.

Quimby, George I. "Culture contact on the northwest coast, 1785–95." *American Athropologist*, New Series, 50 (2): 247–55 (Apr-Jun 1948).

Rosman, Abraham and Paula G. Rubel. "Structural patterning in Kwakiutl art and ritual." *Man* (NS) 25: 620–40.

Shepard, Paul and Barry Sanders. *The Sacred Paw: The Bear in Nature, Myth, and Literature*. Arkana, 1985.

Smith, Marian W. "Petroglyph complexes in the history of the Columbia Fraser region." *Southwestern Journal of Anthropology* 2(3): 306–22 (1946).

Tylor, Edward B. "Remarks on totemism…" *The Journal of the Anthropological Institute of Great Britain and Ireland* 28: 138–48 (1899).

Waterman, T.T. "The explanatory element in the folk-tales of the North American indians." *The Journal of American Folklore* XXVII: CIII (Jan-Mch 1914).

Woodcock, George. *A Picture History of British Columbia*. Hurtig Pubrs., 1980.

Quoted sources

pp. 36-7: adapted and abridged from Evans, Ivor H.N. *Studies in Religion, Folk-Lore, & Custom in British North Borneo and the Malay Peninsula*. Cambridge UniversityPress, 1923, pp. 154, 273–5.

p. 41: Payton, Brian. *In Bear Country: A Global Journey in Vanishing Wilderness*. Old Street Publishing, 2007, p. 30.

pp. 52–3: adapted and abridged from Verrier H *et al*. *Specimens of the Oral Literature of Middle India*. Oxford University Press, 1949, pp. 206, 207, 208; and *Myths of the North-East Frontier of India*, North-East Frontier Agency, 1938, pp. 356–7, 367.

p. 69: adapted and abridged from D.A. Torres, www.cecalc.ula. ve/BIOINFORMATICA/oso/culture_cont.htm.

pp. 73, 85: Muir, John. *The Story of My Boyhood and Youth*. Houghton Mifflin Company, 1913.

pp. 89: Russell, Charles. *Spirit Bear: Encounters with the White Bear of the Western Rainforest*. Key Porter Books, 1997, p. 71.

pp. 100–101: adapted and abridged from Russell, Charles. *Spirit Bear: Encounters with the White Bear of the Western Rainforest*. Key Porter Books, 1997, p. 68.

p. 121: *The Original Journals of the Lewis and Clark Expedition* (1805), New York, 1905, in John M. Holzworth. *The Wild Grizzlies of Alaska*. The Knickerbocker Press, 1930, pp. 223–4.

p. 121: Roosevelt, Theodore. *Hunting Trips of a Ranchman*. G.P. Putnam's Sons, 1885, chapter X, in John M. Holzworth. *The Wild Grizzlies of Alaska*. The Knickerbocker Press, 1930, pp. 316–18.

p. 121. Ord, George. *Guthrie's Georgraphy*. Johnson & Warner, 1815, 2nd American edition, in John M. Holzworth. *The Wild Grizzlies of Alaska*. The Knickerbocker Press, 1930, p. 221.

p. 137: Van Daele, Larry. *The History of the Bears on the Kodiak Archipelago*. Alaska Natural History Association, 2003, p.1.

p. 149: Higgins, E.L. *Kodiak and Afognak Life 1868–1870*. The Limbestone Press, 1981, in Larry Van Daele. *The History of the Bears on the Kodiak Archipelago*. Alaska Natural History Association, 2003, p. 7.

p. 165: adapted and abridged from Birkey-Smith, Kai. *The Eskimos*. Methuen, 1936.

p. 180–81: adapted and abridged from *Memorability of the Three Kingdoms*, 1285; Allen, H.N. *Korean Tales*. The Knickerbocker Press, 1889: 28–40; Montgomery, Sy. *Search for the Golden Moon Bear: Science and Adventure in Pursuit of a New Species*. Simon & Schuster, 2002, p. 104.

Glossary

Alates—reproductive members of a termite colony, a favorite foodstuff of the sunbear.

Allen's rule—a biological rule proposed by Joel Asaph Allen in 1877 that the further south an animal lives, the smaller its extremities in order to minimize heat loss.

Baculum—a bony structure in the bear's penis, which helps to stimulate ovulation in the female and extend copulation.

Bear roots—the nutritious early shoots of sedge and other plants, which bears seek out after their winter sleep.

Biomass—the total mass or organisms within a given habitat, population or sample.

Blubber—the fat found in marine mammals, such as seals and whales.

Bromeliad—a tropical plant (epiphyte, see below) with long, stiff leaves and a fleshy heart.

Bruin—the name given to the bear in the folk story *Reynard the Fox*; its literal meaning is "brown," but it is often applied to any bear.

Cambium—the nutritious layer beneath the bark in coniferous trees.

Carnassial teeth—a pair of lower molars and upper premolars that are specially adapted to cutting/shearing through flesh.

Carnivore—an animal that eats meat.

Cloud forest—moist, high-altitude forest up to 11,500 ft (3500 m), which is shrouded in mist for much of the year.

Cordillera—a series of parallel mountain ranges separated by plateaux; often found in Mexico and South and Central America.

Daybed/daynest—a place where bears rest and sleep between bouts of foraging; created both at ground level and in the treetops, usually with a commanding view, daybeds might be scraped out of earth, beneath tree roots, rocky overhangs, or shady canopies; or they might be made in tree cavities, natural caves, and thickets.

Delayed implantation—a stage in bear reproduction, which allows a fertilized egg to float in the female's uterus until the best conditions prevail for it to implant in the uterine wall and develop.

Den—the nest in which a bear gives birth and/or sleeps for the winter. Dens can be made in caves, rocks, or hollow trees, or dug out of the dirt between tree roots.

El Niño—an irregular warming of waters in the Pacific that occurs around Christmas time and was named for the boy or Christ child. It has been linked to adverse climatic conditions around the world, and is believed to affect light levels.

Epiphytes—plants that grow upon or are attached to other plants for physical support.

Estrus—a period of sexual receptivity in female mammals.

Ethmoid bone—a bone found in the nose; its many projections are covered in sensitive nasal membrane and give bears a particularly acute sense of smell.

Forbs—nongrass species of plants.

Guard hair—an outer layer of long, coarse, waterproof, overlapping hair that protects the soft, wooly underfur from dirt and damp.

Groundnest—a daybed made at ground level (see daybed).

Heat dumping—a means of lowering the body temperature by lying face down on the ground and pressing the belly against the cool earth.

Herbivore—an animal that feeds on plants.

Hibernation—a period of sleep or dormancy during the winter; some bears sleep more deeply and for longer than others.

Keystone species—an animal that plays a vital role in the functioning of the ecosystem; in the bear's case, it helps to disperse seed and open up the tree canopy by breaking off branches for nests.

Lactation—the secretion of milk by mammary glands, essential for suckling the young.

Lantana—an evergreen shrub of the genus Lantana, with orange or yellow flowers.

Lead—a long crack of open water running parallel to the shore in areas where sea ice regularly melts and refreezes.

Mortiño—heather berries found in the páramo (see below).

Montane—mountainous.

Muskeg—a type of bog found in northern Canada.

Nictitating membrane— a transparent inner eyelid that closes to protect and moisten the eye, while allowing continued vision, even under water.

Old-growth forest—ancient, virgin, primeval forest, largely untouched by human activities, characterized by trees that have grown to immense heights and girths.

Omnivore—an animal that eats both plants and meat.

Ovulation—the production of eggs by the ovaries.

Pack ice—large sheets of ice floating in the sea.

Páramo—the grassy slopes of the high Andes in South America.

Permafrost—permanently frozen subsoil found in polar regions.

Phase—a variety of coloration that may be genetic and permanent, or seasonal and temporary.

Plantigrade—able to stand upright with both feet flat on the ground.

Polynya—a temporary pool of open water in areas where sea ice regularly melts and refreezes.

POPs—persistent organic pollutants; a toxic mixture of long-lasting contaminants, including pesticides and industrial chemicals, that work their way up the food chain as they are ingested by various animals. They have adverse effects on health, reproduction, and resistance to disease.

Radial sesamoid—an enlarged bone in the wrist that acts as a thumb.

Sal—a type of hardwood tree found in northern India.

Sapote—a tropical tree that has mahogany-like wood and sweet fruit, a favorite of the spectacled bear.

Scent-marking—the habit of scratching bark, rubbing against trees, and scraping earth to leave smelly markers; these probably serve to warn off trespassers, but also broadcast readiness to mate.

Second-growth forest—areas of forest that have recovered after major damage, such as fire or heavy logging.

Stick/tree nest—made of bent and broken branches, usually in the fork of a strong tree.

Terai—damp grasslands in the Himalayan foothills.

Tundra—a vast, rolling, treeless plain in Arctic and alpine regions, where grasses, sedges, mosses, lichens and dwarf shrubs grow; the subsoil of Arctic tundra is permanently frozen—see permafrost.

Ursid—a member of the bear family, Ursidae.

Zygomaticomandibularis—powerful plant-chewing muscles found in the head of mammals.

Index

Picture Sources

Ancient Art and Architecture Collection/C M Dixon: 117t.
Ardea: Back jacket bl ©Masahiro Iijima, 34t ©Kenneth W Fink; 80t ©Tom and Pat Leeson; 90b ©Tom and Pat Leeson; 136–7 ©Erwin & Peggy Bauer; 144t ©Duncan Usher; 144bl ©Kenneth W Fink; 172tr © Masahiro Iijima, 174–5 ©Masahiro Iijima; 176t ©Masahiro Iijima, 177t ©Masahiro Iijima; 177bl Masahiro Iijima; 178t ©Masahiro Iijima; 178c ©Masahiro Iijima
Bridgeman Art Library: 21bl ©Musee Guimet, Paris, France/ Archives Charmet; 37t Private Collection; 53c ©Victoria & Albert Museum, London, UK/The Stapleton Collection; 100t ©Art Gallery of Ontario, Toronto, Canada/Gift of the J. S. McLean Collection by Canada Packers Inc 1990; 117b ©Victoria & Albert Museum, London, UK; 132t Private Collection/ Peter Newark American Pictures; 165c Private Collection/The Stapleton Collection; 165b ©Hamburger Kunsthalle, Germany; 180t Private Collection; 181t ©Tangun Gahoe Museum, Jongno-gu, South Korea.
British Library, London: 52t.
Corbis: front jacket tc ©Thorsten Milse/Robert Harding World Imagery; bl ©DLILLC; br ©Kennan Ward; back jacket br ©Daniel J. Cox; 5c ©Daniel J. Cox; 6 ©Andy Rouse; 7b ©Hinrich Baesemann/ dpa; 12br ©Redlink; 18tl ©Reuters; 20t ©Zeng Nian; 21br ©Dusko Despotovic; 23br ©Newsphoto/Reuters; 28bl ©Wayne Lawler/ Ecoscene; 32t ©Reuters; 33t ©Reuters/Chor Sokunthea; 34bl ©Ken Bohn/Zoological Society of San Diego; 36t ©Charles and Josette Lenars; 37c ©Jason Reed/Reuters; 39b © Yusuf Ahmad/ Reuters; 51b ©Alexander Rüsche/epa; 60l ©Kevin Schafer; 68t ©Laurie Chamberlain; 69c ©Kazuyoshi Nomachi; 70b ©John Van Hasselt; 71t © Frans Lanting; 75t 83b ©Renee Lynn; 76c ©Stuart; 83b © Renee Lynn; 87t © Raymond Gehman; 87b © Dan Lamont; 91bl © Daniel J. Cox; 92 © Paul A. Souders; 91t © Daniel J. Cox; 92cl ©Richard T. Nowitz; 92cr © Daniel J. Cox; 94–5 © Daniel J. Cox; 97t ©Natalie Fobes; 101t © Francis G. Mayer; 101b ©Bettmann; 103t ©Richard T. Nowitz; 103b © Richard T. Nowitz; 117c ©Francis G. Mayer; 118t ©Vassil Donev/epa; 119b © Sergei Karpukhin; 123t ©Kennan Ward; 126–7 ©Kennan Ward; 133t ©Edward S. Curtis © Stapleton Collection; 135b ©Roy Corral; 139bl ©Horst Ossinger/epa; 142–3 ©Tom Bean; 145bl ©Tom Bean; 145br ©Tom Bean; 149b ©Richard A. Cooke; 151b © Benjamin Lowy; 162bc © Jenny E. Ross; 162br ©Kennan Ward; 164t ©Bettmann; 181c ©Seattle Art Museum; 181b © Royal Ontario Museum; 182b ©Earl and Nazima Kowall.
DK images.com: 11br ©Sallie A Reason/Dorling Kindersley.
FLPA: 3 ©Mark Raycroft/Minden Pictures; 7t ©Gerry Ellis; 10bl ©Gerry Ellis/Minden Pictures; 11bl ©Katherine Feng/Globio/ Minden Pictures; 14–15 ©Pete Oxford/Minden Pictures; 16br ©Mark Newman; 17bc ©Gerry Ellis/Minden; 17br ©David Hosking; 18tr ©Gerry Ellis/Minden Pictures; 18cl ©Katherine Feng/Globio/Minden Pictures; 18 bl; Gerry Ellis/Minden Pictures; 19t ©Gerry Ellis/Minden Pictures; 19b ©ZSSD/Minden Pictures; 22t ©Zhinong X/Minden Pictures; 23t ©Gerry Ellis/Minden Pictures; 24–5 ©Gerry Ellis/Minden; 28br ©Frans Lanting; 32bl ©Inga Spence; 33bc ©Terry Whittaker; 33br ©Nigel Catlin; 34tl ©Jürgen and Christine Sohns; 35b ©ZSSD/Minden Pictures; 37b ©Mark Newman; 38b ©Frans Lanting; 39t ©Terry Whittaker; 42b ©Mark Newman; 49br ©Konrad Worthe/Minden Pictures; ©59t ©Tui De Roy/Minden Pictures; 62–3 ©Pete Oxford/Minden Pictures; 60t ©Tui De Roy/Minden Pictures; 60b ©Tui De Roy/ Minden Pictures; 64br ©Pete Oxford/Minden Pictures; 65t ©Pete Oxford/Minden Pictures; 70t ©Tui De Roy/Minden Pictures; 71b ©Tui De Roy/Minden Pictures; 72–3 ©Mark Raycroft/Minden Pictures; 74b ©Mark Raycroft/Minden Pictures; 76t ©Tim Fitzharris/Minden Pictures; 76b ©Inga Spence; 81bl ©Willem Harinck; 81br ©Konrad Wothe/Minden Pictures; 82c ©Jim Brandenburg/Minden Pictures; 96bl ©Tony Wharton; 96br ©Steve McCutcheon; 97bc ©Frans Lanting; 98br ©Gerry Ellis; 104–5 ©Michio Hoshino/Minden Pictures; 106l ©Mike Lane; 106b ©Mike Lane; 107t ©Michio Hoshino/Minden Pictures; 108c ©Derek Middleton; 112t ©Fritz Polking; 112bl ©Hugo Wilcox/Foto Natura; 112br ©Paul Hobson; 113bl ©Robert Canis; 113bc ©Derek Middleton; 113br ©Wim Weenink/Foto Natura; 115b ©Panda Photo; 118b ©Bjorn Ullhagen; 122b ©Konrad Wothe/Minden Pictures; 124c ©Frans Lanting; 128bl ©Nigel Catlin; 128br ©Steve McCutcheon; 129bl ©Steve McCutcheon; 129bc ©Hiroya Minakuchi/Minden Pictures; 129br ©Paul Hobson; 130c ©Mark Newman; 130b ©L Lee Rue; 134t ©Yva Momatiuk/John Eastcott/ Minden Pictures; 138b ©Mathias Breiter/Minden Pictures; 139t ©Mark Newman; 140t ©Mark Newman; 144br ©Michael Quinton/ Minden Pictures; 145bc ©Mark Newman; 146b ©Mathias Breiter/Minden Pictures; 155t ©Sunset; 160t ©Van Muers/Foto Natura; 160bl ©Michael Quinton/Minden Pictures; 161bl ©Tui De Roy/Minden Pictures; 161br ©David Hosking; 162bl ©Matthias Breiter/Minden Pictures; 163b ©Michio Hoshino/Minden Pictures; 166t ©L Lee Rue; 167t ©Konrad Wothe/Minden Pictures; 168–9 ©Jürgen and Christine Sohns; 170b ©Terry Whittaker; 171bl ©Terry Whittaker; 179t ©John Holmes; 179b ©Terry Whittaker; 182t ©Terry Whittaker; 182c inset; ©Terry Whittaker.
Getty Images: front jacket, bc ©Norbert Rosing; 5t ©AFP; 8–9 ©Lu Zhi; 11 t ©Lu Zhi; 26b ©Roy Toft; 28t ©joSon; 35t ©AFP; 44br ©G R Richardson; 55t ©Rob Elliott/AFP; 69b ©Gareth Cattermole; 75bl ©First Light; 78–9 ©Norbert Rosing; 80bl ©Raymond K. Gehman; 82t ©Norbert Rosing; 84t ©MPI ©85c ©Jon Brenneis; 85b ©Tim Graham; ©102t ©Joel Sartore; 102b ©Ian McAllister; 108b ©Masaaki Tanaka/Sebun Photo; 110–11 ©Klaus Nigge; 115t ©Klaus Nigge; 119t © Steve Winter; 123bl ©Annie Griffiths Belt; 124br ©Joseph Van Os; 131b ©Michael S Quinton; 145t ©Daniel J Cox; 147b ©Tom Walker; 149c ©Jon Freeman; 150b ©Natalie B. Fobes; 151t ©Nevada Wier; 152–3 ©Wayne R Bilenduke; 156t ©Larry Broder; 156br ©Pal Hermansen; ©158–9 Johnny Johnson; 161t ©Ralph Lee Hopkins; 162t ©Wayne R Bilenduke; 163t ©Wayne R Bilenduke; 166b